DOMINICAN EDUCATION 1820–1930

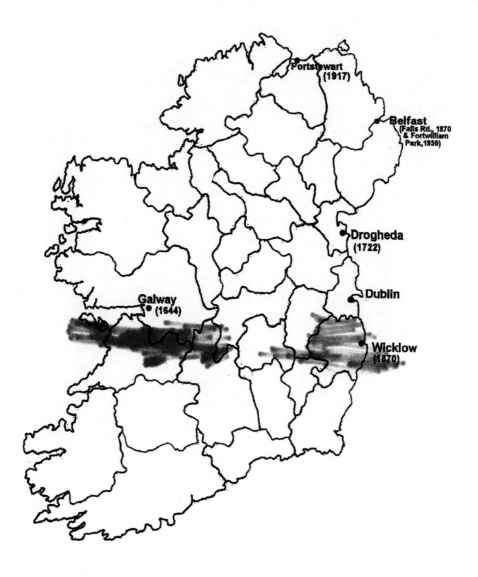

Map 1. Dominican Convents in Ireland.
See Map 3 and Appendix 1 for foundation dates of schools
in the city and county of Dublin 1717–1912.

DOMINICAN EDUCATION
IN IRELAND

1820–1930

MÁIRE M. KEALY OP

IRISH ACADEMIC PRESS
DUBLIN • PORTLAND, OR

First published in 2007 by Irish Academic Press

44 Northumberland Road,	920 NE 58th Avenue, Suite 300
Ballsbridge,	Portland, Oregon,
Dublin 4, Ireland	97213-3786

copyright © 2007 Máire M. Kealy

www.iap.ie

British Library Cataloguing in Publication Data
An entry can be found on request

ISBN 978 0 7165 2888 3 (cloth)
ISBN 978 0 7165 2889 0 (paper)

Library of Congress Cataloging-in-Publication Data
An entry can be found on request

Typeset by Carrigboy Typesetting Services.
Printed by Biddles Ltd., King's Lynn, Norfolk

This book is dedicated with gratitude to all Dominicans
and their lay colleagues living and deceased who
committed their lives to the ministry of education
in Ireland since the seventeenth century.

Contents

Illustrations

Figures

Maps

Tables

Foreword

And that things that are not so ill with you and me as they might have been, is half owing to the number who lived faithfully a hidden life.
George Eliot, *Middlemarch*

I think the above quotation of George Eliot, who in her day had to write under a male pseudonym as women were not accepted as writers, is apt to highlight the story of the great women in this book. In *Dominican Education in Ireland 1820–1930*, Sister Máire Kealy, OP shines a light on the relatively hidden contributions of Dominican Sisters in the field of education. She brings to light the vision, dedication, education and self-sacrifice of women religious, specifically the sisters of the Dominican Congregation, Cabra, Dublin, though not exclusively. The author chooses a time span of over a hundred years – 1820–1930 – in Ireland. She reveals the hidden lives of the sisters in the context of the evolution of education throughout Ireland during this time and provides historical detail, academic appraisal and personal insight into an Ireland easily forgotten today.

In the nineteenth century Irish people were emerging from the restrictions of the penal laws, working towards Catholic Emancipation, enduring and recovering from the Famine years, dealing with massive emigration, struggling for ownership of land and seeking Home Rule. The Catholic Church was coming into its own as a legal, recognized public body in Ireland. This evolution required a whole new definition of relationships between religious and the hierarchy and the transformation of the Dominican Sisters from 'medieval nuns' to modern sisters.

This research shines a torch on the courageous response of the Dominican Sisters to the challenges of the nineteenth-century era in their new convent in Cabra. In 1820 there was only a small group of five sisters and one novice. They had very little money but the first school they opened was a school for the poor. 'This was new and unexplored educational territory for women whose background was that of the landed gentry of Anglo-Irish origin but who were now poor themselves, few in number, ageing, and with an uncertain future before them.' Over the years they became involved in, and often were the leaders of the educational developments at all levels throughout the nineteenth century including pioneering work with deaf children. Having successfully set up primary and secondary schools as well as University and Teacher Training Colleges, they responded to the needs of the new Ireland of the twentieth century in a manner worthy of those sisters who went before them. The book ends with the opening of the first all Irish Medium Secondary School, Scoil Chaitríona in Dublin and with the opening in 1930 of Dominican College Fortwilliam Park in Belfast. Fortwilliam was the first Catholic school to offer a commercial as well as an academic course.

For those interested in women's issues, education, social transformation, the role of the Church and the human story they will find in these pages all elements together with the inspiration and hope that an interesting story can induce. It is written with clarity and honesty dealing with failures as well as achievements in times that were daunting. One is grateful that this hidden, unacclaimed contribution on the part of the Dominican Sisters is acknowledged. Modern day Ireland has inherited much from the 'hidden lives' of these educators and pioneers of the nineteenth and twentieth centuries.

May all who read it be inspired to meet the challenges of education in a multi-cultural and fast-growing secular Ireland today.

Helen Mary Harmey OP
Congregation Prioress
October 2006

Acknowledgements

I wish to acknowledge my indebtedness to the following people without whose help this book never would have been written. *Dominican Education in Ireland 1820–1930* is based on a doctoral thesis presented at Lancaster University in 2005 and so foremost on the list are my joint supervisors, Dr Sarah Barber and Professor Michael Mullett. Their kindness to me personally and their support and guidance in the work were constant and consistent.

The initiative for my writing the history of education in the Cabra Dominican Congregation in Ireland came from Sr Marian O'Sullivan while she was congregation prioress. I thank Sr Marian and her council for their encouragement and for setting me on the fascinating path of research. Sr Geraldine Marie Smyth and her council, her successor, Sr Helen Mary Harmey the present congregation prioress, and her council continued that support, moral and financial, as did the region prioresses and their teams who held office 1999–2005: Srs Margaret Purcell, Helen Mary Harmey and Helen O'Dwyer. All have given me encouragement and support and have shown great interest in the work in progress. Sr Helen Mary has done me the honour of writing the foreword to the book.

The members of my community at Dún Mhuire were ever ready to encourage me and to allow me the time, space and facilities to work. Significant and practical advice and encouragement came unfailingly from Sr Rose O'Neill and Dr Margaret MacCurtain. I am especially indebted to Sr Alberta Lally who together with Srs Terence O'Keeffe, Maureen Flanagan and Veronica McShane, acted as readers and gave helpful suggestions throughout. Sr Francis Lally provided the material on the Dún Laoghaire oratory, while Sr Urban Rodgers helped with her extensive knowledge of the Northern Ireland educational scene.

I am indebted also to Sr Dominique Horgan, congregation archivist, and to all the local archivists in our convents in Ireland who gave me access to the materials relevant to the task. Special thanks are due to Sr Catherine Gibson, archivist of 204 Griffith Avenue, who put the rich store of materials dealing with the foundation of Eccles Street and that community's role in gaining the right to university education to women at my disposal. Srs Breda and Vincent of Dominican Monastery, Siena, Drogheda, allowed me into their archives and extended hospitality to me on more than one occasion. Three people who are no longer with us cannot be omitted from this list: Sr Cécile Diamond, Sr Nicholas

Griffey, and Sr Malachy McKeown. Sr Cécile had done major research into the history of our Congregation but sadly she died before her work was concluded. Her enthusiasm spurred my curiosity and interest. Sr Nicholas Griffey, who in her life-time was an internationally acknowledged expert in the education of the deaf, gave me invaluable help and enthusiastic encouragement in researching the story of St Mary's School for the Deaf, Cabra. Sr Malachy late of the Falls Road community, in Belfast, went to considerable trouble to search out materials relevant to education in Northern Ireland. May these three generous Dominicans rest in peace.

Oral history is valuable if one is fortunate enough to have people who are willing to share their memories of people and events. In the case of Scoil Chaitríona, I was permitted to record the reminiscences of several people who had first-hand knowledge of its foundation. Sr Cajetan Lyons and Sr Aquinas McCarthy, both Dominicans, spent their professional lives teaching in the school and had a life-time's association with the school's foundress, An Mháthair Treasa Ní Fhlanagáin. Three past-pupils from the 1928/29 era gave me their own recollections of the beginnings of the all-Irish medium school: Sr Catherine Whelan, a Daughter of Charity, Máire Ní Mhuireadhaidh, and Máirín Ní Dhomhnalláin spoke freely of their school days and of their impressions of the school in its beginnings and gave me background information about the early days of Scoil Chaitríona. Sadly, Máire Ní Mhuireadhaidh, Máirín Ní Dhomhnalláin, Sisters Catherine and Cajetan, have since died. May they also rest in peace.

Many people outside our Congregation assisted me in various ways. I am grateful for the permission given to use Trinity College Library, Dublin; I thank the staffs of the National Library, Kildare Street, Dublin; the National Archives, Bishop Street Dublin; and Dublin City Council Libraries, for their courteous help at all times. The following archivists were most helpful: Mr David Sheehy, Dublin Diocesan Archives, Ms J. Cox and staff, Cambridge University Library; Dr R. Moad, King's College, Cambridge; Fr Davitt, CM Vincentian Fathers, Raheny; Fr Hugh Fenning, OP, provincial archivist, St Mary's Priory, Tallaght; Fr Fergus O'Donoghue, SJ, and Ms Orna Somerville, Jesuit Archives, Dublin; Canon George O'Hanlon of Down and Connor diocese (Somerton Road, Belfast); Sr Joan McLoughlin, Institute of the Blessed Virgin Mary (Loreto Sisters), St Stephen's Green; Dublin; Sr Ursula Clarke, Ursuline Sisters, Blackrock, Cork; Ms Bernadette Kinsella, Secretariat of Catholic Secondary Schools, Milltown, Dublin; Mr John Morrissey, librarian, and his staff, St Mary's University College, Falls Road, Belfast. My research into the history of Newbridge College, Co. Kildare was made easy by the interest shown and help given by Fr Benedict Kenny, OP community archivist. I am indebted to Nancy Williams, USA, for permission to use excerpts from her poem 'Survival', in her collection *Whooping Crones*.

Visits to the archives in University College, Dublin, Sacred Heart Convent, Mount Anville, Dublin, St Louis Convent and Heritage Centre, Monaghan, Mary

Immaculate College, Limerick and the Sisters of Mercy archives in Booterstown, yielded valuable help and I am grateful to the individual archivists: Miss Kate Manning, UCD, Miss Kate Curry, Mount Anville, Srs Margaret and Mona, St Louis Convent, Monaghan, Mr John Power, Mary Immaculate College, Limerick and Sr Magdalena Frisby in Convent of Mercy, Booterstown, Co. Dublin.

In the preparation of the book for publication, I have had valuable advice and assistance from Ms Lisa Hyde, the representative of Irish Academic Press; the publication is greatly enhanced by Sr Monica Devers' beautiful design for the book cover. A special word of thanks is due to Dr Barbara Walsh who has been supportive with her friendship and help. Barbara designed the maps and Tables 1, 2 and 4, which add clarity to the text.

I am grateful to my own family who have shown a keen interest in the progress of the thesis and have encouraged me throughout. Special thanks are due to my nephew John Kealy, who processed the illustrations in readiness for the publisher and who came to my rescue many times when computer trouble struck. Finally, I owe an enormous and unrepayable debt of gratitude to Srs Louis Marie, Benedict, and Rose Ita and their communities past and present in Nazareth House, Ashton Road, Lancaster, who have given me continuous, welcoming hospitality over the years and have provided a safe, peaceful haven, a home from home, during my many visits to Lancaster.

Notes

1. The title of the book is 'Dominican Education in Ireland 1820–1930', and while there is a brief account of Dominican College, Newbridge, Co. Kildare, a foundation of the Dominican friars, the book is dedicated to the educational work of the Dominican women in Ireland, including the Dominican nuns in Siena Convent in Drogheda. While not part of the Congregation of Dominican Sisters, Cabra, the Siena nuns played a significant and honourable part in education in Drogheda from 1722–1930. Any account of the Dominican women's work in education would be incomplete without their inclusion.

2. Throughout the book the Dominican women who were members of the communities involved in the schools and colleges are referred to as 'nuns', a term which has connotations in canon law: officially nuns are cloistered religious women who take solemn vows and are committed to the contemplative life.[1] Canon 667.2 of the Code of Canon Law states, 'a stricter discipline of enclosure is to be observed in monasteries which are devoted to the contemplative life'. The present day Cabra Dominicans whose origins date back to the two convents in Galway and Channel Row, Dublin, are more properly styled 'sisters'. The 1918 Code of Canon Law defined the status of members of congregations such as the Cabra Dominicans. Canon 667.2 cited above does not apply to them; the Cabra Dominicans take simple vows and are usually engaged in apostolic work. However, in the context of the period in which the book is set, it is more in keeping with the usage of the eighteenth and nineteenth centuries to refer to the Dominican women treated of, as 'nuns'.

3. Religious life presupposes a vowed life; the *Catechism of the Catholic Church* defines a religious vow as a 'deliberate and free promise made to God … an act of devotion in which the Christian dedicates himself [herself] to God or promises him some good work'.[2] Vows can be 'simple' or 'solemn': each type of vow carries its own set of obligations regarding enclosure and inheritance of property. Those who take solemn vows, 'because of the nature of their institute, totally renounce their goods, lose the capacity to acquire and possess goods. … Whatever they acquire after renunciation belongs to the institute.'[3] For the purposes of the present work, an uncomplicated explanation of the difference is that for those with simple vows, strict enclosure is not an obligation, canon law

regarding the ownership of property is less radical, and the Church can more easily dispense one from simple vows than from solemn vows.

1. Canon 667.2 in *The Code of Canon Law,* in English translation (London: Collins, 1983), p.121.
2. 'The Ten Commandments': promises and vows in *The Catechism of the Catholic Church* (London: Geoffrey Chapman, 1944), p.457.
3. Canon 668.5, *Code of Canon Law,* p.122.

Abbreviations

ARCHIVES AND LIBRARIES

AUCD   Archives, University College, Belfield, Dublin 4.
BPP   British Parliamentary Papers
CCSS   Conference of Convent Secondary Schools, Emmet House, Milltown,
       Dublin 14
CUL   Cambridge University Library, Cambridge, England
DDA   Dublin Diocesan Archives, Archbishop's House, Drumcondra, Dublin 9
KCC   King's College Cambridge, England
LHCM   St Louis Heritage Centre, Monaghan
LSG   Loreto Archives, 55 St Stephen's Green, Dublin 2
MAA   Mount Anville Archives, Society of the Sacred Heart, Dublin 14
MIUC   Mary Immaculate University College, Limerick
NAD   National Archives, Bishop Street, Dublin 8
NAF   Newspaper Articles and Features
NLI   National Library of Ireland, Kildare Street, Dublin 2
OPC   Dominican Convent, Cabra, Dublin 7
OPD   Dominican Monastery of St Catherine of Siena, Drogheda
OPE   Dominican Convent, 204 Griffith Avenue, Dublin 9
OPFR   Dominican Convent, Falls Road, Belfast BT12 6AE
OPFW   Dominican Convent, Fortwillliam Park, BT15 4AP
OPG   Dominican Generalate, Westfield Road, Dublin 6W
OPGA   Dominican Sisters, Dún Mhuire, 461 Griffith Avenue, Dublin 9
OPM   Dominican Convent, Muckross Park, Dublin 4
OPN   Dominican College, Newbridge, Co. Kildare
OPR   Dominican Region House, 10 Ashington Grove, Dublin 7
OPS   Dominican Convent, Sutton, Dublin 13
OPSH   Dominican Convent, Sion Hill, Blackrock, Co. Dublin
OPT   Dominican Convent, Taylor's Hill, Galway
OPW   Dominican Convent, Wicklow
PRONI Public Records Office, Balmoral Avenue, Belfast
SCSS   Secretariat of Catholic Secondary Schools, Emmet House, Milltown,
       Dublin 14
SSHA   Society of Sacred Heart, Mount Anville, Dublin 14
SLA   St Louis Convent, Monaghan
SMFR   St Mary's University College, Falls Road
VFR   Vincentian Fathers' Archives, Sybil Hill, Raheny, Dublin 13

Introduction

Dominican ethos in education

Within the general purpose of the Dominican Order the special mission of the Congregation of Dominican Sisters of Our Lady of the Rosary and St Catherine of Siena, Cabra, is the proclamation of the Word of God through living our religious consecration and through education.[1]

It is necessary to grasp the values which for centuries have inspired and animated Dominican educators in order to understand the Dominican ethos in education as a distinctive and characteristic way of conducting an educational establishment. Dominic de Guzman, the Order's founder, was originally a canon of the cathedral of Osma in the north of Spain. Dominic, while travelling in the south of France on a mission with the bishop of Osma, found himself faced with the widespread teaching of a group of people called Albigensians or Cathars, whose preaching work was centred in the area of Languedoc. The Albigensians espoused a medieval philosophy based on the dualistic theory that all being is divided into matter and spirit of which matter is essentially evil, and spirit essentially good. Dominic met many people on his journeys who followed the teaching of the Albigensians. His preaching, in contrast, was based on the Christian theology of the doctrine of the Incarnation of the Son of God in which there was a marriage of spirit and matter, the divine and human. To be effective in spreading the good news of the gospel, Dominic gathered around him a small band of young men who would help in preaching the truth of the gospel to all. From the earliest days of the Order in 1206, Dominic founded a house in Prouilhe, near Toulouse which became the first Dominican convent of nuns.

Dominic realized clearly that to preach the gospel effectively the preacher must have a sound doctrinal training. He therefore dispersed his small band of fifteen followers in 1217, significantly sending seven of them to Paris and Bologna, at that time the main university centres of Europe. In his planning, Dominic developed institutes of study and preaching in collaboration with both of these universities; this was to be the specific approach of Dominicans to the training of their members. There was an emphasis on serious and constant study and contemplation of the Word of God in scripture as a preparation for preaching and teaching. Within the Order, Thomas Aquinas was the greatest exponent of devotion to study and he saw the teacher as the mediator of knowledge:

[co-operating] with the light of reason by supplying the external help to it to reach the perfection of knowledge. ... [i]n the pupil intelligible forms of knowledge, received through teaching, are caused directly by the agent and mediately by the one who teaches.[2]

DOMINICAN ETHOS IN PRACTICAL TERMS

For those aspiring to teach others, intellectual honesty and candour are the first requisites. It is equally important to know that we have not full knowledge of every subject and, above all, we must know how to acquire knowledge. Sr Bede Kearns, a Cabra Dominican, summed up that rooting of the Dominican ethos in the Order's spirituality:

> There is nothing exclusive about the Dominican idea of education any more than there is about the Dominican apostolate of evangelising by preaching. But there is a unique charism inspiring both: a way of education and preaching which springs from the Dominican vision and way of life, the Dominican regard for the person made in the image of God, and for all God's creation.[3]

Education should be for the good of the person. It means developing the powers of soul and body and its aim is the perfection of the person. According to Saint Thomas, it is a precept of the natural law for a person to follow the inclination of his or her nature to be, and to be perfect, to be the best a person can be. Reverence and respect for the unique nature of each one in a lecture hall or classroom are prerequisites of bringing the pupils along to the well of knowledge and inviting them to drink, rather than forcing them to learn without any attempt to help them understand. In the day-to-day work of education, the underlying ethos of Dominican education cannot always be at the forefront of the teacher's mind, but if teachers are imbued with these principles, they cannot but be influenced in their personal way of working and of treating the pupil or student. In dealing with pupils, personal choices are encouraged through discussion so that the minimum of rules and regulations are necessary. Above all, in a Dominican school a love of Truth, which is in essence a love of the person of Jesus Christ who said of Himself, 'I am the Way, the Truth and the Life' is the *raison d'être* of the teacher's endeavours.[4] Ideally, the pupil should leave school with a well-founded knowledge of the truths of the faith, a commitment to the person of Christ, together with a real sense of his or her own uniqueness and personal worth. This sense of personal worth will include an appreciation of one's personal gifts and a good knowledge of the secular curriculum. If the students in some measure are prepared for life according to these standards, then the teacher may feel reasonably happy that the work of the school has been successful.

HISTORICAL BACKGROUND OF DOMINICANS IN IRELAND

The contribution of the Dominican nuns to education in Ireland must be seen against their historical background. The friars came to Ireland with the Normans and had established themselves in Dublin by 1224, three years after the death of their founder Dominic de Guzman. Though religious persecution played its part directly or indirectly in destroying any documentary evidence of Dominican women in Ireland prior to the Reformation (1534), the friars were able to preserve their own history both in written records and through the continuity of their presence in the country throughout the centuries. The first recorded Dominican centre for the education of boys was in 1320 when the archbishop of Dublin, Alexander Bicknor, issued a decree on 10 February for the establishment and administration of a university in Dublin attached to St Patrick's Cathedral.[5] Both Dominicans and Franciscans were involved in this venture, which was recognized by the Church as having canonical status. In the next century, 1428, the Dominican friars opened a school in Usher's Island alongside the Liffey. The area was then a populous suburb of old Dublin and the friars dedicated the school to St Thomas Aquinas. The curriculum brought the boys from courses in grammar, logic and rhetoric, music, geometry and astronomy to courses in theological and legal studies. This school did not have a long life and it was not until the nineteenth century that a stable and enduring college for boys was opened by the Dominican friars.

ST THOMAS'S COLLEGE, NEWBRIDGE

With the emergence of a Catholic middle class in the nineteenth century, there was a demand for secondary education for young Catholic boys. Newbridge College in Co. Kildare opened its doors on 1 March 1852 in what was known in the town as 'The White House' under the direction of Father Nicholas Freyne. By 1895 the number of pupils had increased to 100. The college was a boarding school and from the earliest times competitive sport was encouraged: rugby, soccer, gaelic football and hurling. Fr John Heffernan, in his address to the past pupils in 2002 at the celebration of the school's 150 years of service to education, remarked that the ethos of Newbridge College 'is such that each and every student who enters its doors is special to us and always will be'.[6]

From the beginning the study of music and art were encouraged. Lay teachers 'competent in every department of literature and science' were employed.[7] The curriculum included Greek, Latin, French, Italian, a solid course in English and the sciences. As might be expected, solid instruction in principles of religion was of primary concern to the priest teachers. After the passing of the Intermediate (Ireland) Act in 1878, the boys were entered for the state examinations. The college magazine of 1900 reported successes in first arts of the Royal University and in science and art in the South Kensington board examinations.[8]

Commercial subjects were introduced for those students who wished to pursue a career in the civil service or in the business world.

Newbridge College is today following the tradition so well begun by Nicholas Freyne in 1852, and this short account of the college indicates the similarity of ethos and aims of both Dominican friars and nuns at a time of radical developments in the Irish educational world in the late nineteenth and early twentieth centuries. The synopsis could not, nor is it intended to, do justice to the work of the friars in Newbridge College. While this present book concentrates on the work of Dominican women, it is important to include some reference to Newbridge College in its own right, if only to show that Dominicans, both men and women, played their part in the important developments in Irish education during the hundred and ten years covered in the study.

DOMINICAN WOMEN IN IRELAND PRE-1640

In spite of the lack of historical written records, it is a reasonable assumption that there were Dominican women religious in Ireland in the period 1224–1644. O'Heyne, the eighteenth-century Dominican historian, has recorded the story of the post-Reformation Galway nuns in some detail. His *Irish Domincans of the Seventeenth Century* is the earliest extant published history of the Order in Ireland and fortunately O'Heyne did include some account of its women members.[9] Thomas de Burgo's *Hibernia Dominicana* is another primary source for the eighteenth-century background to the history of the Galway nuns.[10] Thomas O'Flynn, in *The Irish Dominicans 1536–1641*, concentrates on the friars only:

> from their definitive establishment as an independent and corporate body in 1536 through the gradual but systematic destruction of their houses and community existence in the sixteenth century to exciting fresh beginnings in the first decades of the seventeenth.[11]

Hugh Fenning's scholarly work, *The Irish Dominican Province, 1698–1797*, likewise deals with the friars. Fenning includes, throughout his book, accounts of the nuns in Galway, Dublin and Drogheda, and the convent in Waterford. This convent was established in 1736, with two nuns, Sr Anastasia Wyse of the convent in Channel Row, Dublin, and Sr Margaret Brown of the Galway convent. Fenning records that 'the two nuns rented a house in which they began to teach girl boarders', but the nuns did not survive long in Waterford and by the mid-1760s the convent had been closed.[12] Thus, in the eighteenth century, the Domincan nuns were involved in running girls' boarding schools in four places in Ireland: Galway, Dublin, Drogheda and Waterford.

THE GALWAY CONVENT AND ITS OFF-SHOOTS

The first authenticated record of a nuns' monastery which survived the hardships of the seventeenth century is of the Galway foundation in 1643, which was confirmed by the general chapter of the Order in Rome in 1644.[13] The Dominican nuns lived through the vicissitudes of the post-Reformation religious persecution in Ireland and underwent a period of exile in Spain (1652–86); they suffered further persecution on their return to Galway city in the late eighteenth century, but a number of them moved from Galway to Channel Row in Dublin in 1717 and thence to Clontarf on the north side of the city in 1808. Though they met with difficulties in their own lives and in their schools in four centres in Ireland, these women did not cease in their efforts to carry on their apostolate of teaching. For periods of time their schools were closed in both Galway and Dublin; these closures are recorded in the narrative. In Galway they moved into new premises in Taylor's Hill on the west side of the city in 1846, and in Dublin five nuns, most of them elderly, consented to move to Cabra from Clontarf in 1819 as a condition of survival, and survive they did.[14] The Dominican mission of preaching the Gospel through educational service in schools and colleges, begun in Galway in 1644, and continued by communities of the Cabra Congregation which are directly or indirectly off-shoots of that original foundation, continues in Ireland, Portugal, South Africa, Louisiana, Argentina, Brazil and Bolivia, in the twenty-first century. The present study is confined to the educational work of the Dominican women in Ireland, 1820–1930. Sr Rose O'Neill's *A Rich Inheritance,* which relates the story of the Galway convent in Taylor's Hill from 1644–1944, is the first full account of the Dominican nuns' early history in Ireland. O'Neill's work has proved an indispensable source in researching this present book

THE CONTRIBUTION OF THE DOMINICAN LAY SISTERS

One group of Dominican women, the lay sisters, whose names seldom if ever appear in recounting the history of Dominican involvement in formal education in Ireland, cannot be omitted from the story. Lay sisters were taken for granted as having a distinct role to play in communities; their status was a legacy of the past. Practically every order of religious, men and women, in the Church had members whose ministry it was to care for the everyday routine of providing the services necessary for the general maintenance of the convent and schools. Their laborious and demanding work was erroneously considered by some to be a less significant calling than that of the choir sisters, so called because of their obligation to recite the divine office of the Church in choir. Choir sisters taught in the schools and were responsible for administration and leadership within the communities. The lay sisters' separation from the choir sisters, a system of class distinction inherited from another era, was in fact continued for far too long and was tolerated in a society which had a very different value system from that of the twenty-first century.

It is a painful and humbling admission of our short-comings to realize now how very unjust this outmoded system of distinction and separation was to a body of dedicated women without whose willing cooperation no school would have been viable, much less successful. The lay sisters were in many cases a tower of strength to the hard-pressed class-teaching sisters in times of distress, sickness or weariness. The children in the schools often confided in the sisters in the refectory, or dormitory, or in their daily contact with them around the school. The hidden, invaluable ministry of the lay sister in all Dominican schools and colleges is portrayed in the following paragraph written by a past pupil of Cabra boarding school:

> [t]here were two grades of nuns in the convent then, choir sisters and lay sisters. The lay sisters did the domestic work and the choir sisters did the teaching and administrative work. The idea of two kinds of sisters seems wrong to us now in a more democratic if less religious age but one of my best memories of Cabra is of the warmth and kindness and motherliness of those sisters to us small girls lonely for our Daddies and Mammies. Sister Laurence opened the hall door and in my memory she had all those qualities I have just mentioned.[15]

Every convent had not one, but many Sister Laurences. Whatever success may be claimed for Dominican education, it could never have been achieved without the dedication, help and commitment of our many lay sisters over the centuries. Their role in the successful running of the schools and colleges must be acknowledged with gratitude by those who were in full-time teaching in the schools and colleges and who depended on the collaboration of the lay sisters and their dedication to their vocation in the Order.

HISTORIOGRAPHICAL CONTEXT – WOMEN'S EDUCATIONAL ISSUES

The historiographical context of this study is seen as part of the nineteenth and early twentieth-century development of policies initially involving the British government and its political administrators in Ireland, not only in education but in politics and church–state relations. D.A. Kerr notes that there was a change in the Irish Catholic Church after 1800; there was, for one thing, an increase in the number of prosperous Catholic farmers who were the main support of the clergy. The rural community identified with the Catholic clergy who took an active part in the political life of the country – 'the men on horseback accompanying the priest as he led them to the polls'. Kerr adds, '[e]ducation at all levels remained a priority for the clergy'.[16]

The era of the Penal Laws left the Catholic bishops with a legacy of suspicion and fear of proselytism and the domination of the Catholic population through a state-controlled system of education. Following Catholic Emancipation (1829) and the Famine in Ireland (1847–49), Catholics were becoming more confident in their own ability to help themselves, by forming alliances and groups which would put forward the ordinary people's concerns, as distinct from the concerns of the ascendancy class which dominated politics in the time of Grattan's Parliament. The work of Daniel O'Connell, the Young Irelanders, and in later years, the Land League, the era of Parnellite politics, Sinn Féin and the Gaelic League, gave the people a sense of their own nationhood, with a cultural identity distinct from the ideas and ideals which came from Great Britain.

The appointment of Paul Cullen as Archbishop of Armagh in 1849 and later to the archbishopric of Dublin (1852), brought further change to the Irish Catholic Church. Emmet Larkin sums up the change in liturgical and popular devotional practices as a 'devotional revolution'.[17] In 1849 Cullen returned from Rome where he had been rector of the Irish College and where he had influence in Vatican circles; it was intended that Cullen would instigate further reforms in the practices of Irish Catholicism, and put an end to the real and perceived abuses which were reported to the authorities in Rome by Bishops O'Shaughnessy of Killaloe and Murphy of Raphoe. The Synod of Thurles (1850), called by Cullen, concerned itself with the proper administration of the sacraments, the regulation of the lives of the clergy, and the encouragement of the laity to practices of piety, which would instil in them a sense of veneration for the sacraments and a love of the beauty of ritual and a sense of mystery.

The Synod reforms were put into practice by means of parish missions and the introduction of devotional exercises which included the rosary, forty hours' adoration of the Blessed Sacrament, benediction of the Blessed Sacrament, devotion to the Sacred Heart, novenas and triduums, pilgrimages to holy wells and shrines, processions and retreats. Sodalities and confraternities were set up to encourage regular reception of the sacraments and instruction in the doctrines of the Catholic Church. Sacred music, hymn-singing, candles, ornamental vestments, the use of incense, the wearing of medals, all became widespread. Archbishop Daniel Murray of Dublin had earlier paved the way for Cullen's reforms and had already introduced many of the devotional practices associated with Cullen in his own life-time as archbishop. Larkin contends, however, that whatever measure of reform was achieved by the Catholic Church in Ireland in pre-Famine days was confined to the 'respectable' class of Catholics to which families such as the Cullens and their relatives the Mahers of Carlow belonged.[18] It should be noted in passing, that the Maher family mentioned here gave three Dominican nuns of that name to the order in Cabra in the nineteenth century, besides some Moran and McDonnell cousins.

The legacy of suspicion and fear from the days of the Penal Laws, already referred to, is palpable when one examines the reactions of some of the members of the Catholic hierarchy to the proposals for a state-aided system of national education. John McHale, Archbishop of Tuam (1791–1881), while initially allowing his schools to accept state aid, later withdrew and became one of the bishops most notably opposed to the establishment of the national schools. A careful watch was kept especially by Dr William Walsh, Archbishop of Dublin (1841–1921), on the implementation of the Intermediate Act of 1878, and the Catholic Church was keenly desirous of having a state-aided Catholic university. The bishops' main grievances were: restrictions on religious teaching and practices in national schools; the inadequacy of state grants in secondary schools; and inequality with non-Catholics in the provision of university education and teacher-training facilities. On behalf of the majority of the bishops, resolutions on these grievances were adopted. The three signatories to the resolutions, Drs Logue of Armagh, MacCormack of Galway, and Woodlock of Ardagh and Clonmacnoise, demanded of the government that,

> their Educational grievances, which have extended over 300 years, and which have been a constant, ever-growing source of bitter discontent, be at length redressed; and they appeal to all sections of Parliament, without distinction of political parties, to legislate promptly and in a just and generous spirit in this all-important matter.[19]

Emmet Larkin, in his books on the formation of modern Ireland as an independent state, offers the theory that the Catholic Church in Ireland through its hierarchy, and in conjunction with the nineteenth-century political leaders, came to an accommodation in the creation of that state.[20] Larkin writes,

> the Irish state could not perhaps have been made real and certainly not stable, before 1886 if the Irish Church had not been accommodated. If the Irish church, moreover, had not accepted the accommodation when it did, the character of the Irish state would have been a great deal different from what it eventually did become. ... When the Irish state finally emerged in 1921 as legal as it was real ... it could proceed with greater confidence to the rapid consolidation of the coup so recently made against the remnants of British rule in Ireland.[21]

The result of this accommodation was the strong influence that the Catholic bishops exerted over many aspects of Irish life. For more than half a century prior to 1921 the bishops helped to establish a system of state-aided primary and secondary schooling for Catholics which was favourably disposed towards the Church. They watched over the system and safe-guarded the Catholic Church's rights; that system survived throughout the nineteenth and twentieth centuries and, taking an over-all view, in its time served the country well. The writings of Caitríona Clear, Mary Cullen, Mary Daly, Maria Luddy and Margaret MacCurtain, twentieth-century pioneers in studies of women's history in Ireland, and especially in their recognition of the importance of the role played by women religious, have been mined for information about women's concerns from the mid-nineteenth century onwards. The demand for university eduation for women arose as one facet of the general demand for a Catholic university in

Dublin. The Dominicans were not alone in seeking university education for Catholic women; the Loreto and Ursuline nuns worked for this also and in this they all played their part in the campaign for women's rights in the educational field. It is intended that this book, besides forming a part of Dominican history, makes its own contribution to both the history of education in Ireland and to the history of women religious. The provision of educational services for women developed from the generally accepted early nineteenth-century norm of their education as good wives and mothers, to the era when women eventually won access to higher education. The logical outcome of that development meant that women thus educated could then take their place in the professions, including politics, academic life and the world of commerce.

SOURCE MATERIAL

Theses and diploma dissertations for master's degrees written on aspects of Dominican women's involvement in education are noted. Two studies of the education of the deaf in St Mary's Cabra have proved very helpful, especially Joseph Cunningham's 'Father John Burke C.M.' (1978), which researched Burke's development of language teaching methods in deaf education in the school in its earliest years.[22] Regina Duggan (1998) took 'Post-primary Education of Deaf Children' as her subject – a thesis which extended the research into the late twentieth-century developments in the education of the deaf.[23] While her thesis covers a period outside the scope of the present work, Duggan's research of the background to the thesis was very helpful. Finbar O'Driscoll and Elaine Barry dealt with the Dominican nuns' work for the provision of a college for the higher education of women. Both O'Driscoll's 'Dominican Convents in the Diocese of Dublin and their Contribution to the Higher Education of Women 1882–1924' (1982), and Barry's thesis, 'St. Mary's University College and the University Question for Women, 1893–1909' (1995), were confined to the work of the Dominicans in relation to university education.[24] Camilla Roche (1980), in her thesis 'Founded for the Future: the Educational Legacy of Mary Ward', while covering the educational work of Mary Ward (1585–1645) and its influence on the Loreto educational ethos, included a study of the Loreto nuns' contribution to education in Ireland in the years leading to and following the Intermediate Education (Ireland) Act 1878 and the consequent drive towards women's university education.[25]

An interesting aspect of the whole movement in women's higher education is the parallel, but not coordinated, campaigns for university education for women, in the nineteenth and early twentieth centuries run by the Ursulines in Cork, the Loreto nuns in St Stephen's Green and the Dominican nuns in Eccles Street. The Loreto nuns worked tirelessly for this aim, especially under the leadership of Mother Michael Corcoran (1846–1922). Edel M. Murphy (1999) has made a study of 'The Contribution of Dominican Sisters to Education in the Town of

Dún Laoghaire, Co. Dublin'.[26] Dominican post-primary provision in the North of Ireland 1870–1995 is covered by Geraldine Matthews in her M.Ed. dissertation.[27]

The primary sources used here are the general archives of the Congregation held in Cabra, which has a rich collection of papers, including correspondence relating to many aspects of the educational activities of the Dominicans in Ireland. It was fascinating to find there, among other valuable material, a register of all the students who passed through St Mary's University and High School, 1893–1911, numbering in excess of 700: a number which included both university students and secondary pupils. The local archives of Dominican Convent Cabra, the mother-house of the Congregation, and the convent archives in Siena Convent, Drogheda, provided a wealth of material in the research. Dominican College, Eccles Street, archives, now held in the new convent in 204 Griffith Avenue, Dublin and to which I was allowed frequent and generous access, is a treasure-trove of primary source material. Its papers deal with the work done for women's university education in Eccles Street, in Merrion Square, and for a short period in Muckross Park, Donnybrook.

I was fortunate in being able to gain access to archives outside the Dominican convents, which proved to be of great assistance in supplementing the information gleaned from the Dominican primary sources. The Dublin Diocesan Archives provided valuable material among the papers of the various archbishops who headed the archdiocese in the period 1820–1940. The archives of the Institute of the Blessed Virgin Mary (Loreto Sisters) in St Stephen's Green were of particular interest, since both Loreto and Dominican nuns were striving towards the goal of establishing a Catholic university college for women. The archives of the Society of the Sacred Heart in Mount Anville, Dublin, and those of St Louis Convent, Monaghan, helped to make some interesting comparisons between the schools of both those orders and the Dominicans' schools in the nineteenth and early twentieth centuries.

My thanks are also due to the Vincentian Fathers, whose archives in Raheny helped me to flesh out the connection between the Vincentian priests and the Cabra community in the foundation of St Mary's School for the Deaf. A very important section of the primary sources for St Dominic's Training College was found in the archives of Cambridge University Library and King's College Archives, Cambridge. This collection has never, to my knowledge, been used before in any study of the Irish Dominicans' work. I am grateful for being allowed access to both these institutions and to John Power, Librarian, for allowing me access to archival materials in Mary Immaculate Training College, Limerick; Sr Loreto O'Connor's account of the Limerick college, *Passing on the Torch*, was also used to make a comparative study with St Mary's Training College, Belfast. Table 1 sets out the location of all the Dominican schools and colleges in Ireland from 1820–1930.

Location of School	Poor School (Pre-Stanley)	National School (Post-Stanley)	Girls' Junior School (including some boys)	Girls' Secondary Day School	Girls' Secondary Boarding School	Special School for the deaf	Boys' Preparatory Boarding School	Boys' Preparatory Day School	Commercial College	Third level University (U) and Teacher Training (TT)
Taylor's Hill, Galway	Unknown c.18th C	1848	1859	1858	1859					
St Mary's, Cabra, Dublin	1820	1841/1846	c.1835	c.1933	1835	1847				
Siena, Drogheda, Co. Louth	c.1722	1852		1840	1840					
Sion Hill, Blackrock, Dublin	1860 + Industrial Class 1865		1840 + Boys	1840	1840					1930 TT
88 Lr Mount St, Dublin				1836	1836					
34, Usher's Quay, Dublin				1842						
Kingstown/ Dun Laoghaire	1847	1848 + Industrial Class	c.1850	1850	1850					
Wicklow Town		1870 + Industrial Class	1870	1870	1870		1887			
Falls Road, Belfast		1871	1870	1870	1870					1900 TT
19 Eccles St, Dublin			1882	1882	1882			1898	1930	1884 U 1909 TT
28 Merrion Sq., Dublin				1893						1893 U
Muckross Park, Dublin			1900	1900						1900 U
Sutton, Dublin			1912 + Boys	1912	1912					
Portstewart, Co. Derry			1917	1917	1917					
Scoil Chaitriona, Eccles St, Dublin				1928	1928					
Fortwilliam Park, Belfast			1930	1930					1930	

NOTES

1. *Constitution of Irish Dominican Sisters, Cabra* (Private publication, 1947), Constitution 1, p.26.
2. Thomas Aquinas, *Questiones Disputate de Veritate*, Vol. II, translated J.V. McGlynn (Chicago 1952), p. 85.
3. B. Kearns, *The Dominican Approach to Education* (Unpublished pamphlet, OPE. n.d.).
4. New Testament, John, 14: 6.
5. Anon, 'The Dominicans of Newbridge', *Newbridge Quarterly, Christmas 1947* (Newbridge College, 1947), p.2.
6. J. Heffernan, *Newbridge College Annual* (Newbridge, 2002), p.34 and following.
7. Ibid., p.36.
8. *Newbridge College Magazine,* Summer 1900, p.91.
9. J. O'Heyne, *The Irish Dominicans of the Seventeenth Century.* First published in Latin as *Epilogus Chronologicus* (Louvain: 1706), reprinted with English translation and appendix by Ambrose Coleman OP, (Dundalk: Wm. Tempest, 1902), cited as *The Irish Domincans.*
10. T. de Burgo, *Hibernia Dominicana, sive Historia Provinciae Hiberniae Ordinis Praedicatorum* (Cologne: Mettermich Press, 1762, supplement, Cologne, 1772, reprinted, Farnborough, 1970).
11. T.S. O'Flynn, *The Irish Dominicans 1536–1641* (Dublin: Four Courts Press, 1993), p.xiii.
12. H. Fenning, *The Irish Dominican Province, 1698–1797* (Dublin: Dominican Publications, 1990), pp.152–4 and 355–7.
13. R. O'Neill, *A Rich Inheritance: Galway Dominican Nuns, 1644–1994* (Galway: Dominican Sisters, published privately, 1994), p.9. (Cited hereafter as O'Neill, *A Rich Inheritance*).
14. For an account of the Dominican nuns in Dublin prior to 1820, see M.M. Kealy, 'The Dominican Nuns of Channel Row, 1717–1820' (unpublished MA dissertation, Lancaster University, 1998), cited henceforth as 'Nuns of Channel Row'.
15. M.F. Lucey, (née Roynane), 'School Days in Cabra Recalled 1936–1940', in *Dominican Sisters, Cabra, 1819–1994; Celebrating 175 Years* (Cabra: Dominican Convent, private publication, 1994), pp.23–6 (23).
16. D.A. Kerr, 'The Catholic Church in Ireland', *Ireland after the Union.* Proceedings of the second joint-meeting of the Royal Irish Academy and the British Academy, London, 1986 (Oxford : Oxford University Press, 1986), p.42.
17. Emmet Larkin, 'The Devotional Revolution in Ireland 1850–75', *American Historical Review* 77 (1972), pp.626–52.
18. Ibid., p.639.
19. Archbishop of Dublin, [William Walsh], *Statement of Cheif Grievances of Irish Catholics in the Matter of Education, Primary, Secondary, and University* (Dublin: Browne & Nolan, 1890), pp.345–8.
20. Emmet Larkin, *The Roman Catholic Church and the Creation of the Modern Irish State, 1878–1886* (Philadelphia, PA: The American Philosophical Society, 1975), *passim.* Larkin, *The Roman Catholic Church in Ireland and the Fall of Parnell, 1888–1891'* (Raleigh, NC: University of North Carolina Press, 1979), *passim.*
21. Larkin, *The Roman Catholic Church and the Creation of the Modern Irish State, 1878–1885* pp.xxi, xxii.
22. J. Cunningham, 'Father John Burke, C.M. 1822–1894' (Unpublished dissertation submitted for Diploma for Teachers of the Deaf, University College, Dublin, 1978).
23. R. Duggan, 'Evaluation of the Senior Cycle Curriculum and its effectiveness in the Preparation of Deaf Students for Life after School' (Unpublished M.Ed. thesis, University College, Dublin, 1998).

24. F. O'Driscoll, 'Dominican Convents in the Diocese of Dublin and their Contribution to the Higher Education of Women 1882–1924 (Unpublished M.Ed. dissertation, Trinity College, University of Dublin, 1982). E. Barry, 'St Mary's University College and the University Question for Women 1893–1909' (Unpublished MA thesis, University College Dublin, 1995).
25. C. Roche, 'Founded for the Future; The educational legacy of Mary Ward' (Unpublished M.Ed. dissertation, Maynooth College, 1980).
26. E. Murphy, 'The Contribution of Dominican Sisters to Education in the Town of Dún Laoghaire, Co. Dublin' (Unpublished M. Ed. thesis, University College, Dublin, 1999).
27. G.M. Matthews, 'Dominican Post-Primary Education in the North of Ireland 1870–1995' (Unpublished M.Ed. dissertation, University of Ulster, Jordanstown, Northern Ireland, 1996).

1

Primary Education

The early history of the Dominican nuns of Cabra in Dublin and their involvement in education must be placed in the context of the political, social and religious history of nineteenth-century Ireland and, in particular, to the Catholic bishops' attitude to the state's involvement in the control of schools. The Catholic Church in Ireland was emerging from centuries of persecution, which was particularly virulent in the eighteenth century. The passing of the Penal Laws relating to the practice of their faith bore heavily on the Catholic population, denying their property rights and the right to have a Catholic education for their children. The general tenor of the laws relating to education was to deny schooling to Catholics, or if they were allowed access to schooling, it was in return for renouncing their religion, acknowledging the Established Church as the one true church, and attending its services on Sundays.[1] To overcome this legislation it was not uncommon for the children of better-off Catholic families, boys in particular, to be smuggled out of the country to schools and colleges in France, Spain and Belgium. Though many of these boys were in training for the priesthood, not all proceeded to ordination and some of these young men returned to Ireland to take up positions as professional laymen. However, for the majority of the population, a specifically Catholic education was not available; though at the beginning of the nineteenth century, as Dowling observes, there was a 'great number of small independent pay-schools in towns up and down the country run by men who probably sought wider opportunities for their talents'.[2]

From the late eighteenth century onwards, legislation was progressively introduced to rescind the Penal Laws and to alleviate the difficulties which Catholics had in providing education for their children. In 1782 the independent Irish Parliament, 'Grattan's Parliament', repealed the Acts under which Catholic teachers were subject to heavy penalties if they engaged in school teaching. The 1782 Acts allowed Catholics to teach at school, albeit subject to certain rigorous conditions.[3] The teachers were obliged to swear an oath of allegiance to the crown, were forbidden to teach Protestant pupils, or teach in Protestant schools and, until further legislation in 1792, they were obliged to take out licences to teach from the bishops of the Established Church of the dioceses in which they worked.[4]

Meanwhile, numbers of Catholics in eighteenth-century Ireland were threatened by a systematic campaign of proselytization. The Irish Protestant charity school movement began early in the century; the schools founded under that umbrella were in some instances financed by voluntary subscriptions, and religious instruction in them was in the hands of the various Protestant denominations only. In 1724 George I nominated Hugh Boulter (1672–1742) to the primacy of the Established Church as Archbishop of Armagh. Gilbert, his biographer, sums up Boulter's stated policy as that of securing what he styled, "'a good footing", for "the English interest" in Ireland ... to repress the efforts of the Protestants in Ireland towards constitutional independence and to leave the Roman Catholics subjected to penal legislation'.[5] Boulter went on to found a society for 'instructing and converting the younger generation' of Catholics and in 1730 addressed '[a] humble proposal for obtaining his Majesty's Royal Charter to incorporate a society for promoting Christian knowledge among the poor natives of the kingdom of Ireland'. In a lengthy petition to the crown Boulter repeated a traditional jibe about the ignorant Irish; it is important to quote Boulter at some length. He wrote:

> [i]n many parts of the Kingdom there are many Tracts of Mountainy and Coarse Lands ... almost universally Inhabited by Papists ... The Generality of the Popish Natives appear to have very little sense or Knowledge of Religion, but what they implicitly take from their Clergy ... and are thereby kept not only in gross ignorance, but in great Disaffection to your Sacred Majesty and Government. Among the ways proper to be taken for converting and civilising these poor deluded people, ... one of the most necessary, and without which all others are like to prove ineffectual, has always been thought to be that a sufficient number of English Protestants Schools be erected and established, wherein the children of the Irish natives might be instructed in the English tongue, and the fundamental principles of True Religion, to both of which they are generally great strangers.[6]

Boulter's derogatory language serves to strengthen the obvious bias against Catholics and is evidence of his intention of using the schools for proselytizing the pupils. His petition for a royal charter was granted in 1733. The official name given to his society was 'The Incorporated Society for Promoting English Protestant Schools in Ireland (1733)'.[7] The schools were funded by a royal bounty of £1,000 a year, which was later increased; unofficially, they were known as charter schools. Other Protestant groups which depended on charitable subscriptions included the Association for Discountenancing Vice and Promoting the Knowledge and Practice of the Christian Religion (1792) and The Society for Promoting the Education of the Poor in Ireland (1786). Known from its location as the Kildare Place Society, this latter society was non-denominational, at least throughout its early years. In contrast to the spirit of

Hugh Boulter's earlier and markedly anti-Catholic 'humble proposal', some Dublin citizens were responsible for founding the Society; among the founding members were Samuel Bewley, a merchant, William Guinness of the brewing family, and John David La Touche of the banking family. In their founding meeting, a number of resolutions were passed reflecting the values of the Enlightenment, among which was one that summarized the society's conciliatory philosophy: 'that for the accomplishment of the great work of educating the Irish poor, schools should be built upon the most liberal principles, and should be divested of all sectarian distinctions in Christianity'.[8]

In the Kildare Place schools the Bible was read without note or comment, in contrast with the practice in commitedly Protestant schools, where the interpretation of biblical texts followed that of the Established Church. Less than a century later, the question of neutral readings of Scripture was to confront Irish Catholic educationalists. In 1870 the Commission of Irish Education Inquiry examined the Catholic bishops, Murray of Dublin, Kelly of Tuam, and Doyle of Kildare and Leighlin, on the subject of reading the Bible without note or comment. Dr Murray testified that in some instances the Kildare Place Society acted 'with less danger than others', but that of late the Society had connected with other societies which were less impartial. Dr Doyle of Kildare and Leighlin gave the format of the first commandment as an example of biblical inter-pretation that was objectionable to Catholics. According to the Church of Ireland this commandment is divided into two sections: 'I am the Lord thy God who brought you out of the land of Egypt, out of the house of bondage', and, 'Thou shalt not make any image of anything in heaven, or upon the earth, or in the waters', and they omit what should follow: *'to adore and worship'*. The Authorised Version places a full stop after the commandment not to make images, so that, according to the doctrine of the Established Church, it appears that God has expressly prohibited the making of all statues and images and pictures, for whatever purpose or end. Dr Doyle explained that in Catholic doctrine that is not the intent of God's commandment. The meaning of it is this: that we shall not make to ourselves any graven thing or image to bow down before it and worship it. The omission of the italicized words gives, in the Catholic view, a false interpretation.[9]

For some years the Kildare Place Society was supported by Protestants and by some Catholics, but it ceased to hold its neutral position in regard to proselytizing and its schools came eventually to be seen by the majority of Catholics as yet another proselytizing agent. Dowling describes the steps by which these schools progressively alienated Catholics:

> [t]he Bible was being interpreted after his own fashion by any teacher who wished to do so, and in some instances was being used by the teachers as a weapon against the Catholic faith; books of a controversial nature were introduced and the Kildare Place Society was subsidising other bodies, such as the London Hibernian Society and the Baptist Society, which were

well known to be engaged in proselytism. Catholics therefore withdrew their support ... and appealed to parliament to provide a system of education such as would not interfere with their beliefs.[10]

After the Act of Union between Great Britain and Ireland in 1801 and during the following thirty years, the government initiated a series of enquiries into the condition of education in Ireland with a view to establishing a system of national education which would be acceptable to both Protestants and Catholics. Akenson recounts the creation of a national educational structure and the stresses to which it was subjected:

> [a]ny attempt to uncover the administrative outline of the national system of education [in Ireland] in its first twenty years is necessarily a confusing job. During this period the bureaucracy grew into an intricate assemblage of professional administrators. ... Without an understanding of the administrative configuration of the national system of education, it is impossible to understand the system's subsequent history, especially the twisting of the system by religious groups. ... The national system was created at a time in which the bureaucratic pattern of the entire British civil service was beginning to undergo reform and expansion.[11]

Clearly, official views concentrated on the advisability of providing a suitable and worthwhile system for the schooling of children, but the national system of education which eventually evolved in Ireland had its more distant origins in a plan introduced by the then Chief Secretary for Ireland, Thomas Orde. In 1787, Orde's plan for education was introduced into the pre-Union Irish Parliament, but was never implemented. Nevertheless, once the question of a national plan for education had been raised in this way by Orde, it was followed up by a number of government enquires during the first thirty years of the nineteenth century. Part of the difficulty in having a clear idea of the sequence of events is demonstrated by the sheer number of commissions on education that were set up by the lords lieutenant, and the subsequent numerous reports that were issued between 1806 and 1828. Lack of clarity is compounded by their terminology – key terms being used interchangeably and inaccurately.[12]

GOVERNMENT REPORTS

Between 1806 and 1812, the government set up a commission of enquiry to investigate the condition of education in Ireland. Fourteen reports were issued by this body between 1809 and 1812. While the first thirteen reports dealt with the existing charitable and foundation schools – royal, diocesan, charter, parish and 'classical' (those schools in which Latin and Greek were taught were known as classical schools), the fourteenth report was of great importance for its influence on Irish educational practice during the nineteenth century. The commission concluded that a permanent body of education commissioners should be appointed, which, when established, was often referred to as the 'board of education'; this 'board of education' was to administer parliamentary grants, create new schools where needed and have these schools under its control. This was a signal for state intervention in education in Ireland and a requirement for the provision of elementary education for the poor. Teacher-training institutions would be necessary if the state were to provide an efficient system of education. From the Catholic perspective, the most far-reaching and crucial statement made by the commission was:

> we are encouraged ... to hope, that if a scheme for such improvement [of schools in Ireland] were ... carefully executed it would meet with very general success. ... We conceive this to be of essential importance in any new establishment for the education of the lower classes in Ireland, and we venture to express our unanimous opinion, that no such plan, however wisely and unexceptionably contrived in other respects, can be carried into effectual execution in the country, unless it be explicitly avowed, and clearly understood, as its leading principle, that no attempt shall be made to influence or disturb the peculiar religious tenets of any sect or description of Christians.[13]

The board established in 1813 as a result of the commissioners' recommendations of the previous year did not entirely fulfil the hopes of Catholics: for one thing, it dealt exclusively with the existing endowed schools, which catered mainly for the middle class. The fourteenth report of 1812 had recommended the creation of a national system of education for the poor, but this was not implemented. Furthermore, a national system of education in Ireland, if it were to be truly representative, needed the approval of the Roman Catholic clergy and laity.

In response to Catholic demands, lay and clerical, a Royal Commission on Irish education was appointed in 1824. It published nine reports. In the second of these, apart from the Kildare Place Society schools, nine other groups of schools were listed that were regarded as suspect by Catholics. 'It is evident', the Commissioners reported, 'that the Objects and Proceedings of the Society have given rise to a very natural Persuasion in the minds of the Roman Catholics that its members are actuated by a Spirit of Hostility to their Church'.[14]

The Catholic Archbishop of Dublin, Dr Daniel Murray, gave evidence before this commission, making two crucial statements which had repercussions among some other members of the hierarchy later on. The first was to the effect that he had no objection to 'common' literary (that is, non-religious) instruction being received by the Catholic pupils from Protestant teachers. Secondly, the archbishop did not object to the provision of religious instruction by Catholic teachers who were approved by their bishops.

The Commission also found that there were numerous popular schools in Ireland, not all Catholic in orientation, but not subject to any control or inspection. These schools were 'popular' in so far as they were supported by the parents who sent their children to them and were owned by the schoolmasters (or schoolmistresses) who taught in them.[15] They included the remaining famous, illegal and informal 'hedge schools', taught by travelling teachers. Other schools were 'pay schools', set up in some towns for the education of children whose parents did not want either the education offered in the charity schools or in those of the Kildare Place Society. The authors of the report saw these irregularities as sufficient cause for state intervention and regulation. J.L. Foster was one of the five commissioners appointed by the crown in 1824. He had no Catholic sympathies and had been elected to parliament for County Louth on the basis of his opposition to Catholic claims.[16] In a letter to the board, Foster set the scene for some aspects of Irish education with its

> [i]tinerant schoolmasters ... who appear to prevail in the south and west in such considerable numbers. Men who ... set up schools during the summer months in temporary hovels, or transfer the scene of their instructions once or twice a week from cabin to cabin ... pursuing this system during the fine weather and disappearing regularly ... at the commencement of winter. ... Hardly any other country is so amply provided with the means of education but when we take into consideration, not merely the quantity, but the quality of these means [of education], the extent [of the disorder] becomes an additional and imperious reason for interference and alteration.[17]

RECOMMENDATIONS OF THE SELECT COMMITTEE: 1828

Following the reports of previous Commissioners of Irish Education in 1807–12 and 1825–27, the new Select Committee in 1828 favoured establishing a system of education in Ireland in which no attempt should be made to influence or disturb the religious beliefs of any one denomination. The Select Committee set out six main recommendations:

1. Literary instruction should be given in common to Catholics and Protestants in the same school or class. This was to be termed 'united education'.[18]
2. It was made clear that there should be facilities for religious instruction to be given by clergy of each denomination.
3. Parliament was to provide grants for education to supplement local contributions and help to build and support primary schools.
4. A Board of Commissioners was to be appointed by the government; the Board would distribute the grants.

5. The teachers' qualifications were to be tested by examination in a model school under government control.
6. There would be a system of inspection under the aegis of the Board of Education.[19]

The reaction of the Catholic clergy to these recommendations was mixed. At the beginning of the nineteenth century the Irish Catholic clergy were, according to one commentator, 'timid and conservative ... it was not until after 1820 that the priest cast off altogether the habitual stoop which had so long been the disgraceful distinctive of his order'.[20] This, clearly, is a generalization: the evidence is that the members of the Catholic hierarchy were certainly not 'timid' in asserting their claims and, in particular, in voicing their reaction to the efforts of the government to establish state-financed primary schools in Ireland. The Catholic bishops' reactions to educational initiatives by the government is a continuous theme in the history of Irish education in the nineteenth century. It is not possible to evaluate how the system worked without examining the political decisions made which affected both the organization and financing of education and the controversial issues of the time.

The Catholic bishops in Ireland were very well aware of, and alert to, anything which might militate against the Catholic education of youth. Dr Murray's statements to the Commission of 1824 seemed to open a new way for Catholics to participate in 'combined', 'mixed' or 'united', education, that is Protestants and Catholics being educated together in secular subjects but having separate religious instruction given by approved persons of the children's own faith. However, not all Murray's colleagues in the hierarchy shared his liberal views on that score. The Archbishop of Dublin was supported by some of the other Catholic bishops, particularly by Archbishop William Crolly of Armagh and Bishop John Doyle of Kildare and Leighlin, while a minority, led by Archbishop John McHale of Tuam, and Bishop William O'Higgins of Ardagh and Clonmacnoise, were very much opposed to allowing the state to organize or finance schools for Catholics. McHale and O'Higgins had a great distrust of government interference in the running of the schools, and especially so if the schools were to be 'mixed' in the sense outlined above. In contrast, though given certain religious safeguards, Bishop Doyle took the view that if children of differing religious persuasions were to live together in harmony as adults, they should be educated together as children. This argument about mixed education continues in educational circles in Ireland, particularly in Northern Ireland, to the present time.

ARCHBISHOP MCHALE'S REACTION TO THE SELECT COMMITTEE

Archbishop McHale's attitude was at first favourable to accepting the 1828 proposals, but in time he became vehemently opposed to combined education.

Events in his archdiocese account for his change of mind. Unlike Murray, Crolly and Doyle, McHale and O'Higgins lived in dioceses which were impoverished, giving both bishops reason to be suspicious of the real purpose of any government scheme. Two examples of proselytism supported by financial inducements in McHale's archdiocese of Tuam will show why the archbishop was so suspicious of any government scheme, which he believed would be used in a biased manner, and which caused his change of mind. These experiences, among others, made him perhaps more cautious than those other bishops towards government initiatives. The first incident occurred in the 1830s, in Slievemore, a small village on Achill Island. Edward Nangle, a clerical member of the Irish Church Mission Society, set up an orphanage, a hospital, schools, a church, a hotel and a printing press. It is true that employment was generated by these enterprises, but Edward Nangle made many converts to Protestantism from among the poor Catholics of the village and surrounding countryside.[21] In the same archdiocese, the Irish Church Mission Society, a Protestant evangelizing body, was set up in the 1840s and actively encouraged the people to convert to the Protestant Church.

PROSELYTIZING IN CO. MAYO

A more serious form of intimidation and manipulation occurred in Tourmakeady, a poor district on the shores of Lough Mask in Co. Mayo, where there was only one Catholic school. The Plunket family came to the area of Tourmakeady in 1831. In 1839 Thomas Plunket was appointed Protestant Archbishop of Tuam and founded two Protestant schools on his own estate in the area. Plunket insisted the Catholic tenants attended these schools. Positive inducements in the form of food and money were offered in return for the tenants' compliance with Dr Plunket's wishes, otherwise they were threatened with eviction. In this campaign, Plunket was helped by his sister Catherine, who was known locally as 'Cáit an Bhracháin', or 'Stirabout Kate', from her custom of giving food, particularly porridge, to the poor, as an inducement to them to convert to Protestantism.[22] This particular incident serves to illustrate a form of intense pressure used to induce poor people to convert to Protestantism. Such practices were widespread in many parts of the country, especially during the Famine period (1845–50). The Tourmakeady and Slievemore experiences provoked great anger in McHale because he, in contrast to Murray, Doyle and Crolly, belonged to a younger generation of clergy who were deeply influenced by the cause of Irish nationalism. As Connolly puts it, the 'old-fashioned deference to [the] state by men like Murray and Crolly was already being superseded ... by a more combative and independent outlook'.[23]

STANLEY'S EDUCATION BILL 1831

Following Catholic Emancipation in 1829, expectations rose with regard to the provision of schools funded by government grants for education. In 1831 the House of Commons voted £30,000 for primary education in Ireland; at the same time a sum of £30,000 was withdrawn from the Kildare Place Society, a tacit admission by the government that the Society was not in fact acting in a neutral manner towards the teaching of religion in their schools. The Chief Secretary for Ireland, Lord Edward Stanley (later Earl of Derby), was promoted to cabinet and in October 1831 set out a scheme based on the 1828 Select Committee's recommendations. Stanley's instructions for implementing these guidelines were written in the form of a letter to the Duke of Leinster, who had been suggested as a possible president of the Board of Commissioners of Education. Stanley set up the Board by a Bill introduced into parliament in 1831.[24] Political circumstances at the time made it difficult for Stanley to have a statute passed setting up the Board: Akenson writes, '[o]f course parliament could dictate the conditions under which the money it granted was spent, but in practice the House of Commons could give little of its time to discussing Irish education'.[25] In theory, the prime minister and parliament of the United Kingdom were the lawful legislators for Ireland. However, in this case, as has been argued by Akenson, 'parliament actually had little influence on Irish national education during the early years of its development'.[26]

Stanley as chief secretary was, in theory, Lord Lieutenant Anglesey's assistant, but in fact, was an equal partner with him. The national education system was created therefore not by an act of parliament, but by the instructions of an Irish chief secretary. As Akenson indicates also from the evidence of another letter, this time from Lord Anglesey to Lord Stanley, we can surmise that setting up a state-funded educational system for all denominations in Ireland was fraught with anxieties about the reaction to any such scheme:

> [i]t is probable that the duke [of Leinster] would not very often attend but his name would be very useful and at once stop any jealousy that might be between the 2 churches by naming Whately [the Protestant Archbishop of Dublin] as president, altho' he would usually officiate as such.[27]

It is evident that there was connivance between Stanley and Whately to control the Board of Commissioners, leaving Stanley's education system subject to influences which were outside the control of the government. Whately's role as a 'stand-in' president for the Duke of Leinster could not have been reassuring for Catholics. In later years, Archbishop William Walsh of Dublin quoted excerpts from Whately's diary which bear out this conjecture. Whately made his opinion clear:

I believe ... that if we give up mixed education, as carried out in the system of the National Education Board, we give up the only hope of weaning the Irish from the abuses of Popery. But I cannot venture openly to profess this opinion. I cannot openly support the Education Board as an instrument of conversion. I have to fight its battles with one hand, and that my best, tied behind me.[28]

Whatley's 'opinion' echoes Boulter's outburst of 1730 and confirms the fixed purpose of influential Established Church bishops of weaning the Irish from the abuses of Popery.

Stanley's guidelines were far-seeing even by today's standards, in suggesting that no church would have direct control over the schools; that was true in theory, but Whately's diary revealed that there was pressure being brought to bear on the Catholic members and he claimed that the national education 'is gradually undermining the vast fabric of the Irish Roman Catholic Church'.[29] The first managing Board would have a majority of non-Catholics; the two Catholic members were Archbishop Murray of Dublin and Mr Anthony Blake. Blake was the treasury remembrancer – an exchequer official responsible for collecting debts due to the crown – and the first Roman Catholic to be appointed to a British government commission of inquiry.[30] It is worth reflecting that at the time, Catholics looked on some aspects of the Stanley system with disfavour, but they also knew that some system of education was a real need in Ireland and that they themselves could not provide any satisfactory scheme without financial aid from the government. According to the Jesuit historian P.C. Barry, most of the Catholic bishops were willing to accept the Stanley system, 'reassured especially by the guarantee [given by Chief Secretary Stanley] that proselytism would not be tolerated'. In the case of the Catholic bishops, pragmatism won the day and the National System 'became a help rather than a hindrance to the Church'.[31]

Given the acceptance of Stanley's Education Bill by the majority of the Catholic bishops, it is not surprising that the greatest adverse reaction came initially from the two main Protestant denominations, the Established Church in Ireland and the Presbyterians of Ulster. The Established Church refused to join the Stanley scheme but set up its own schools; it did not want to share control of education, and some of its members proposed that the Established Church should have sole control. The Presbyterians for their part did not want to share control of it with the commissioners; one of their objections was that men of all denominations were included in the membership of the Board of Commissioners. Both the Established Church and the Presbyterians feared the influence of the Roman Catholics. An anonymous commentary on Lord Stanley's letter instructing the Board of Education, *The Christian Examiner and Church of Ireland Magazine*, stated that the Anglicans objected to the use of the schools 'for the purpose of the teaching of peculiar dogmas, superstitious rites, blasphemous fables, and all the errors of popery'. They further contended that 'the system ... is a conspiracy ... to keep the light of God's word from ever shining on the Roman Catholic child'.[32] With such antagonism between the religious denominations, it is surprising that Stanley's Education Bill enjoyed the success it did in the long term.

Archbishop William Walsh (1841–1921), Dr Murray's successor, and his fellow bishops strongly objected to the system of training given in the Model Schools;[33] it was a 'mixed' system, Protestants and Catholics together, with no training given in the teaching of religion.[34] The bishops would also have liked more freedom to have religious emblems and images displayed in the children's classrooms and the time of prayer in the schools less restricted. However, they saw the possibility of using the system to their own advantage and the three bishops, Murray of Dublin, Doyle of Kildare and Leighlin, and Crolly of Armagh, all accepted the scheme, with reservations, from the beginning and encouraged their clergy to set up grant-aided schools in their parishes. Archbishop McHale of Tuam – true to form – was suspicious of the scheme from the outset, though he did allow some schools to be established in his diocese. However, from 1838 onwards he again vehemently opposed the system, and severed the connection between the schools in his diocese and the government system of education. This outcome is to be expected given McHale's instinctive distrust of the system; Ulick Bourke notes that McHale regarded the national system of education 'as a vast scheme for proselytizing'.[35] McHale could be forgiven for this, taking into account the comments of Archbishop Whately already cited, together with further comments by him, reported in *The Packet News*, a newspaper of the time: 'Popery in Ireland', Whately had written, 'is a mixture of Foreign Politics and False Religion ... we must prevent them from indoctrinating the minds of our people with the former'.[36] The dispute between the two archbishops was reported to Rome; in 1841 the Holy See eventually settled that each bishop should decide on the best course of action in schooling in his own diocese. At that time in Ireland, the atmosphere regarding the Stanley scheme was fraught with fears and suspicions on all sides. Again, as Costello emphasizes,

> McHale regarded the whole organization as an insidious method of prose-
> lytism, and ... the powers of the Commissioners ... as an infringement of
> the authority of the bishops. The Protestants were sincerely shocked by
> [the system's] virtual exclusion of the Bible from the curriculum.[37]

The reactions of Whately, Murray and McHale were but symptomatic of those fears and suspicions.

To sum up the success of the Stanley system: it may be held that the National Schools system in Ireland underwent in time such modifications that, having begun as a non-denominational system of primary education, it in fact became denominational. Demographic and practical reasons dictated that, in the main, Catholics attended only schools managed by local parish priests, while children of the Protestant denominations attended schools managed by their own clergy or church boards of management. Stanley's National School system eventually became acceptable to all the churches and continued in its essential form until well into the twentieth century. The religious teaching orders, including the Dominicans, were, for the most part, influenced and encouraged by the bishops to accept and work the system to the advantage of the Catholic families. In the next section of this chapter the history of the Dominican poor schools in the pre-Stanley era is recorded and discussed.

DOMINICAN PRIMARY EDUCATION

(a) Pre-Stanley connection: the Poor Schools

In the years following the introduction of the Stanley Scheme, Dominican nuns in Ireland were managers of six primary schools under state control. Table 2 sets out the convents in which these schools were located and indicates those which had been 'poor schools' prior to 1831. The number of these schools is small relative to the nuns' over-all involvement in education at all levels. These six schools – Taylor's Hill, Galway, Siena Convent Drogheda, St Mary's Convent, Cabra, Dublin, Kingstown, Wicklow and Falls Road, Belfast – were not the only primary educational establishments provided by the Dominicans. Attached to practically all their convents were private, fee-paying, primary schools. These private schools catered for those parents who wanted what was considered a more exclusive education for their children. Dominicans referred to their private primary schools as 'junior schools' and this term is used throughout the book in reference to them. In this section of the chapter, there is a brief account of the place played by the Dominican Poor Schools prior to their changing to the Stanley Scheme. Following this there is a combined account of the schools under Stanley and of the Dominican private junior schools. Finally, St Mary's (primary) School for the Deaf in Cabra is a uniquely successful initiative by the Dominicans which called for a very special commitment on the part of the community. St Mary's School for the Deaf is treated of at the end of the chapter.

As has been shown, the poor schools run by some charitable groups of lay people and religious, both before and after Stanley in 1831 in Ireland, were begun because of the obvious lack of basic education for poor Catholics. The schools managed by the various Protestant bodies were not acceptable to the parents of Catholic families, nor had the poor access to the schools that charged a fee for tuition. In the case of the three Dominican poor schools which were begun in Galway at an unknown date in the eighteenth century and two others, one in Drogheda, Co. Louth (c. 1722) and one in Cabra, Dublin (1820), we may assume that the nuns' motivation for their beginning was a desire to provide a Catholic education for the poor girls in their localities and to teach them the rudiments of literacy and numeracy, together with some practical skills which might help them to earn a living. In their convent in Galway, in Kirwan's Lane (which later extended into Cross Street), the nuns conducted a school for the poor in the eighteenth century, but in 1815,

Table 2. Primary schools under Dominican management 1722–1930

Location of School	Poor School (Pre-Stanley)	National School (Post-Stanley)	Girls' Junior School (including some boys)
Taylor's Hill, Galway	Unknown date 18th C	1848	1859
St Mary's, Cabra, Dublin	1820–41 and 1858–83	1841–58 and 1883	c.1835 Boys' Prep. School; 1908
Siena, Drogheda, Co. Louth	c.1722	1852	Date unknown
Sion Hill, Blackrock, Dublin	1860 + Industrial Class 1865		1840 + Boys in 1865
88 Lr Mount St, Dublin			1837
34, Usher's Quay, Dublin			1842/3–1867
Kingstown/ Dun Laoghaire	1847	1848 + Industrial Class	c.1850
Wicklow Town		1870 + Industrial Class	1870
Falls Road, Belfast		1871	1870
19 Eccles St, Dublin			1882 + Boys
28 Merrion Sq., Dublin			1893 + Boys
Muckross Park, Dublin			1900 + Boys
Sutton, Dublin			1912 + Boys
Portstewart, Co. Derry			1917
Scoil Chaitriona, Eccles St, Dublin			
Fortwilliam Park, Belfast			1930

[t]he last warden of Galway, the Dominican, Dr Edmund French, invited the Presentation Sisters to Galway to take over a school run by the pious ladies in Kirwan's Lane. He wished to ensure continuity of this work for the poor. The Dominican school was still in existence in 1817, but must have been relinquished after this date.[38]

No record of the running of the school is extant. By the beginning of the nineteenth century the premises there had become dilapidated and unsuitable for use as a school. Rose O'Neill, in her account, gives as a reason for the closure of the poor school the scarcity of recruits to the religious life: in 1800 there were only eight nuns in the community.[39] The Dominicans left the Cross Street convent in 1845 and moved to their present location in Taylor's Hill on the west side of the city. Here they began another poor school for the children of the families fleeing from the effects of the Famine in Connemara, who were coming into the city in search of food and shelter. The nuns began the school to prepare the children for the reception of the sacraments and they also taught the skills of knitting and sewing. The Taylor's Hill poor school went 'into connection' with the Commissioners' Board of Education in November 1848.

The second Dominican convent poor school was situated in Drogheda, Co. Louth. Siena Convent, as it is called, is an eighteenth-century re-foundation of an older pre-Cromwellian Dominican convent. Catherine Plunkett was one of those nuns, who, with her blood sister Mary, and Mary Bellew the foundress of Channel Row Convent in Dublin, left the Galway community in 1717. Having lived in Belgium for five years, Catherine was requested by the Irish Dominican provincial, Stephen MacEgan, to re-found the convent of nuns in Drogheda in 1722. The nuns had a poor school in Drogheda, and De Burgo, the Irish Dominican historian, wrote of it in 1726:

> [o]ur sisters' of Drogheda have … numerous pupils whom they excellently instruct in religion and morals. The convent is regarded by the generality of persons as a Boarding House for Ladies and a school for the daughters of 'Papists'.[40]

In the nineteenth century the nuns, like their sister Dominicans in Galway and Dublin, applied to the Commissioners of Education for recognition of their poor school and its teachers under the Stanley terms. They came into connection with the Board on 19 March 1851.

There are very few records of the poor school in Cabra Dublin. St Mary's Dominican Convent was chronologically the last Dominican convent to open a poor school. The nuns moved from their convent in Clontarf to Cabra in 1819 and under the prioress (Anne) Columba Maher, their first educational action was to open the poor school early in 1820. The *Annals of the Dominican Convent Cabra* record that between 1820–23, 'a school was opened immediately for the poor of the neighbourhood'. This school, according to the *Cabra Annals*, 'has always been to the nuns an object of special predilection'.[41] Columba Maher's term of office ended later in 1820 and she was succeeded by Mother Magdalen Butler, who determined to bring about a fundamental change in the life of the community, a change which had profound consequences for the nuns, one of which was to bring their poor school into the Stanley System in 1841. The account of Magdalen Butler's departure from the community in Cabra to make a new foundation in Mount Street Dublin is treated of later in the chapter.

(b) Dominican national schools, post Stanley

The transition from poor school to national school was made for each of the three older Dominican convents, Cabra, Galway and Drogheda, for different reasons. The Cabra community under Mother Magdalen Butler was shocked to realize that its convent and school were not mentioned in the first report of the Commission on Education, 1825. This omission caused the nuns great anxiety and hurt. They reasoned that if the archbishop had not recorded their school in his report to the Commission, their future development and growth as a community was in danger. It was only five years since their change from Clontarf; the move to Cabra was made in the hope of a more secure life and that new postulants would join the community. Survival must have been uppermost in their minds; their funds were low and they numbered only five nuns. *Cabra Annals* notes: '[t]he poverty which had been the trial of the nuns for many years past continued to mark their lot during the period of their establishment in Cabra'. This non-recognition of the Cabra school by the archdiocese was a new worry and again the *Cabra Annals* sets out the nuns' thinking:

> [w]hile new convents and new institutions were springing up in the diocese [of Dublin] under the wise guidance of the saintly Archbishop, the Most Rev. Dr Murray, the venerable community of Cabra was still struggling for existence, still hoping against hope. It had been in Dublin for over one hundred years, it had carried on a boarding school ... at a period when all Catholic schools were banned by law. ... However in spite of all this, at the time of which we write, the existence of this very community seems not to have been known in the Archdiocese.[42]

Why was the Cabra school omitted from the 1825 list? The quotation above is clearly a *cri de cœur* from the nuns protesting that after more than 100 years of dedicated work in Dublin under the most difficult circumstances, they were totally ignored. The Dominican women were not under the jurisdiction of the archbishop of Dublin, and therefore, they reasoned, Dr Murray omitted their school from his list. There were three schools in the Dublin archdiocese included in the archbishop's list: the Carmelite school, St Teresa's in Warrenmount; the Poor Clare school in Harold's Cross and the Presentation school in George's Hill.

Table 3 shows the convent schools named in the 1825 list.

Table 3. Convent schools in Ireland 1825 ('Archbishop's list')

No.	Place	County	Religious Order	Number of Girls	Free or Pay School
1	Carlow	Carlow	Presentation	300	Free
2	Clonmel	Tipperary	Do	300	Do
3	Cork	Cork	Do	157	Do
4	Do	Do	Do	100	Do
5	Do	Do	Do	120	Do
6	Do	Do	Do	570	Do
7	Do	Do	Ursuline	170	50*
8	Clonegal	Wexford	Not stated	30	Free
9	Doneraile	Cork	Presentation	220	Do
10	Drogheda	Louth	Do	240	Do
11	Dublin	Dublin	Carmelite	115	Do
12	Do	Do	Presentation	175	Do
13	Do	Do	Poor Clare	213	Do
14	Dungarvan	Waterford	Presentation	300	Do
15	Galway	Galway	Do	395	Do
16	Kilkenny	Kilkenny	Do	200	Do
17	Killarney	Kerry	Do	350	Do
18	Limerick	Limerick	Presentation	320	Do
19	Mountrath	Queen's Co.	Confraternity	85	Do
20	New Ross	Wexford	Carmelite	130	Do
21	Ranelagh	Dublin	Not stated	100	23*
22	Thurles	Tipperary	Ursuline	150	32*
23	Tullow	Carlow	Not stated	200	Free
24	Thurles	Tipperary	Presentation	140	Do
25	Tralee	Kerry	Do	180	Do
26	Waterford	Waterford	Ursuline	130	Do
27	Do	Do	Do	30	Some Pay
28	Do	Do	Presentation	430	Free
29	Do	Do	Do	200	Do
30	Wexford	Wexford	Do	180	Do

Source: Commission on Education in Ireland First Report 370–9415 C20 F 1825, p.87.
Parliamentary Papers, National Library, Dublin.
* Number of paying pupils.

Like the Dominicans, both the Carmelite and Poor Clare communities were in the tradition of the medieval mendicant contemplative orders, but the Carmelites and Poor Clares had gone under the Dublin archiepiscopal jurisdiction before 1825. It might be argued that the Dominican schools in Cabra and Drogheda were excluded because both these convents were at that time under the jurisdiction of the Master General of the Order in Rome. This was the accepted line of authority for those women religious who were in this tradition of mendicant contemplative orders: the time had come when none of these convents could continue as it had. However, a change in thinking within these three women's orders in Dublin in the eighteenth and early nineteenth centuries was underway. The Poor Clares were under the jurisdiction of the Franciscan friars until the 1750s, when they changed to that of the Archbishop of Dublin. The Carmelite nuns, similarly, were under the jurisdiction of the Carmelite friars; from 1813 they too had a poor school (St Teresa's), in Warrenmount, in the Liberties area of Dublin. In 1814 these Carmelites 'transferred their obedience to the diocese' [of Dublin]. 'They attracted vocations and set a standard of religious observance that was the admiration of the other convents'.[43] Séamus Enright relates how the Poor Clare nuns in Dorset Street, Dublin, were 'the first of the old religious communities to respond to the needs of the poor and, in the process, re-invented themselves as a religious community'. Enright holds that the Poor Clare, Carmelite and Dominican nuns in the early nineteenth century were obliged to change their way of life to survive; their disconnection from the male branches of their orders was, according to him, the price they had to pay for survival.[44]

The Dominicans in Cabra would have been well aware of the success of the Carmelites after their transfer of jurisdiction; Mothers Magdalen Butler and Columba Maher also felt that the Dominican friars were not as diligent in their care for the welfare of the community as the nuns would have wished. This alleged neglect, when combined with the publication of the report of the Commissioners of Education, Cabra's omission from the list of schools, and the example of the Warrenmount Carmelites, tilted the balance in favour of a change in jurisdiction; Magdalen Butler and her community set about making themselves known to the archbishop. In 1830–31 the process was put into action. Magdalen Butler applied to Rome requesting permission for the transfer of the Cabra community from the canonical jurisdiction of the Dominican Order to that of the Archbishop of Dublin.[45] The negotiations took some years; a special Brief of Pope Gregory XVI was signed in December 1831 and was received in January 1832 by Archbishop Murray. The requested transfer of government for the Dominican community of Cabra was made.[46] From this date, Archbishop Murray of Dublin, and his successors, were responsible for the canonical jurisdiction of the Cabra community and the community's formal canonical ties with the Dominican Fathers were broken.

The effects which this change of jurisdiction had immediately on the educational establishments attached to Cabra, and in later years on its daughter

Figure 1. Brief of Pope Gregory XVI to Dominicans in Cabra 1831

Transfer of Jurisdiction from the Master of the
Order to the Archbishop of Dublin
Copy of the Brief of Pope Gregory XVI
10 December 1831.

Cum Moniales Ordinis S. Dominici Monasterii S. Mariae de Cabra Prope
Dublinum pluribus adductis gravibus rationibus omnino necesse esse
exposuerint ad tranquillitatem recuperandam, ad disciplinam Monasterium
ipsum jurisdictioni subjeci R.P.D. Archiepiscopi Dublinensis, S.
Congregatio Glis de Propaganda fide habita die 28 Novembris anno 1831,
referente Emo. ac Rmo. D. Carolo Maria Episcopo Praestino S.R.E.
Cardinali Pedricino S. Congnis. Praefecto, rebus omnibus mature perpensis
consideratisque testimoniis veritatem totius rei confirmantibus, censuit ac
decrevit supplicandum SSmo. Dno. Nostro pro deputatione R.P.D. Danielis
Murray, Archiepiscopi Dublinensis in Visitatorem Apostolicum memorati
Monasterii ad beneplacitum Sedis Apostolicae suspensa interim remanente
in illud jurisdictione Superiorum Ordinis Praedicatorum.

Hanc autem sententiam S. Congnis. SSmo. D.N. Gregorio PP.XVI
relatam in audientia diei 4 Decembris anno 1831 habita a R.D. Cajetano
Martucci S. Congnis. Officiali in absentia R.P.D. Castracane Secretarii
Sanctitas sua benigne in omnibus probavit et literas Apostolicas in forma
Brevis de ea re expediri jussit.

Datum die 10 Decembris an. 1831.

Source: Annals of Dominican Convent, Cabra (Dublin) p.88

houses, is clearly important. The Pope's Brief stated in effect that by the
plenitude of his power, His Holiness Gregory XVI constituted the Archbishop of
Dublin, Dr Daniel Murray, to be the Apostolic Visitator and ecclesiastical
superior of the Dominican nuns in Cabra, Dublin. The Brief was dated 10
December 1831. In the years following 1832, the community in Cabra increased
in numbers and its schools flourished: 'according to the Community Register,
twenty-two subjects made profession within ten years after the change of
government had been made, and thirty-one in the following years.'[47] One of the
immediate consequences of the change was that the chaplaincy to the community was transferred from the Dominican friars to the Vincentian Fathers in
Castleknock, a factor which was to be important in the foundation of St Mary's
School for the Deaf in Cabra in 1846. To the Cabra community, the increase in
the community membership must have seemed sufficient justification for their
transfer of jurisdiction. The first official reference to the Cabra poor school in the
records of the Commissioners of Education is in 1841. Archbishop Murray was
a member of the Board of Commissioners; he was a supporter of the national
school system and he, presumably, strongly advised the nuns to apply for
recognition by the Board.

Taylor's Hill Galway and Siena Convent Drogheda remained under the jurisdiction of the Master of the Dominican Order. Both convents applied for recognition of their poor schools to the Board of Commissioners in 1848 and 1851 respectively. Both schools were accepted under the usual conditions. In terms of their schools, this meant that it was the Dominican Provincial or his delegate who conducted the school business with the Board of Commissioners for the Galway and Drogheda schools, while the prioress of Cabra was manager of her own school. Although later functioning under the archbishop's control, three other Dominican schools were part of the Stanley Scheme: Kingstown began as a poor school in 1847 and was quickly connected to the national school system in 1848; and both St Catherine's National School, Falls Road Belfast and Dominican Convent School, Wicklow were recognized under the system from their foundation in 1870.

DOMINICANS' DIFFICULTIES WITH STANLEY SCHEME

Cabra

When the Dominican schools became part of the government-run system, the relationship between the nuns and the Board of Commissioners of the Stanley Scheme was not always an easy one. A particularly clear example came in 1857–58; a dispute arose between the two parties over the precise delineation and definition of religious practice. On that occasion, the school inspector reported that pupils at the Cabra school were making the sign of the cross on the striking of the clock each hour. The inspector claimed that this practice was contrary to the government Regulations for Schools, Section III: I, setting out the required hours for religious instruction at school and specifying that these were to be observed irrespective of religious denomination. This school-time was to consist of 'literary and moral education' using such extracts from Scripture as were specified by the Board.[48] The reading of Scripture, beyond those excerpts sanctioned for the teaching of literary and moral education, was to be confined to those times set aside for religious instruction and the same applied to prayers, which would in Catholic practice have involved the making of the sign of the cross. The woman dealing with the Board at this time was Mother de Ricci Maher, elected prioress and *ex officio* manager of the Cabra school. She was a niece of Mother Anne Columba Maher and she was judged to have many of the great qualities of mind and heart of her aunt, including the same genius for government. Mother de Ricci was not a lady easily intimidated. The Board presented her with an ultimatum: it required the rule prohibiting religious exercises except at the time set apart for that, to be strictly complied with, and should the practice be continuing when the inspector next visited, all grants would be withdrawn. This order was dated 12 February 1858.[49] Six weeks later the Board recorded that 'Mrs. Maher' had refused to carry out the Order of the Board, and from the end of March that year, all grants were cancelled and the school struck off. The report made an interesting distinction in de Ricci's response to it. The school was struck off because she had refused to enact the Order. However, she was reported to be unable 'conscientiously' to 'prevent the pupils from making the sign of the cross when the clock strikes and *furthermore declines* to carry out the Board Order, Section III, 5 which states,

> [t]he reading of Scriptures, either in the authorised or Douai version, is regarded as a religious exercise, and as such is confined to those times which are set apart for Religious Instruction. *The same regulation is also to be observed respecting prayers* [emphasis added].[50]

There is little doubt that the nun-teachers, with the knowledge of the manager, Mother de Ricci Maher, were breaking Section III, 5 of the Board's regulations. This incident, at least on a strict interpretation of 'prayers', contravened the Board's rules and regulations. The issue of the teaching of religion was clearly very contentious and engendered suspicions between Protestants and Catholics. The Board was legally obliged to uphold and enforce the regulations of the commissioners of national education where the teaching of religion was concerned. A close watch was kept in the early stages of Stanley's Education System for breaches of these rules. Both parties were also acting from a sense of duty: the nuns giving the pupils a habit of remembering the mystery of Redemption, while the inspector adopted a very strict interpretation of Section III, 5 of the regulations. In view of de Ricci's refusal to obey, the Board had no option but to stop their grants and salaries. Rather than compromise her principles about religious education and practice, de Ricci Maher was happy to allow Cabra Convent National School to forego the government's financial aid. The Board withdrew the grants and salaries but the school reverted to the status of a poor school, with financial help from the Dominican community. While there is no further mention of the school in the annals, the Cabra account book has entries for annual payments of £20 'for the Poor School' for the years 1872 to 1882 inclusive, an indication that the nuns had kept the school in operation in the years between 1858 and 1883.[51] The Report of the Commissioners of National Education for the year 1858 has the following entry about schools struck off their list. It says in part:

> [l]ist of one Hundred and Twenty-two Schools struck off the Roll during the year 1858 ... Parish of Castleknock, Roll no. 3108 Cabra Female School. 185 on roll; average daily attendance, 109. Reasons for striking off and cancelling grants, manager declining to comply with Board's rules.[52]

Clearly, the reason for the withdrawal of funding to the Cabra convent national school was not any imputation of inefficiency or deficiency in teaching or school provision, but an issue of religious conscience. However, when Mother de Ricci Maher was again in office as prioress in 1882 she applied to the Commissioners of Education to have the poor school in Cabra taken back into the National Schools system. In the years between 1858 and 1882 de Ricci had ample time to reconsider the wisdom of her strong opposition. When she applied to the Commissioners of Education to have the poor school taken back into the National School system, the response from the Commissioners was not an unqualified acceptance. The prioress had to make a formal application, answer a list of eighty-two questions, some of which concerned religious observances, and sign a declaration that she would obey the rules and regulations of the Board.[53] From December 1882 forward, the poor school regained the status of a national school and the nuns continued quietly to educate the children from the area, a ministry which still continues into the twenty-first century.

Galway and Drogheda

Galway Dominican national school management also had its difficulties with the School Board. In 1848 Fr Rush, the Dominican Prior in Galway, applied to have the Taylor's Hill school recognized by the National Board. There were 215 pupils on rolls and the children came from a population described as: '[l]arge and perhaps one of the poorest in Ireland'.[54] Fr Rush's thinking was that a school under the Board was in a better position to safeguard the religion of the children than one which was under the control of other denominations. By 1855 the Dominican nuns in Galway ran into difficulties with the Board's inspectorate. The report of 13 December 1855 states that 'the manager's attention is called to the low proficiency of pupils in Grammar, Geography, and Arithmetic and to the want of neatness and accuracy in accounts and also to the offensive condition of the out offices'.[55] Further warnings of a similar nature were given by the inspector in 1856 and 1857. The community was at a low ebb at that time and was given help by their Dominican Sisters in Drogheda. Three nuns came from Siena Convent to Taylor's Hill to help in the school and in the community. This did not bring about any notable improvement in the running of the national school and in 1859 the school was struck off the Board's register and the grants were cancelled.[56]

Interpreting what happened to the national school in Taylor's Hill in 1859 at the time of its closure is difficult. Mother Josepha O'Halloran and her two companions from Siena Convent, Drogheda, were able to help the Galway community open both a fee-paying boarding school and day school in 1858 and 1859 respectively, but they seemingly were unable to bring about the improvements necessary to keep the national school open. It appears they made a decision that, given the poor state of the nuns' financial position and the depletion in numbers at the time, the practical solution was to open schools which would bring an income to the community. There were only six nuns in the community at the time. Both the Sisters of Mercy and Presentation had well-established national schools in Galway and so the need for the Dominican school was not as great as it had been in the Famine years.

1. Dominican community, Cabra, 1893

Left to right in all rows. *Back:* Srs. Pius, Benvenuta, de Paul, Catherine, Juliana. *Centre:* John, Angela, Aloysius, Monica, Joseph, Berchmans, Columba. *Front:* Mothers Dominic Purcell, de Ricci Maher (prioress), Bertrand Maher.

This is not the entire story. O'Neill has given a detailed account of the disagreement among members of the Taylor's Hill community about the desirability of transfer of jurisdiction over their community to the bishop of the diocese, as had been done by the Cabra nuns in Dublin.[57] The success of the Cabra community in attracting vocations after their transfer to the jurisdiction of the Archbishop of Dublin and the increase in the number of boarders in their school was well known in Taylor's Hill, Galway. A series of letters from some members of the Taylor's Hill community to Cardinal Cullen, Archbishop of Dublin, sought the transfer of that community from the Order's jurisdiction to that of the Bishop of Galway, Dr O'Donnell.[58] The matter was eventually settled by a majority decision of the community in Taylor's Hill to remain under the jurisdiction of the Dominican Master General. The effect of the unrest generated within the community in Galway during the decade of the 1850s must have had an adverse effect on the efficiency of the teaching nuns' work in the schools, and this – together with illness and deaths among the nuns – must have been a contributory cause for the closure of the national school in 1859. In 1855, Siena Convent national school was criticized also for the 'low proficiency of the pupils and the large amount of time devoted to vacations'.[59] In this case, the manager, Mrs Donnellan, replied that the Board's directions would be carefully attended to, but the reason for the school closures was not for holidays but was due to the 'destitution' of the children.[60] Within a year Siena Convent also had withdrawn from connection with the Board. They too opened fee-paying day and boarding schools and concentrated their efforts on these, rather than on the national school.

The overall relationship between the Dominicans and the Board of Education in the early years of each school's existence was not good. It may be that in the first thirty years of the Stanley Scheme the authorities were intent on enforcing the rules and regulations strictly, especially in the case of Catholic schools. Reporting to the Chief Secretary in 1858, the Commissioners drew attention to the fact that 120 schools had been struck off the Board's roll. The reasons assigned were varied: manager declining to comply with the Board's rules; house unsuitable; average attendance insufficient; school retained by dismissed teacher. It would be difficult to claim that the Dominicans were singled out for unfair treatment in any of these instances.[61]

NATIONAL SCHOOLS' TEXTS AND CURRICULUM

The curriculum in the national schools was that set out by the Board of Commissioners of Education. The records show that grants were given for the purchase of books; these texts were prescribed by the Board or, if other books were used for teaching purposes, the permission of the Board was required for their use. St Catherine's national school in Belfast seems to have been the only Dominican national school which took advantage of the Board of Education grants for teaching extra subjects. Irish, French, Latin, instrumental music, geometry and algebra were offered and were subject to examinations set by the Board's inspectors. The Dominican schools in Kingstown, Wicklow and Belfast did not have the same degree of adverse comment by inspectors as did the Galway and Drogheda schools. Kingstown and Wicklow both tried to incorporate industrial subjects in the national school syllabus; these classes consisted of teaching sewing with the use of machines. The Board of Education gave financial assistance to schools which had these classes and the nuns gave their unpaid services. The Dominican school in Wicklow experimented with a small hosiery enterprise with limited success from 1901–04. They sought advice from the Irish Sisters of Charity in Foxford, Co. Mayo, whose woollen mills were thriving and well-known. The advice from Mother Arsenius Morrogh-Bernard was that the hosiery industry was not a viable proposition and so the classes in Wicklow were discontinued.[62]

In the 1864 Report of the Commissioners of National Schools, the Dominican convent school Kingstown is recorded as having a number of lay teachers and twelve monitresses to assist in their school. The Report stated:

[t]here are 12 nuns in constant attendance. These are indefatigable both in teaching themselves and in superintending the teaching of the monitresses. ... Their (monitresses') acquirements are of a high order, and they have received practical instruction in method and organization from one of the Board's organizers.[63]

In 1869 a report recorded that a capitation allowance was given; the monitors and industrial teachers were paid personal salaries amounting in total to £102.10. They must have had some success in this field of education, for the industrial classes lasted in Kingstown for forty years. By 1889 the scene had changed: the inspector's report noted that, 'on the occasion of her visit to the school, this department was not in working order'.[64] It was reported also that the industrial class had not been properly set up and the teacher was not considered to be properly qualified.

St Catherine's National School on Falls Road, Belfast, was opened in 1870, the same year as the Wicklow Dominican school. The Powis Commission, which was set up in 1869, published its report in 1870; one of the outcomes of the report was the system known as 'payment by results'. Payment of teachers' salaries was made up from local subscriptions, fees from pupils and government gratuities. It was argued that the payment-by-results method would act as an incentive and a teacher's place on the salary scale was in future determined by the result of an annual government inspection and examination in each school. It was at this turning point that the Wicklow and Belfast Dominican schools came into being. While in Wicklow the nuns tried out their industrial classes, the Belfast school offered extra subjects such as Irish, French, Latin, instrumental music, geometry and algebra. The nuns in Falls Road hoped to give the pupils something more than the traditional 'three Rs' of primary education. The success of the 'payment-by-results' is reflected in the inspector's report in 1876, when he remarked on the children's 'proficiency in music and elementary French'.[65] Reading the inspector's report, it is clear that while the school was praised for the pupils who were examined, it also shows that from an attendance of 218 children, only eighty-six pupils were presented for examination. This was a downside of payment-by-results: some teachers were tempted to neglect the less able pupils while giving extra tuition to those who would make a good impression on the day of the examination.

The records of St Catherine's School are meager and there are none for the last years of the nineteenth century. Those which are there for the early years of the twentieth century show that the school continued to serve the people of the Falls Road area. Lay teachers were employed, and in the 1920s the curriculum was expanded to include nature study and elementary science. It is curious that while the schools in the south of Ireland tried to give some training to the pupils in industrial work – mainly sewing – the Falls Road school, situated in an area which had many mills and factories, favoured a more academic curriculum including French, music, mathematics and science.

THE INDUSTRIAL SCHOOL IN SION HILL – A TRANSIENT EPISODE

The industrial school which is most interesting was that in Dominican Convent, Sion Hill. The school's existence was forgotten or ignored down through the years and it was unusual in its foundation and in its early closure. In 1860, without giving any reason for opening a school for the poor, *Sion Hill Annals* describes the building of a new west wing for the boarding school with additional accommodation in the east wing for the community, and then simply states, '[w]e also built a Poor School detached from the Convent'.[66] The National Archives has no record of a request from Sion Hill for recognition of the school under Stanley, so presumably the nuns financed it themselves. *The Complete Catholic Registry, Directory & Almanack* for 1860 records that Sion Hill had 100 poor children in its school.[67] In 1862 the number was the same. The school did not last: by 1865 mention of it had disappeared from both *The Complete Catholic Registry* and the *Sion Hill Annals*. However, a new development followed within the year 1865; an attempt was made to provide for older children of the area who had no opportunity for further education. In August of that year *Sion Hill Annals* notes: '[I]ndustrial school opened. Machines and work materials cost £30'.[68] *The Catholic Directory* observed in its entry: '[i]ndustrial school recently opened at which all orders are gratefully received and executed promptly'.[69] However, *Sion Hill Annals* reported the closure of the industrial school in December 1867: '[i]ndustrial school closed not having support'.[70]

The episode poses some questions: in particular, why did the Dominican community in Sion Hill decide to take up these new works, the poor school and the industrial school, which lasted less than five years, and for whom were the nuns making provision? It appears as if perhaps the poor school merged into an industrial school as the children grew older. The need for some such establishment in the 1860s is obvious from the writer Weston S. Joyce's account. In 1869 he wrote of the parish of Booterstown: '[c]onditions for the poor were deplorable with numerous crowded cabins', which housed the people of all the labouring class.[71] There was no employment in winter; the poor depended on summer work, attending the bathers in Blackrock. Ó Maitiú also confirms that there were 'long-established settlements with comparatively sizable working-class populations, in particular … in the Blackrock village and Williamstown village areas'.[72] This social background would have been sufficient reason for some of the nuns at least to feel a certain responsibility for helping poor people in the immediate area of the convent. Joyce also mentions deplorable conditions in nearby Merrion. Williamstown and parts of Blackrock were contiguous to the Sion Hill convent grounds and therefore access was easy for children attending the schools there. Provision had been made by the Sisters of Mercy in 1838 in the Booterstown area of the parish, for a national school and orphanage; presumably that school catered for the children who lived further away from Sion Hill. The Dominican Convent, though in the parish of Booterstown, is sited between Merrion Avenue and Cross Avenue. Close by in 1860 there was a mixture of small villages, Williamstown, Booterstown itself, and the growing town of Blackrock, which was given the status of township in 1863.[73]

Map No. 2 shows the location of Sion Hill relative to the surrounding villages.

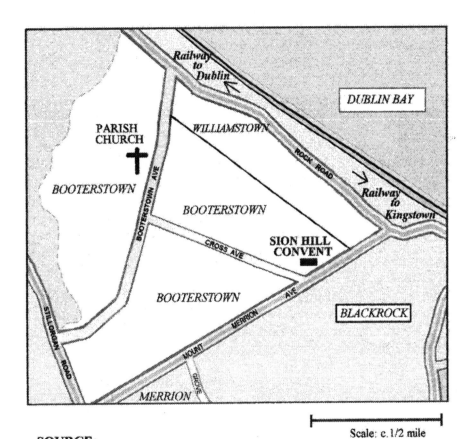

SOURCE:
Map based on N.A.I., Ordinance Survey Maps
C37/5 Booterstown and Union of Stillorgan and Kilmacud (1837)

Map 2. The location of Sion Hill convent in relation to Booterstown, Williamstown and Blackrock, Co. Dublin. 1837–1868

A plausible explanation for the opening and short duration of the poor school and its industrial off-shoot can be given by analysing the internal affairs of the community in Sion Hill over the preceding decade. Mother Bertrand Furlong is perhaps the key to the question. Monica Furlong, in religion Sr. (later Mother) Bertrand, entered Sion Hill in February 1843. In 1846, while as yet just two years professed, she was made mistress of novices. From that time forward Mother Furlong was in a position of authority and influence in the community. Her election as sub-prioress came in July 1854, and in October of that year she was elected prioress. She remained in that office until two months before her death in December 1864 while not yet 50 years of age. During her regime of ten years, the boarding school prospered and numbers in the day school increased.

There were twenty-nine members in the community in 1860, a sufficient number to sustain the extra work involved in the new ventures. Perhaps the Sion Hill nuns may have been invited to open the school, but there is no record known to me of any such request, and since the nuns did not apply for connection of their school within the Stanley system, it seems unlikely that the archdiocese had put forward the idea. The Dublin archdiocese would probably have suggested that the school would benefit from being connected with Stanley. This would be in keeping with the archdiocesan's qualified approval of the national school system. Perhaps the Sion Hill community, knowing of Cabra's difficulties with the Board of Education, may have been nervous of committing themselves to Stanley and decided to be independent and fund the school from their own resources. Mother Furlong, with or without the consent of her council, may herself simply have made the decision to open the school. If this were the case, Mother Furlong had the resources and the personnel at her disposal to expand their ministry in 1860. An argument for the short duration of both schools, poor and industrial, may have been the community's dissatisfaction with, or even opposition to, this decision.

A deliberate stand had been taken in Sion Hill in 1846 to cater for the middle class.[74] Less than twenty years later it would appear that the decision was over-ridden by a prioress who may not have had the good-will of the community. Reading the *Sion Hill Annals* more closely, one could argue that while there were ample resources, both financially and in personnel, to undertake the new venture in 1860, the situation changed rapidly, leaving the community no option but to close the poor school after three or four years. Between 1861 and 1866 four nuns, including Mother Furlong herself, died from tuberculosis. From 1863 there are references to the poor health of the prioress, who was bedridden for the greater part of the two years preceding her death. Some of the community blamed her for not resigning but she justified herself as being 'guided by ecclesiastical authority', an attitude which points to a strong personality who did not submit to the wishes of others, even when her own health and the good of the community was in question. This in itself points to a division of opinion within the community and it must be pointed out that Mother Furlong's successor, Mother Clare Elliott, was also a strong-minded woman who had been sub-prioress to Mother Furlong.

Mother Clare Elliott was elected prioress for the first time in 1864, and she also held that office almost continuously until August 1903. Possible dissension in the community, and particularly with Mother Elliott, about the poor school, the commitment to the education of the middle class, and the thorny question of the prioress's resignation, were all factors which must have had an effect on the internal morale of the community. The annals openly stated that it was 'a period of great difficulty for the community'.[75] The original educational policy stated by the community in 1836 was, '[t]he establishment of a Day School for children of the middle class to be carried out on the same principles as the Boarding School at Cabra'.[76] Mount Street school took boarders after some time and, when the school transferred to Sion Hill in 1840, the number of boarders had declined to six. A short paragraph from the *Sion Hill Annals* for 1845 is worth noting here:

> [o]n leaving Mount Street the Foundresses changed their original plan and opened the School at Sion Hill *for the children of the upper classes* at a pension of £50 per annum all extras included. For some time this succeeded pretty well though we never had a large school. At length we found that our efforts to keep our school so extremely select by *excluding children of the middle class*, offended and estranged many of our friends, and we did not receive sufficient support from the upper classes to enable us to continue this system. The Foundresses, however, were not disposed to change their views and so the School gradually declined.[77]

In 1846 the pension of the school was reduced to £30 per annum and the prioress determined '[t]o receive children of the middle class ... while the school still *retained its character for being select*'.[78] In the light of such strong statements about the nuns' school policy, it is not surprising, therefore, that the poor school was probably a contentious issue and that for those reasons it was closed in August 1865.

In summary: the idea of opening the school in 1860 may have been put forward by Mother Bertrand Furlong with the support of a minority in the community; Mother Furlong's prolonged illness and her absence from active duty deprived the school of the moral support of the person who most favoured it; more revealing perhaps is the sentence in the *Sion Hill Annals* that follows immediately on the announcement of the opening of the industrial school in September 1865: '[a] school opened for a respectable class of boys'.[79] The deduction may legitimately be made that Mother Elliott was now in charge, Mother Furlong was dead, and the decision about the poor school was reversed. The opening of the school for 'a respectable class of boys' so soon into Mother Elliott's term as prioress, amounts not to a statement of a policy shift but rather a return to the nuns' original policy as noted above, which leaves no doubt about the nuns' determination to keep to their original decision of providing education for the middle class. In fairness to the Sion Hill community of the day, we must concede it was the work for which they were best suited by training and tradition. This lengthy record is given of the poor school and the industrial class in Sion Hill because there is no full written account of their existence, except for the brief references to them in the Sion Hill annals. It also underlines the fact that in most Dominican convents, the nuns' ministry in education was intended by the nuns themselves to be mainly for a middle-class clientele.

CATERING FOR LOCAL NEEDS – AN ASSESSMENT

Except in the case of the Kingstown school, the Dominican nuns' attempt at providing 'industrial' classes in their primary schools in the nineteenth century met with small success. The Wicklow national school, after its initial attempt at the production of hosiery, seems to have made no further effort to provide classes of this kind. Sion Hill's venture hardly got off the ground. The Kingstown school was the most persevering, surviving for forty years and, apart from Kingstown, the Dominicans' most successful efforts with industrial classes were in St Mary's School for the Deaf in Cabra. In general, the Dominican national schools in Kingstown, Belfast and Wicklow were on average working well, with some falling off in standards from time to time. Apart from the industrial classes, no remarkable educational developments were pioneered; the nuns who taught in these schools were dealing with large classes and poor facilities and, in general, were caught up in the day-to-day running of the schools. The economic and social expectations for, and of, the majority of pupils attending national schools in the late nineteenth and early twentieth centuries were not high. For most of the pupils, life after national school meant employment, if any, was in low-paid jobs in domestic, farm or factory work. The nuns, while trying to prepare them for that life, gave the pupils the best education available to them in the climate of the time in which they lived.

The nuns themselves had no experience or training in teaching advanced technical subjects, nor had they the business expertise to make a financial success of even a small enterprise such as the experiment in hosiery-manufacture in Wicklow. Each of the four Dominican national schools catered for the local population of children. A survey of the occupations of the fathers of the pupils in Cabra, Wicklow and Belfast reflects the type of work available in each place. The Cabra area, in the nineteenth and early twentieth centuries, was on the outskirts of Dublin city but was not yet part of it. Its people were mainly farmers; over 60 per cent of the pupils of the national school were from labourers' families while most of the remainder came from tradesmens' families. In Belfast, the majority of pupils in St Catherine's National School were from mill workers' families, as borne out by the quaintly named occupations associated with the manufacture of linen goods – roughers, bundlers, hacklers, fentors.[80] In contrast with the Dublin and Belfast pupils, the occupations of the fathers in Wicklow were labourers, sailors and railway employees, as might be expected from a sea-side town with a railway station; in addition, Wicklow had a farming community in the surrounding area. Kingstown was not only a sea-side town but a busy port with a railway station. The occupations of the labouring class there were associated with shipping, fishing and railway work. The source material for Siena Convent national school in Drogheda has no record of the fathers' occupations, but the extreme poverty of the children who attended in the early days of the school is noted. The fathers' occupations, if they had any, must have been those of a poorly paid labouring nature.

THE TWO-TIER SYSTEM: A QUESTION OF CLASS?

To use twentieth-century parlance, the Dominicans had a two-tiered approach to primary education: the national schools and the private fee-paying junior schools. In these junior schools there was no state intervention or legal requirements relating to curriculum, teacher qualifications, or inspection; there were no financial endowments for salaries or school grants. The managers of the junior schools were free to choose the curriculum, text-books, amount of time given to teaching and, especially, freedom to have the schools conducted according to the religious ethos and practices of the Catholic Church. Because the numbers in the classes were fewer than those in national schools, the parents' assumption was that in the private schools more attention was given to each child. These were the factors which appealed to parents in their choice of school, considerations which explain their willingness to pay school fees at primary level.

Parents may have been influenced by the assumption that social mobility for their children depended on getting a 'good start in life', or as Francis Stevens put it, the private schools 'bestowed ... certain marks of an in-group', which varied from the 'essentials of learning to inessentials, such as graceful manners'.[81] Extra subjects were introduced that were deemed to develop social skills and talents, such as dancing, music, art (drawing) and fine needlework. Elocution, drama and stage productions involving singing and dancing were also considered to be important parts of the curriculum. Most junior schools held an annual parents' day or had an end-of-year concert, when the pupils received prizes for their progress in studies and displayed their social skills in music, dancing, recitation and dramatic productions. This was important both for the reputation of the school and as an occasion when the parents could assess the values and achievements of the school. It also acted as an advertisement for new pupils and as an incentive for parents to send the children to the secondary school attached to that particular convent. In this way the girls' junior schools acted as feeder schools to the secondary schools. Catering for the boys aged five to seven years was part of a policy to be family orientated and to ensure the viability of the schools, which were dependent almost wholly on the pupils' fees. Indeed, one of the features of these junior schools was the loyalty of certain families to a particular school. This was evident as the years passed: generations

2. Junior boarders, Cabra, 1882

of girls, from the grandmothers' generation, through to the next generation of daughters and grand-daughters, attended the schools and continued the family tradition of attending a Dominican school. Such loyalty was not unique to parents whose children attended Dominican schools but was given also to other orders of teaching nuns throughout the country.

In the years 1820–1930 Dominican convents in Ireland increased from two in number to eleven. Of these eleven, ten had private primary schools while six had national schools. Even among the six, two – Siena Convent Drogheda, and Taylor's Hill Convent Galway, respectively – closed their national schools permanently in 1856 and 1859, as already noted. A proposition might be put forward that the Dominicans in their educational work could be perceived as favouring private primary schools rather than national schools, which catered for the more deprived members of society. The answer is patently clear: the schools were intended for the 'better-off' children in society. This policy of concentrating on private junior schools, secondary boarding and day schools, lies in the history of Dominican women in Ireland. The clients of their earlier boarding schools were the daughters of the Anglo-Irish gentry. The clients of their earlier boarding schools were the daughters of the Anglo-Irish Catholic gentry. Later, the Dominicans in Cabra accepted, with reservations, the Stanley system with its strict demarcation between secular and religious education. The initial call to provide education for the poor came to the communities in Cabra, Dublin, Taylor's Hill, Galway, and Siena Drogheda in times of extreme poverty, deprivation of Catholic education and no state system to give financial support. The geographical areas in which these three convents were situated were close to large numbers of poor people or, as in the case of Taylor's Hill, where there was a transient population of poor migrants in famine times. The approach of the nuns in each of the three communities was initially a response to an urgent need in areas where no other group of religious was as yet established.

Hardiman's *History of Galway*, published in 1820, praised the Presentation nuns who had arrived in the city in 1815. It has already been recorded above that the Dominican poor school in Kirwan's Lane was handed over to the Presentation nuns at that time. Enright cites Hardiman as 'chiding' the three orders of nuns already in Galway, for not 'adopt[ing], even on a limited scale, this humane plan'. Dominicans, Poor Clares and Augustinians were the orders in question; the humane plan was 'the education of so many of its [Galway's] most helpless and most generally neglected members'.[82] In Dublin, Teresa Mulally (1728–1803), founded a school for poor girls in George's Hill in 1786. Teresa was an admirer of Nano Nagle (1728–1784). Nano, who founded the Presentation Sisters in Cork, had set up poor schools and was supportive of Teresa Mulally's work in Dublin. Yet Teresa did not approve of the Presentation nuns changing their constitutions and giving time annually to retreats and prayer. She saw this withdrawal for prayer, even if only for a short period each year, as taking time from the school-work to which they had committed themselves. This was the tension which at times the Dominicans found difficult: Teresa Mulally had considered joining either the Dominicans or Poor Clares as a vowed religious.

One may gain an insight into the Dublin people's perception of the Dominican nuns in Channel Row – and of the Poor Clares in King Street – during Teresa Mulally's lifetime. Burke Savage in his biography of Mulally, *A Valiant Dublin Woman*, relates how Teresa consulted a priest friend about her future and 'the attraction she felt towards religious life'. At that time, around 1766, the Dominicans' only convent in Dublin was in Channel Row, not far from Mulally's home in Phrapper's Lane off North King Street:

> [t]he Dominicans were in Channel Row, and the Poor Clares in North King Street and Dorset Street. ... As [Teresa's] sterling character was well known, each of these Convents was anxious to gain so suitable a subject. [Teresa] hesitated; she was not sure that her vocation was a contemplative one. True, the Dominicans and Poor Clares *had been pressed into active service, and taught some girls of the wealthier classes; but active work for the poor was as yet unknown*. ... [Yet]; strong as was her attraction to the religious life, *she felt she should not desert the poor among whom she lived*.[83]

Enright sets out the difficulties of the 'conflicting needs of the school and religious life', but the Presentation nuns were able to sustain their commitment to the education of the poor, 'which remained at the heart of their mission'.[84] This last phrase speaks for itself. Here we have two religious orders coming to the ministry of teaching from different perspectives. Teresa Mulally felt she could not 'desert the poor' by entering either the Dominican or Poor Clare convents. The obvious perception of the people of Dublin was that the Dominicans in Channel Row, while dedicated to education, did not extend that dedication to the poor. Thus it could be said that the Dominicans came to the education of the poor in Galway, Cabra and Drogheda by accident rather than by design, whereas the Presentation nuns had the poor 'at the heart of their mission'. Although an Apostolic Brief of 1805 imposed the rule of enclosure on the Presentation nuns, they continued to make the education of the poor their central ministry.[85] Nano Nagle's legacy to them was safe.

In contrast with the Dominicans, the new Irish religious orders of the eighteenth and nineteenth centuries, specifically, but not exclusively, answered the educational needs of the poor. Nano Nagle's Presentation Sisters in Cork (1718–84), Catherine McAuley's Sisters of Mercy in Dublin (1781–1841), Teresa Mulally's Presentation school in George's Hill, Dublin, Mary Aikenhead's Sisters of Charity (1787–1812), and Margaret Aylward's Sisters of the Holy Faith (1810–89), all began their educational work in Dublin with an emphasis on the children who were most needy. Both Teresa Mulally and Nano Nagle realized that their schools for the poor needed an order which was not constrained by the rule of enclosure, to which both Dominicans and Poor Clares were subject: note Burke Savage's phrase about them: '[they] had been pressed into active service'.[86] Enclosure did not allow them to work outside the convent precincts. In fact, more than 100 years later, in 1870, when news of the Dominicans' coming to Wicklow town was broken to the local people, it was made known that the townspeople's preference would have been for an order of nuns who would visit their homes and comfort and minister to the sick. It was obviously the thinking of the people in Wicklow town that the Dominicans, although having a reputation as good educators, were too far removed from the daily concerns of the people. Like Nano Nagle, Margaret Aylward, foundress of the Sisters of the Holy Faith, had a clear vision of her ministry when she formulated her own school philosophy:

> [the schools] are free to the poor, in fact the poorest have the first claim to admittance; they are free also from government control ... They are named Catholic schools, being entirely under the guidance of the Church and under the guidance only of her authority.[87]

The primary commitment of Nano Nagle, Teresa Mulally and Margaret Aylward was to the education of the poor, and they were prepared to go where the need was greatest. Throughout the period covered by this study, the Dominicans had a concern for the poor in their own particular localities and provided schools for them. Nevertheless, they concentrated on their fee-paying boarding and day schools. Their commitment to fee-paying schools was underlined also by opening their junior schools to young boys of primary school age. In Cabra and Wicklow there were preparatory boys' boarding schools for that age-group; in Sion Hill day-boys were admitted to the junior school up to the age of about seven years, while in Eccles Street a separate school, St Thomas' Academy, for boys of pre-First Communion age was opened in 1898. We have here a very good example of the difference between the Dominican approach to education and that of the newer orders. The emphasis on service to the poor which was a hall-mark of Nano Nagle, Teresa Mulally, Catherine McAuley and Mary Aikenhead, was not as strong nor as all-embracing among the Dominicans. The Dominicans' history, that of enclosed nuns with a strong leaning towards the Dominican motto, *'contemplare et contemplata aliis tradere'* – 'to contemplate and to give to others the fruits of contemplation', pre-determined the path they had taken in the eighteenth century – the education of the upper and middle-classes. This path was followed through into the nineteenth and early twentieth centuries, but when the need arose to serve a disadvantaged section of society – to educate deaf children – the Dominicans answered the call.

ST MARY'S SCHOOL FOR DEAF GIRLS, CABRA 1846–1930

This section on St Mary's School for Deaf Girls, Cabra, is separated from the account of the 'ordinary' primary schools because of its importance and unique place in the history of Dominican education in Ireland. It was a pioneering work for Dominicans, filling a very great gap in the education of deaf girls in Ireland in the mid-nineteenth century. It was not by chance that in 1848 a call came to the Cabra nuns to enter into this altogether different ministry. There was a very definite choice made by the nuns to answer this call, instigated through the mediation of the Vincentian Fathers, in particular through the influence and persuasive power of Fr Thomas McNamara (1801–92) a Vincentian, working in Phibsboro, Dublin. From the time of their transfer to the jurisdiction of the Archbishop of Dublin, the Cabra Dominicans were under the spiritual direction of the Vincentians and so were well known to Fr McNamara for their work both in their national and boarding schools in Cabra. When St Mary's School for the Deaf was established in 1846, the national and boarding schools had been in operation from the 1820s and 1830s respectively.

The Dominican Sisters of the Cabra community, in launching the new venture for the education of the deaf, moved into new paths. They had no knowledge or expertise in the specialized field of teaching the deaf; they had no experience of dealing with children with a disability that called for new teaching methods and for a whole new approach to communicating with their students. Their new school would call for a knowledge of technical issues, not least of which was the adoption of an appropriate sign language, a matter which today is fraught with controversy among professionals in the field. Crean gives an account of the debate on signing and oralism in his book, *Breaking The Silence*.[88]

The challenge

When the nuns undertook the education of the deaf in the Cabra school in 1846, they were concerned to help the children attain that independence and dignity which were their right as human beings made in the image of God. They were concerned that the deaf children should be given an education which would challenge them to use whatever potential they had, and which would foster their innate abilities to the maximum level possible. Bearing in mind this ethos, it is not surprising that the Dominican community in Cabra agreed, in the mid-nineteenth century, to undertake this very specialized work of educating deaf girls. Sr Nicholas Griffey (1916–2002), whose work for the deaf in Cabra spanned more than sixty years, wrote ' ... deafness from birth causes spiritual starvation unless education is available'.[89]

When Sr Nicholas was interviewed, the strength of her conviction of the importance of religious education for the deaf came through very strongly. She worried about the lack of provision of religious instruction for them in some of the schools she visited outside Ireland. Her conviction spurred her on to seek further training for herself and other teachers, so that in Cabra the pupils of St Mary's would get the best possible education, including religious education.[90] The pupils who were to be helped by the school, were those handicapped by their inability to acquire language without specialised help. This incapacity to realize their full potential affected them in their personal lives, in their career prospects and in gaining a knowledge of their religion. While teaching whatever is necessary for the development of their pupils as educated adults, the nuns' primary aim in conducting a Catholic school is to bring the pupils to a knowledge of God, of the mystery of salvation and their true destiny as children of God with a capacity for everlasting happiness in the life to come. The Dominicans realized that the form of education which they were providing was an opportunity for them to help the children who came to the school with their handicap of deafness to come to this realization of their true destiny as human beings. Indeed, in Ireland in the nineteenth century some deaf children in Ireland were hidden away by their families through a false sense of guilt and shame: it was not unknown that, in a few cases, a deaf child was either kept apart from socializing with family members and relatives or even, in one or two extreme cases, given shelter in an out-house.[91]

Charles Orpen, pioneer in the education of the deaf in Dublin

Education of the deaf in Dublin was pioneered by Dr Charles Orpen, a medical doctor who lived in North Great George's Street and practised in Dublin in the first half of the nineteenth century.[92] Orpen was influenced by the work of the Institute for the Deaf and Dumb established in Birmingham in 1813 or 1814. Orpen himself, through reading and study, addressed the problem of how to teach a deaf person to speak. He became acquainted with a Dublin deaf boy, Thomas Cooney, on whom he tested out his own theory. Orpen had some success with Thomas Cooney and, following on this success, the Protestant bishops and leading laymen in Dublin established the first school for the deaf, in 1816. Griffey noted that Orpen 'did much to awaken public interest in the education of Irish deaf children'.[93] Orpen's school was transferred from its original site in Smithfield to Claremont in Glasnevin. It had a small enrolment of boys and was endowed by the Church of Ireland. Some Catholic children were also enrolled in Orpen's school, though there was strong Catholic opposition towards Protestant schools, which Catholics suspected of proselytism. It was inevitable that, sooner or later, some influential Catholic would press for a Catholic school for deaf boys and girls. That person was Fr Thomas MacNamara, a priest of the Vincentian community in Phibsboro, Dublin.

Fr Thomas McNamara CM

Claremont is not far from Phibsboro, where the Congregation of the Mission, popularly known as the Vincentians, has a community house and church. Fr Thomas McNamara became aware of the Claremont school and its enrolment of Catholic children, and realized that there was no provision for the education of Catholic deaf boys and girls in Dublin. (A Catholic co-educational day-school for the deaf had been founded in Cork in 1822. The school lasted about twenty-five years until its closure owing to lack of funding.) Apart from the Dominicans, other religious opened schools for deaf girls later in the nineteenth century: the Sisters of Mercy of St Mary of the Isles, Cork, from 1858 to 1900, administered two schools for deaf girls in the city and again in the 1930s, but it was not until 1840 that Fr McNamara took some practical measures to open a school for the deaf in Dublin.[94] McNamara's first move was to visit *Le Bon Sauveur* school for the deaf in Caen, Normandy. *Les Filles du Bon Sauveur* congregation was founded in 1730 by Anne Leroy and had as its mission 'the maintenance of *Les Petites Ecoles* to teach poor girls working skills and to visit the sick'. After the French Revolution, they re-formed in 1805, and it was then that they specialized in teaching the deaf and dumb.[95] Impressed by what he saw in Caen, and by the teaching methods of the French nuns, Fr McNamara appealed to a Dublin parish priest, Monsignor Yore, to help him set up a committee to be known as the Catholic Institute for the Deaf, to raise funds for the venture and to interest themselves in the new school. Eventually, Archbishop Murray of Dublin became president of the committee, with Monsignor Yore as chairman and Fr McNamara as secretary; the committee had a lay and clerical membership totalling twenty-six. At the committee's first meeting, on 5 January 1846, it was decided to ask the Dominican nuns in Cabra to undertake the work.

Fr McNamara, in a letter to the archbishops and bishops of Ireland explained, '[i]t was thought well to commence with the female department [for the education of the deaf] and accordingly ... I addressed myself to the good Daughters of St Dominic, at Cabra'.[96]

St Mary's School for the Deaf – the beginnings

According to Fr McNamara, Mother Columba Maher, the prioress of Dominican convent, Cabra, was 'a large-hearted lady, always ready with earnest zeal for every good work'.[97] When Columba Maher put Fr McNamara's proposal before her community, it was agreed to undertake the education of deaf and dumb girls, or 'deaf mutes' as they were then called. Fr McNamara was conscious that Columba Maher, in underaking the building of a new school, had to consider that a large demand was made on the Community funds'.[98] Two members of her community, Sr Vincent Martin and Sr Magdalen O'Farrell, were chosen as potential teachers for the new school. At Fr McNamara's suggestion, the two Sisters were sent to Caen, where they spent eight months in the School for the Deaf observing the method and becoming familiar with it. As Fr McNamara wrote in his memoirs:

> [i]t will always be a memorable circumstance in the history of the Institution that the Sisters of St. Mary's who were selected to commence it, were sent to that establishment to learn the system of deaf mute teaching in operation there. Thus the project in the course of providence found its practical realisation in the very place it was first conceived and the respected community of Le Bon Sauveur were happy to receive the Sisters of St. Mary's ... and afforded them hospitality free of all charge during their stay.[99]

Sisters Vincent and Magdalen worked in the school by day and in the evening they studied and discussed what they had learned. Since the system which the Sisters were studying in Caen was a French-language one, adaptations were needed to make it suitable for an English-medium school. Srs Vincent and Magdalen spent many hours adapting the sign language to suit the specific needs of Irish children. At the suggestion of the authorities in Caen, two deaf girls accompanied the Sisters: Agnes Beedem and Mary Anne Dogherty, both from Dublin city. The girls were brought to Caen so that, on their return, there would be at least two pupils who had been given some training in sign language. Agnes and Mary Anne would help with teaching the fifteen new girls who were admitted to the school at the end of August 1846.[100] Throughout the first 100 years, some of the pupils became teachers through a monitress system of pupil-teacher training.

Development of language teaching

At first, the programme worked well, but the sign language adapted by the Sisters was soon found to be inadequate for complex language patterns. Fr Thomas McNamara and a fellow Vincentian priest, Fr John Burke, devised a more comprehensive programme of sign language, based on the Caen system. Burke, in particular, 'studied the writings of the best among the continental educators of the deaf – de l'Epée, Abbé Sicard and others – and adapted their system to the requirements of the English language'.[101] He also took a keen interest in the educational methods being developed in the Cabra school and, besides devising the programme of language, Fr Burke organized the system in the school and acted as chaplain to the pupils. His constant preoccupation was to achieve the best possible means to educate them. He was not content merely to teach sign language, but also set out to help in the development of each child intellectually through the growth of language and expression. Fr Burke was intolerant of low teaching standards and upbraided the staff for accepting less than the best from their pupil-teachers.

Towards the end of his life Fr McNamara wrote his memoirs and his own account of the founding of the school for the deaf. He modestly wrote throughout in the third person, never mentioning his own name but referring to the visits of 'the Superior' of the Vincentians to Caen.[102] If Fr McNamara was the inspirer of the foundation of St Mary's, Fr Burke was the person who ensured that the teaching given in the school was of the highest quality. The Dominican Sisters gave of their expertise, taught in the school and cared for the children in after-school hours. By 1877 the number had increased to 211, and in 1879 Archbishop McCabe, successor to Cardinal Cullen, laid the foundation stone of a new wing, which provided accommodation for a further ninety pupils. The school's fame spread: towards the end of the century teachers from other schools for the deaf in Halifax, Nova Scotia and from London came to visit St Mary's. In 1912 Hugh Myddelton, a teacher of the deaf in London, wrote in appreciation of the work: 'the language results are the very finest I have seen and I have learned much from the methods. As a teacher of the deaf this is one of the most helpful days I have ever experienced.'[103]

Sign language and oralism

Technically, the method of language teaching used by the staff in Cabra and adapted from the Caen method was described as a 'manual pronunciation of words' and consisted of natural gestures and conventional sign language based on finger-spelling. These signs had built-in grammatical inflections and linguistic markers. The teachers in the Cabra school, under the direction of Fr Burke, developed this further into a structured system of language teaching.[104] The spoken word was never used, even though some of the pupils had residual hearing. When speaking about this silent approach to the teaching of the deaf, Sr Nicholas remarked, 'we ended up as a closed community ... and within the

Congregation, we were a closed community'.[105] The nuns who taught in St Mary's School for the Deaf were to a certain extent cut off from the full community life of the other nuns. This was so because the education of the deaf required the constant presence of the nuns with the children, and, as a consequence, those who were teaching in the school had far longer hours of teaching and supervision than was usual in day or boarding schools.

The Milan Congress 1880

An educational congress held in Milan in 1880 recommended that all schools for the deaf should use oralism – that is, lip-reading, speech reading and writing. The congress passed a resolution, 'the oral method ought to be preferred to that of signs for the instruction and education of the deaf and dumb'.[106] For the deaf, this meant watching the movements of the lips, facial expression and body language to interpret the speech of others. When oralism became widespread in schools for the deaf (though not in St Mary's after the Milan congress), there were two schools of thought – to keep to the manual method or to use 'total communication', that is sign language together with the oral method. This debate grew into a controversy, and indeed heated argument on the subject continues to this day. Cabra kept to the manual method for a century. Even in 1936, at a time when the total communication method had gained widespread currency, children were admitted to the Cabra school on the assumption that they would be taught exclusively through sign language. In fact, if left to their own devices, deaf children will use natural signs: signs that are handed down from one generation of children to another, though they obviously may vary from group to group. Sign language is a purely visual language and includes dramatic gestures, mimicry and body language. Some researchers claim that it has structure and grammar and that it has properties common to all spoken languages. Irish sign language in everyday parlance is called ISL, and in the United States this type of sign language is known as American Sign Language (ASL). Both have been documented. Deaf pupils who use ISL as their first language must learn to read and write in English,which is a completely different language form.[107] The Cabra school, however, was probably unique in the early 1930s and early 1940s in that manual communication continued to be the only method used in the school.

This study of St Mary's School for Deaf Girls 1846–1930 does not include the great controversy which emerged in the later decades of the twentieth century about the relative merits of the oral versus the signing system of communication in the education of the deaf. In teaching only through sign language, the Dominican nuns went against the accepted practice of European educators of the deaf in the late nineteenth century by ignoring the decision of the Congress of Milan, by which the oral method then became the norm for most European schools for the deaf. The Dominican nuns, after their initial training in Caen in 1846, did not visit the Continent to refresh their methods and perhaps

3. Lay staff, St Mary's School for Deaf Girls, Cabra

were not in communication with other educators of the deaf. The Cabra school increased in numbers, and the thinking in Ireland was that sign language was best suited to the needs of the children. It was not until 1951 that Srs Nicholas Griffey and Mary Tolan from Cabra visited *Le Bon Sauveur* school in Caen. On their return to Cabra, the oral method of teaching the deaf was adopted in St Mary's School.

Influence of the Caen school

Apart from the teaching of language and communication skills, *Le Bon Sauveur* school influenced the curriculum in St Mary's Cabra in a very practical way. Hufton writes:

> [t]he educational package offered by the *petites écoles*, accentuated literacy less than it did catechetical instruction which would allow the pupil to resist heresy. Second came survival skills, that is spinning, sewing, lace-making and embroidery. The girl who was [a pupil] of one of these establishments ... received the equivalent of an apprenticeship and ... she could expect a good place in service.[108]

The example of the school in Caen may have influenced the Dominicans in St Mary's School for Deaf Girls, when a vocational department was set up in Cabra in 1863. Unlike the industrial classes attempted in the Dominican national schools in Wicklow, Kingstown, and in the industrial school in Sion Hill, the

Cabra venture was much more successful and continued into the late twentieth century. Not all deaf pupils were able to return to their homes when their primary education was complete: these girls were catered for and got employment in the workrooms in Cabra and remained in residence, some for the remainder of their lives. Others who were capable of independent living were employed in the clothing industry in Dublin and other towns. Lace-making, embroidery, dressmaking and tailoring were taught and special workrooms were built to accommodate the staff. Other past-pupils who had the ability and wished to train as teachers of the deaf availed themselves of a training course set up in the school by the nuns in 1854.

St Mary's School for the Deaf, Cabra, has been in existence since 1846. To an outsider, the Dominicans in the period 1846–1930 conducted a very large institutional type of school for deaf girls. While the nuns were courageous in undertaking such a daunting task and in sending their young nuns to train in Caen in 1846, they did not follow up this formal training with succeeding groups of nun-teachers until after the Second World War. The isolation of the school may be the reason for the nuns' failure to take up the oral method advocated by the Congress in Milan. Even so, by the standard of the time they gave generations of deaf girls the best educational opportunities available to them.

CONCLUSION

This chapter has set out the history of the Dominican women's national and private, primary schools in Ireland, including the school for deaf girls, in the period 1820–1930. Some schools began initially as poor schools which in time became connected with the Stanley Scheme; others came as new foundations connected from their beginnings to Stanley. The school for deaf girls in Cabra was *sui generis*, an entirely new venture for Dominicans in Ireland. The Dominican national schools were not unusual in any way from other Catholic schools, except insofar as the particular ethos of a congregation or order differed from others. The inspectors' reports for the national schools varied in their evaluations: there were periods when the schools were commended for their teaching and at other times the teaching was considered to leave much to be desired, or the provision of facilities was not up to the standard demanded by the inspectorate. These adverse reports resulted in the closures of the schools in Taylor's Hill in 1859 and Siena Convent, Drogheda in 1860. The nuns in Cabra convent decided to withdraw from the national system when there was a conflict of opinion between the inspectorate and the nuns about religious education and its place in the day-to-day running of the school.

While the national schools were important in the ministry of the Dominican women, one is forced to concede that these schools did not claim the same attention as the secondary schools and especially the secondary boarding schools. The Cabra community had the foresight to send some members to Caen to train as teachers of the deaf. However, there is no record of formal training for those nuns who were engaged in the national schools in the early years of the Stanley Scheme, until St Mary's Training College was set up in Belfast in 1900. It cannot have been by coincidence that St Catherine's national school in Belfast was the only Dominican national school which took advantage of the grants given for the teaching of Irish, French, Latin, instrumental music, algebra and geometry in the early twentieth century. There is no record of any other Dominican national school doing so. St Catherine's was a teaching practice school for St Mary's Teacher Training College, and the argument could be made that the nuns there were more conscious of the availability of grants and perhaps also there was a pool of student teachers who taught these extra subjects.

In 1930 there were eleven convents of Dominican teaching nuns in Ireland; Siena Convent, Drogheda, resumed the full contemplative Dominican life in that year. The Dominicans had by tradition catered for the education of the middle-class children rather than concentrating on the education of the poor. The choice was not theirs to make until circumstances changed for them in 1820 when they moved to Cabra. The opening of the poor school in Cabra was to take the nuns in a new direction with their involvement in the national school system in Kingstown, Wicklow and Belfast. In general it can be said that the Dominican nuns continued to give more attention, if judged by the number of their fee-paying schools, to the middle-class families who could afford to pay for their children's education. One must consider the background from which the seventeenth-century Dominican nuns came: a group of women who were of Anglo-Norman anscestry. Their thinking was formed by their personal family histories, by their membership of a medieval enclosed religious order whose thrust was towards contemplation. It is relevant to recall here Burke Savage's opinion of the Channel Row Dominicans which was quoted earlier in this chapter: 'the Dominicans ... had been pressed into active service, and taught some girls of the wealthier classes; but active work for the poor was as yet unknown'.[109]

The newer orders had the freedom to go about the towns and cities to carry out their work for the poor. Their stated charism or particular call was to meet the growing need for schools and services for the poor and in this they were very successful. The Dominicans on the other hand guarded their lives of enclosure with an emphasis on contemplation allied to a life of action. They were in a sense remote from the busy hustle of life among the people. While catering in four specific instances for the poor, the Dominicans concentrated their energies on their original ministry to the middle classes. In Chapter 2, it will be seen how they expanded their schools both boarding and day, in the secondary sector between 1820 and 1930, while keeping the four national schools in Cabra, Kingstown, Wicklow and Belfast, St Mary's School for the Deaf in Cabra and the private junior schools in most of their convents.

NOTES

1. For religion and education in nineteenth-century Ireland, see D.H. Akenson, *The Irish Education Experiment; The National System of Education in the Nineteenth Century* (London: Routledge & Kegan Paul, 1970).
2. P.J. Dowling, *A History of Irish Education: A Study in Conflicting Loyalties* (Cork: Mercier Press, 1971), pp.80–1. Cited henceforth as Dowling, *History of Irish Education.*
3. British Parliamentary Papers (BPP), 1710, 8 Anne, c.3 and 1782, 2 George III, c.4.
4. P.S. McGarry, 'Penal Laws', *Catholic Encyclopedia* (New York: McGraw-Hill, 1966), Vol.3, pp.66–8.
5. J.T. Gilbert, 'Hugh Boulter (1672–1742)', *The Dictionary of National Biography,* Vol. II (Oxford: University Press, 1921–22), p.915.
6. M.G. Jones, *The Charity School Movement* (Cambridge: Cambridge University Press, 1938), p.234.
7. Maureen Wall, 'The Penal Laws', in G. O'Brien (ed.), *The Collected Essays of Maureen Wall* (Dublin: Geography Publications, Templeogue, 1989), pp.6–7.
8. H. Kingsmill Moore, *An Unwritten Chapter in the History of Education* (London: Macmillan & Co., 1904), pp.1–2, cited henceforth as Moore, *Unwritten Chapter.*
9. British Parliamentary Papers (BPP), 1825 (433), xii, *First Report of the Commissioners on Irish Education Inquiry,* p.771 and following.
10. Dowling, *History of Irish Education,* p.112.
11. D.H. Akenson, *The Irish Education Experiment: the National System in the Nineteenth Century,* eds T.W. Moody, J.C. Beckett, Studies in Irish History series, Vol. VII (London: Routledge and Kegan Paul, 1970), p.123.
12. For example, the group of men chosen in 1813 to oversee the endowed schools was given the title of 'commissioners of education' but were often referred to as the 'board of education'. These commissioners of 1813 continued to function after the national system was founded, but they continued to be known popularly as the 'board of education'. The new set of appointees was called 'commissioners of national education in Ireland'. In this study the terminology follows Akenson, *Irish Education,* p.124, n. 'Commissioners' refers specifically to the men appointed by the lord lieutenant to oversee the national system and 'board' is used to refer to the central establishment of the system of national education in Ireland, include commissioners, secretaries, inspectors and clerks.
13. BPP, 1812–13 (21), vi, *Fourteenth Report of the Commissioners of the Board of Education in Ireland,* p.2.
14. BPP, 1825 (433), xii, *First Report of Commissioners of Education Inquiry (Ireland),* p.6.
15. Dowling, *A History of Irish Education,* p.106.
16. Akenson, *Irish Education ,* pp.94–5.
17. BPP, 1813–14, iv Letter of John L. Foster to Board of Education, Ireland., p.341.
18. The terms 'united education', 'mixed education' and 'combined education' were used to denote schools in which literary instruction was to be given to Catholics and Protestants together.
19. BPP, 1828 (341), iv, *Report from Select Committee on the Subject of Education in Ireland,* p.341.
20. Moore, *Unwritten Chapter,* p.11.
21. Television Documentary, 'Léargas', Radio Telefís Éireann, 27 February 2001.
22. T. Ó hÉineacháin, 'Tuar Mhic Éide', Radio Telefís Éireann, 8 November 2000.
23. Seán Connolly, *Religion and Society in Nineteenth-Century Ireland* (Dundalk: Dún Dealgan Press, 1985), p.13.
24. BPP. 1831, I, A Bill for the Establishment and Maintenance of Parochial Schools, and the Advancement of the Education of the People in Ireland, p.286.

25. Akenson, *Irish Education*, p.125.
26. Akenson, *Irish Education*, p.126.
27. Ibid.
28. The Archbishop of Dublin [William Walsh], *Statement of the Chief Grievances of Irish Catholics in the Matter of Education*. (Dublin: Browne & Nolan, n.d.), p.10. Cited henceforth as Walsh, *Chief Grievances*.
29. Ibid.
30. Akenson, *Irish Education*, p.94.
31. P.C. Barry, 'The Holy See and the Irish National Schools', *Irish Ecclesiastical Record* (Maynooth: St Patrick's College, August, 1959), pp.90–105, (90, 104).
32. *The Christian Examiner and Church of Ireland Magazine* 2 series, iv, (No. 26, October 1835), p.686 and 3 series, ii (No. 26, Nov. 1837), pp.867–83, (London: William Curry). Both of these quotations are cited in Akenson, *Irish Education*, p.190.
33. Model schools were set up under Stanley's scheme as practising schools for the student teachers; the regular staff members were expected to have very high standards in their teaching methods.
34. Walsh, *Chief Grievances*, p.197.
35. Ulick Bourke, *Life of Archbishop McHale* (New York: Kennedy, 1902), p.57.
36. NLI Mss. 7649, 7650, 7651, Larcom Papers: nineteenth century collection of newspaper clippings on Irish affairs, particularly those relating to education and the Irish Catholic Church prelates.
37. N. Costello, *John McHale, Archbishop of Tuam* (Dublin: Talbot Press, 1939), p.64.
38. O'Neill, *A Rich Inheritance*, p.37.
39. Ibid., p.35.
40. T. de Burgo, *Hibernia Dominicana, sive Historia Provinciae Hiberniae Ordinis Praedicatorum* (Cologne: Metternich Press, 1762; supplement, Cologne 1772), p.361.
41. OPC, *Annals of the Dominican Convent Cabra: with Some Account of its Origins, 1647–1912.* Compiled by Mother Imelda Kavanagh (Dublin: published privately 1912), p.83. cited henceforth as *Cabra Annals*.
42. OPC, *Cabra Annals*, p.87.
43. Information given in conversations with Sr Marie Feeney, archivist, Poor Clare Convent, Harold's Cross, and Mother Brigid, Prioress, Carmelite Monastery, Hampton, Drumcondra, in 2004.
44. S. Enright, 'Women and Catholic Life in Dublin, 1766–1852', in J. Kelly and D. Keogh (eds) *History of the Catholic Diocese of Dublin* (Dublin: Four Courts Press, 2000), p.273.
45. OPC, *Cabra Annals*, pp.86–95. A more comprehensive account of Cabra's canonical separation from the Dominican Fathers is part of an on-going study by Sr Maura Duggan, a member of the Cabra Dominican Congregation.
46. OPC, *Cabra Annals* pp.92–3. See Figure 1, p.31. Copy of Brief of Gregory XVI.
47. OPC, *Cabra Annals*, p.96.
48. BPP 1834 (500), xl. *First Report, Commissioners of Education, Ireland*, Appendix 1 of Report.
49. NAD ED2.121, Folio 93, Cabra Convent School.
50. NAD, ED2/121, Folio 93, Cabra Convent School.
51. OPC *Account Book, 1872–1940*.
52. BPP, 1858, Vol. 25, No. 2 *Report of Commissioners of National Education*, Appendix, p.216.
53. NAI ED/32, Cabra Convent School.
54. NAI ED1/34, No. 87, Taylor's Hill, Galway.
55. NAI, ED2/136, Folio 84, Taylor's Hill, Galway.
56. O'Neill, *A Rich Inheritance*, p.74.
57. Ibid., Chapter 5, pp.54–75.

58. DDA Files 325/1, and 325/8, Cullen Papers, correspondence with nuns in Dominican Convent, Taylor's Hill, Galway, 1852–1860, Nos. 138, 169, 213, 218, 222, 223, 237, 247.
59. NAD ED2/104, Folio 92, Siena Convent School.
60. NAD ED9, Folio 92, Siena Convent School.
61. BPP, *Report of Commissioners of National Education,* Vol. 25, 1858 Appendix, p.216.
62. OPW, School Report Books, 1907–1923. K. and C. O Céirín, *Women of Ireland* (Kirwara, Galway: Tir Eolas, 1996), pp.159–60. In 1892 Mother Arsenius Morrogh-Bernard, an Irish Sister of Charity, began production of flannels, tweeds, blankets and other woollen goods with great success in Foxford, Co. Mayo.
63. BPP *Report of Commissioners of National Education 1864* Vol. IV, Accounts and Papers, Convent Schools, p.283.
64. NAI, ED9/File 5235, Kingston Convent School.
65. PRONI, 'Observations and Suggestions of District Inspector', St Catherine's Primary School, Falls Road Belfast, 1876.
66. OPS. *Book of Annals, Sion Hill Convent, Blackrock, Co. Dublin* (Dublin: Browne & Nolan, 1904), p.29. These annals will be referred to henceforth as *Sion Hill Annals.*
67. *Complete Catholic Registry, Directory and Almanack* 1860–66 (Dublin: Mullany, 1860–66) and following issues, referred to henceforth as *Catholic Directory.*
68. OPS, *Sion Hill Annals,* p.40 'Industrial school' in the case of the Sion Hill school, meant, presumably, a day school as distinct from a boarding school.
69. *The Catholic Registry* 1866, section on religious orders of women in the Dublin archdiocese.
70. OPS, *Sion Hill Annals,* p.52.
71. W.S. Joyce, *The Neighbourhood of Dublin,* (Dublin: Skellig Press, 1988, new edition), p.32.
72. Séamas Ó Maitiú, *Dublin's Suburban Towns, 1834–1930* (Dublin: Four Courts Press, 2003), p.150.
73. B.H. Blacker, *Brief Sketches of the Parishes of Booterstown and Donnybrook* (Dublin: Herbert, 1860), p.257.
74. OPS, *Sion Hill Annals,* p.12.
75. Ibid., pp.34–5.
76. Ibid., p.1.
77. Ibid., p.11. Emphasis mine.
78. Ibid., p.12. Emphasis mine.
79. Ibid., p.40.
80. D.C.I. MacAfee (ed.), *Concise Ulster Dictionary* (Oxford: University Press, 1996). J. Wright (ed.), *English Dialect Dictionary,* (Oxford: University Press, 1961) Vol. 5. Roughers did the preliminary preparation of the cloth when it was in the 'rough' or initial stages of manufacture. Hacklers spun the thread; stacking the woven cloth was the job of bundlers; fentors made openings or slits in the garments.
81. F. Stevens, *The New Inheritors* (London: Hutchinson, Educational, 1970), pp.166–7.
82. S. Enright, 'Women and Catholic Life in Dublin, 1766–1852, in J. Kelly & D. Keogh (eds), *History of the Catholic Diocese of Dublin* (Dublin: Four Courts Press, 2000), p.198.
83. R. Burke Savage, *A Valiant Dublin Woman* (Dublin: Gill & Son, 1940), p.54. Emphasis mine.
84. Enright, 'Women and Catholic Life in Dublin', p.271.
85. S.M.P. O'Farrell, 'Nano Nagle, Woman of the Gospel' (Cork: privately published master's thesis, University College, Cork, 1996), pp.215–36.
86. Burke Savage, *A Valiant Dublin Woman,* p.54.
87. J. Prunty, *Margaret Aylward, 1810–1889* (Dublin: Four Courts Press, 1999), p.102.
88. E. Crean, *Breaking the Silence, Education of the Deaf in Ireland, 1816–1996* (Dublin: Irish Deaf Society, 1997).

89. N. Griffey, *From Silence to Speech* (Dublin: Dominican Publications, 1994), p.22.
90. Information based on the tape-recorded interview with Sr Nicholas (March, 2000), referred to henceforth as Griffey's interview.
91. Griffey's interview.
92. C. Hope, *The Treble Almanack* (Dublin: Hope, 1835), List of Medical Practitioners.
93. Griffey, *From Silence to Speech,* p.72.
94. R. Duggan, 'Evaluation of the Senior Cycle Curriculum and its Effectiveness in the Preparation of Deaf Students for Life after School' (Unpublished M.Ed. thesis, University College, Dublin, 1998), pp.36–8.
95. O. Hufton, *The Prospect Before Her* (London: Harper Collins, 1995), p.390 and following.
96. T. McNamara, Letter addressed to the Irish hierarchy, quoted in the *Annals of Cabra,* pp.109–11.
97. Ibid., pp.109–11.
98. OPC, *Annals of Cabra,* p.111.
99. VFR, T. McNamara, 'Memoirs of the Congregation of the Mission in Ireland, England and Scotland 1867'. (Unpublished manuscript; pages unnumbered). Cited henceforth as McNamara, *Memoirs.*
100. T. Broderick and R. Duggan, *St. Mary's School for Deaf Girls, 1846–1986* (Dublin: St Mary's School for Deaf, 1996), p.16.
101. J. Cunningham, 'Fr. John Baptist Burke C.M., 1822–1894 (unpublished dissertation, Diploma for Teachers of the Deaf, University College, Dublin, 1978), p.3. Cited henceforth as Cunningham, 'Fr. John Burke'.
102. McNamara, *Memoirs,* p.157.
103. Griffey, *From Silence to Speech,* p.16.
104. Cunningham, 'Fr. John Burke', p.8.
105. Griffey's interview.
106. Crean, *Breaking the Silence,* p.22.
107. Griffey's interview.
108. Hufton, *The Prospect Before Her,* p.391.
109. Burke Savage, *A Valiant Dublin Women,* p.54.

2

Secondary Education[1]

Females go in a different direction[2]

The government's success with the primary schools under Stanley's Education Scheme of 1831 and the acceptance of the schools by the Churches, Protestant and Catholic, gave an incentive to interested parties, both political and clerical, to press for some kind of state funding for the many secondary schools which had sprung up around the country, especially in provincial towns. After the Famine years of the 1840s, conditions improved for tenant farmers who were now able to get more favourable leases for their land. These prosperous farmers, together with the merchants, traders and shop-keepers in the towns, all of whom now benefited from the increased money-flow, were able to send their children to the boarding schools which had been opened by the religious orders in Dublin and in the provincial towns.

By the 1870s, some Dominican nuns and other religious orders of women were eagerly awaiting any opportunity to further the cause of girls' secondary schooling but, as with the boys' schools, the question of funding was crucial. The religious, both men and women, who were running the schools, were for the most part financially dependent on the income from the low fees charged and in many cases fees were waived. Were it not for the donations of people who knew and were appreciative of their work, the schools could not have survived. To a lesser degree, the Protestant population also needed more financial help for the continuation of their schools. McElligott explains the situation:

> the eagerness with which the religious orders undertook the work of teaching had one paradoxical effect: it both lessened and increased the need for government intervention. On the one hand, the orders were in effect beginning to build a system of education which was eventually to supply the needs of over 90 per cent of the island's inhabitants. Hence the government could argue that it need do nothing. On the other hand, these same schools were soon to find the burden of providing money too much for them and so *had* to seek government aid.[3]

GOVERNMENT NEGOTIATIONS WITH THE CATHOLIC HIERARCHY

Necessity made the Catholic hierarchy negotiate with the government: they wanted to keep control of the schools while at the same time getting funding from the state for maintenance, building and staffing. Serious discussions began between the representatives of the Catholic hierarchy and the politicians and civil servants in Dublin and London. The land agitation of the 1870s made the government aware of the importance of the goodwill of the Catholic clergy to keep the political climate cool: it was in that context that the government moved to put a system in place which would partially finance the schools.

Patrick Keenan was a man who had had considerable experience in the educational field. His career included teaching in Blackrock College, Dublin, and some years as a training college professor, while later still he served as an inspector of schools under the Board of Education. In 1871 Keenan was appointed Resident Commissioner of National Education. He had made a study of a government system of funding schools which was in operation in Trinidad. This Trinadadian model allocated grants to each school in proportion to the number and proficiency of the students who passed an examination satisfactorily. Edward Howley, also a teacher in Blackrock College, used Keenan's findings and published *The Universities and Secondary Schools of Ireland with Proposals for their Improvement*. The first draft of the government plan was based on Howley's book.[4]

The demand for state funding was growing, especially from Cardinal Cullen who 'steadily opposed the undenominational system of education'.[5] In 1871, the Cardinal wrote a pastoral letter to the people of his archdiocese, in which he demanded that the monopoly of public money by 'schools in which you and we have no confidence and many of which are directly hostile to the Catholic religion', should be re-directed and used without religious distinction, for the benefit of all the intermediate schools in Ireland. The government required that examination results should be the criterion for the state funding of the schools and Cullen agreed to this. In a letter to Gladstone, cited by McElligott, Cullen wrote:

> the Catholics of Ireland have suffered in the past and are still suffering serious grievances in reference to education. They now expect that their wrongs will be redressed and that through your powerful influence some compensation will be made for past injustice, by establishing a system of public instruction of which Catholics rich and poor may avail themselves for their children without exposing their faith and morals to danger.[6]

Gladstone himself chose to address the matter of university education in Ireland instead of pursuing the more urgent question of intermediate education, as secondary education came to be called from that time onwards. In fact he lost on the university issue and parliament was dissolved in 1874. Home Rule, land reform and education were issues which occupied the minds of parliamentarians in relation to Ireland in the late 1870s and throughout the remainder of the century.

APPOINTMENT OF CHIEF SECRETARY, HICKS-BEACH

The Conservatives, in office under Disraeli in the years 1874–80, did not look favourably on Home Rule nor on Land Reform, but as Victoria Hicks-Beach points out in her book on Sir Michael Hicks-Beach:

> the feature of the new Parliament was the appearance for the first time of a solid body of fifty-four Irish members, pledged to the policy of Home Rule, and prepared under Isaac Butt, to press their claims in season and out of season.[7]

In 1874 Disraeli, who was aware that the political climate in relation to Ireland was fraught with difficulties, appointed Sir Michael Hicks-Beach as Chief Secretary for Ireland in 1874, warning him of the attitude in England to sectarianism in education and declaring that 'any measure, which advances or sanctions Denominational Education in Ireland will array the whole of England against it, except a portion of the clergy and a few country gentlemen'.[8] Funds were made available from surplus money, earlier allocated to the Established Church, which had been disestablished in 1869; in 1876 Keenan, the Resident Commissioner, was made aware of this arrangement. The Catholic hierarchy through their spokesman, Bishop George Michael Conroy of Ardagh and Clonmacnoise, made known their anxieties about interference by the state through inspection – fears that the Catholic schools could not compete with the amenities in well-endowed Protestant schools and that any inspection would point up the deficiencies in the Catholic schools. In 1876 Bishop Conroy wrote to Hicks-Beach:

> I trust that your plan for the improvement of Intermediate Education will not include a demand of the right to inspect Catholic Schools *otherwise than by testing their results in the examinations*. We should be jealous of such inspection; and to claim the right of making it, would signally interfere with the success of the proposed scheme.[9]

By 1877 Keenan succeeded in bringing the Catholic Church along with him and was ready to submit his plan to the cabinet. Conroy informed Hicks-Beach that 'the general feeling is that your plan is excellent in its outline and in most of its details'. In Hicks-Beach's letter to Cullen, Hicks-Beach explained that the word 'students' was intended to include girls, though he suggested that the value of payments, prizes, and exhibitions to girls might be lower than for boys.[10] We see in this an example of the prevailing attitude towards the education of girls. It was Hicks-Beach's inclusive definition of the term 'student' which drew this response from Cardinal Cullen:

> [i]n the intermediate schools the boys begin to train themselves for the army or navy, for the bar or magisterial bench, for the medical or surgical

professions, or for other occupations to which men alone can aspire; females go in a different direction and require other sorts of training and teaching; and it seems strange that regulations for the two classes should be united in the one bill.[11]

LACK OF GOVERNMENT FUNDING FOR TEACHERS

A serious fault in the memorandum prepared by Keenan in 1877 for Chief Secretary Hicks-Beach was the lack of provision for the payment of teachers in the proposed schools. It was particularly difficult for the Catholic schools and colleges which were dependent for the most part on the services of the religious as unpaid teachers. They could not afford to pay many lay teachers and this in turn left a legacy of poorly paid teachers in the Catholic schools. The involvement of so many religious in the schools meant that teaching posts were almost exclusively held by priests, brothers or nuns. Cardinal Cullen commented that the absence of provision for the payment of teachers would be a burden on Catholics who had no endowments to draw on and who could not afford to pay teachers' salaries at a reasonable economic rate to their lay teachers. Whatever were the shortcomings of the memorandum, the Cardinal gave it his qualified approval, provided the bill on which it was based did not clash with Catholic interests or doctrine. In June 1878 the Intermediate Education (Ireland) Bill was introduced in the House of Lords. The Bill went through both houses of parliament without too much controversy and An Act to Promote Intermediate Education in Ireland was given the royal assent in August 1878.[12]

The Act was not perfect and there were a number of issues which were not resolved. In particular, there were no grants for the building, furnishing or equipping of schools. Though the schools were to receive money based on examination results, there were no guidelines laid down for the use of such money. The Act recognized the right of girls to inclusion in its terms, but no additional financial provision was made for them. The thorny question of inspection of the schools was not clearly defined. As a result, no inspections were carried out. The Catholic hierarchy favoured inspection only if it did not involve the internal management of the schools. A Board of Commissioners of Intermediate Education was established in 1878, representing the Church of Ireland, Catholic and Presbyterian Churches.

PROGRAMME FOR EXAMINATIONS 1879

The first task of these Commissioners of Intermediate Education was to set out a programme of studies for all the schools coming under their jurisdiction, to decide on the method of examinations, and to give the terms of reference for the appointment and the duties of examiners and superintendents, whose responsibility it would be to set the examination papers and to supervise and examine the pupils throughout the country. The standing committees of the Catholic Headmasters' Association, representing the leading religious orders and the diocesan seminaries, and the Schoolmasters' Association (Protestant), met the Commissioners. Significantly, there was, as yet, no representative body for Catholic headmistresses. The result of the meeting with the Commissioners was that a programme of examinations was drawn up for 1879. Payment was made to the schools on the results of the examinations, and prizes and exhibitions were awarded to pupils of outstanding ability. There were three grades: junior, middle and senior. A preparatory grade was instituted in 1892 and lasted for about twenty years, at which point it was decided that the pupils were too young to be put under the strain of a public examination. Dowling comments, 'the schools could now, if efficient, command a steady additional income, while intelligent pupils could by their own industry pay their way through a secondary school.'[13] Prior to the introduction of the Intermediate examinations, many schools had entered their pupils for the examinations of the Science and Art Department, South Kensington, the examinations for the Civil Service, and examinations under the old Queen's University, similar to those set up by the universities of Oxford, Cambridge and London. The examinations of Queen's University ended in 1879.

IMPORTANCE OF THE 1878 ACT

From an educational point of view, the Act to Promote Intermediate Education in Ireland failed to ensure that inspection took place in the schools, while the system of payment by results lent itself to cramming and excessive inter-school rivalry. Accordingly, changes were made to the Act in 1900. In spite of its short-comings, the Act was of immense social importance. Boys and girls who, prior to the passing of the Act, would not have had the opportunity for secondary education, could now attend schools where the fees were low or, if the pupils were academically able, they could finance themselves through the system of prizes and exhibitions. Thus they could now aspire to opportunities which had previously been closed to them; for the boys, entrance to university opened the way to careers in the professions or to the higher civil service. For the girls, however, university education was not to be an option for another decade.

THE DEBATE ABOUT WOMEN'S EDUCATION

The delay in introducing university-oriented education for girls in Ireland can be attributed in part to the Victorian image of the ideal woman leading a sheltered life and acting as the guardian and manager of the home, which was her domain. Victorian women were not expected to compete with men intellectually and therefore education for women demanded only that they should have the accomplishments necessary for their role in society. Burstyn, in her book on women's education in Victorian times, writes that, '[c]leverness in women, was measured by social success. Women achieved influence over men indirectly, by listening to them, agreeing with them or, occasionally, offering an opinion of their own'.[14] In the case of Irish Catholic women, a strong commitment to their religion was demanded in addition to this ideal of womanhood.

The immediate task of the Commissioners for Education in 1878 was the implementation of the Intermediate Act. Daniel Murray's and Paul Cullen's combined terms of office as archbishops of Dublin spanned the years 1823–78, the half-century preceding the passing of the Intermediate Education (Ireland) Act in 1878. Although the education of Irish Catholic girls was of prime importance to both archbishops, neither envisaged a secondary education system which would prepare young women for gainful employment or for higher education. Equal status for boys and girls in the new system was not on their agenda. Murray and Cullen and other bishops were supportive of the education given prior to 1878 in the existing convent boarding schools of the Loreto, Ursuline and Dominican orders, and in the schools of the new Irish congregations of the Sisters of the Presentation, Sisters of Mercy, Irish Sisters of Charity and also the Brigidine Sisters.

It was at the request, direct or indirect, of the local bishop that new foundations were opened by the nuns; in the case of the Dominicans, all the convents founded from Cabra in the nineteenth century were given prior episcopal approval. The bishops also welcomed the new French congregations which came to Ireland between 1770 and 1870, as witness the geographical spread of the convents through all four provinces of the country; some had opened more than one convent. In the period preceding the passing of the Intermediate Education Act in 1878, at least nine French teaching congregations came to Ireland. By 1878 they were firmly established and their schools were well received.[15] Donal Kerr credits Murray with identifying 'the much-neglected education of the people as a major need'; the archbishop set about finding religious men and women who would undertake that work.[16] Thanks largely to Murray, by 1840 the number of orders of religious women in Dublin had increased to seven, having between them fifteen convents, each with a school attached. The Jesuits were also supported by Murray in providing education for boys of middle-class families. Ignatius Rice, at the request of Murray in 1812, opened a Christian Brothers' school in Hanover Street in Dublin for the free education of boys.[17]

INCREASE IN NUMBER OF CONVENT SCHOOLS 1865–90

In 1865 the number of religious in Dublin had increased to eleven orders and forty-three convents and by 1890 had further increased to seventeen orders with a total of eighty-seven convents. This was an increase of ten new congregations of women and of seventy-two convents in the Dublin archdiocese alone over a period of fifty years. Not all of these eighty-seven convents had schools; some congregations of religious women had a combined ministry of health care and education. Kerr writes that Murray, 'prudent and cautious though he was, welcomed anyone who had something useful to do for the diocese and people of Dublin'.[18] The Sisters of Mercy and the Irish Sisters of Charity, the latter known today as the Religious Sisters of Charity, were engaged in the archdiocese mainly in primary schools. The Presentation Sisters had a secondary school in Clondalkin, County Dublin from 1857; all the other Presentation schools in the archdiocese of Dublin at that time were primary schools. At the time of Murray's death, in 1852, Dublin had 220, mostly national, schools which Catholic children could attend without fear of proselytization.

Cardinal Cullen's great ambition and enthusiasm was for the establishment of a Catholic university in Dublin, and while he took a very active part in the debates about state support for secondary education, he was not favourably disposed towards new ideas for expanding the curriculum in girls' schools. Evidence of this was shown by his opposition to Hicks-Beach's inclusion of girls in the new Act of 1878. Were it not for the lobbying and urging of Anna Maria Haslam, Isabella Tod and their group, girls might not have been included in the Act.[19] Their part in the debate will be treated of below. The comment of Dr Nulty of the diocese of Meath seems to sum up the opinion of many of his contemporaries, that examinations were unsuited for 'the respectable middle-class female youth of Ireland, who will be the wives and mothers of farmers, graziers, merchants, manufacturers and professional men of the coming generation'.[20]

EARLY NINETEENTH-CENTURY CONVENT SCHOOL EDUCATION

What was the curriculum of the convent education so favoured by the bishops? *The Catholic Directory* 1873 carried advertisements for the schools of St Louis Convent in Monaghan, Dominican convent schools in Kingstown, Wicklow and Sion Hill, and the Brigidine convent schools in Abbeyleix, Queen's County and in Tullow, Co. Carlow. The Brigidines and Dominicans used the same kind of wording to sum up the education offered prior to the introduction of the Intermediate Education (Ireland) Act of 1878, with phrases such as, 'all elements of an English education … the course comprises English, History, Geography … and all the accomplishments necessary to complete the education of a Young Lady'. The description of the school was usually couched as 'Kingstown Boarding School for Young Ladies'. The St Louis Convent in Monaghan used an expanded version:

> [T]he deportment and manners of the pupils are scrupulously attended to, no efforts are spared to give the Young Ladies habits of order and neatness,

that they may return to their families not only accomplished but helpful and intelligent in all the duties of a woman's sphere.[21]

There was no mention of either science or mathematics, except for some basic arithmetic; neither was Latin taught in girls' schools. Whatever the wording, the formation of the 'Young Lady' was clearly what the Catholic hierarchy expected of a convent boarding school education and that was what was given. Neither religion nor religious instruction is mentioned explicitly in any of these schools' notices; a convent education was inherently a religious education; there was no need to stress the obvious in a Catholic directory.

INFLUENCE OF PROTESTANT WOMEN EDUCATORS

The banner for secondary and higher education for girls in Ireland was carried by women of various Protestant denominations, but there was no woman from a Catholic background publicly agitating for an expansion of educational opportunities for girls. Four ladies in particular were determined to provide secondary education for a broader population of girls than those whose families could afford a place for their daughters in boarding schools: Anne Jellicoe (1823–80) was from a Church of Ireland background; Anna Maria Haslam's (1829–1922) family was Quaker; Margaret Byers (1832–1912) and Isabella M.S. Tod (1836–96) were both Presbyterians. These leaders of the Irish campaign for the social and educational advancement of women were influenced, in some measure, by their sister-campaigners in England, particularly by the work of the educationalists Frances Buss of the London Collegiate School and Dorothea Beale of Cheltenham Ladies' College.[22] There was a difference in the approach in each country. In Ireland, in general, the concentration was on the question of political independence for the whole nation and not just for women's franchise. Jellicoe, Byers, Haslam and Tod were interested in equality of education and saw it as a crucial element in the furtherance of the women's cause in Ireland, though not to the exclusion of more overt political action. In educational circles, these pioneering women were very successful; Haslam and Jellicoe founded the Irish Society for the Training and Employment of Educated Women (later the Queen's Institute) in 1861. Later Haslam, Byers and Tod were instrumental in having girls admitted to both the Intermediate examinations and to take the degrees of the Royal University of Ireland.[23]

Byers established the Ladies' Collegiate School in Belfast in 1866, renamed Victoria College in 1897, the year of Queen Victoria's diamond jubilee. The Collegiate School became a highly regarded educational institution where girls could pursue their courses to university level. The pupils were prepared for the examinations and successfully entered for them. Jordan writes, 'the biggest obstacle to girls' education was the sort of social pretensions which made the gentry ... and professional men reluctant to allow their daughters to mix with the children of respectable shopkeepers and well-to-do farmers'.[24] This kind of social snobbery was not alien to parents of Catholic girls either.

TOD, HASLAM, BYERS AND JELLICOE

Of the four ladies who campaigned for better educational opportunities for girls, Jellicoe, according to Anne O'Connor and Susan Parkes, does not fit in to the mainstream of educational reformers of this period in the sense that she was not interested in the wider question of feminism and women's rights. The only women's right for which she contended was, to quote her own words, 'their right to be educated'.[25] Tod, Haslam and Byers had the more public profiles; they campaigned on an educational and political front. Mary Cullen lists Haslam's interests as married women's property rights; improved female education and access to higher education; access to better paid and a wider variety of employments for middle-class women, including the professions; opposition to double standards in the response to prostitution; and participation in political life.[26] Isabella Tod had even wider concerns, which involved her in campaigning for the women's franchise while at the same time working tirelessly for girls' secondary and university education. Luddy points out that Tod's involvement in the National Association for the Promotion of Social Science (NAPSS) 'provided an important platform for activists, many of them women, who wished to reform society'.[27]

Tod was also very much involved in the political sphere in Ulster. Armour says she was 'the moving spirit behind the foundation of the Ulster Women's Liberal Unionist Association', an organization which rallied Ulster Unionist women to 'give moral support ... to the cause of the Union'.[28] Through her writings, Tod contributed to the debate on education, submitting articles on education to journals such as the *Dublin University Review* and *Englishwoman's Review*. An example of her style and concern for equality of treatment of all girls, rich and poor, can be read in an article which she had published in 1889. Tod was reacting to a new rule of the National Board of Education, which laid down that girls who had passed the fifth standard in the national school, should thereafter spend the remainder of their time in [national] school in 'industrial education'. Tod objected strongly, making the following points: the new rule would halt the mental development of the girls at a very young age; children of many different classes attend national schools in Ireland and those who were better-off financially would leave the school after fifth class and thus reduce the mix of ability among the pupils. Many schools would then cater for the very poor and these girls would be denied the benefits of the stimulus of the more able pupils. Tod took particular exception to needlework being the main subject of this new industrial education: 'plain sewing which every woman requires for home use does not need that such a heavy sacrifice be made for it'. Above all, a girl 'must have her mind so far trained as to learn *how to learn*'.[29] This was the great objective of the campaigners for girls' secondary and university education: the expansion of the girls' school curriculum to bring it into line with that of the boys. Tod's influence and connections with so many strands of the politics of her time – anti-Home Rule; reform of the Land Acts; the franchise – all gave her added authority when campaigning for parity of treatment of girls with boys. In Tod's opinion, what was available to one group should be available to all.

ALEXANDRA COLLEGE

The influence and example of Isabella Tod and Margaret Byers in Belfast spurred Anne Jellicoe in Dublin to establish similar institutes for girls. Jellicoe was associated with two educational enterprises in Dublin in the 1860s: the Queen's Institute (1861) and Alexandra College (1866). Though the Queen's Institute lasted just twenty years, it served a very great need indeed in women's education during its short life-span; it was regarded in its time as 'one of the most practically useful establishments in Ireland'.[30] Jellicoe saw the necessity for practical training for girls and the openings which such education would offer to those interested in independent careers. The curriculum of the Queen's Institute catered for the training of telegraph clerks, including the study of commercial subjects, with an emphasis on foreign-language correspondence. Lithography, sewing-machine work and wood-engraving were also included. However, more successful and even more enduring was the establishment of Alexandra College (1866), a joint foundation of Anne Jellicoe and the Church of Ireland Archbishop of Dublin (1864–84), Dr Richard Chenevix-Trench (1807–86). Alexandra College was modelled on Queen's College, Harley Street, London. But whereas the Queen's Institute in Dublin could cater only for 'distressed gentle-women', Jellicoe had a broad vision of a women's college which would not only provide for the practical skills of the commercial world but would also train young women for teaching careers, whether as governesses or in schools. Alexandra College thus provided a sound liberal education for young middle-class women and was the first college of its kind in Ireland. Jellicoe's success indirectly 'provided the stimulus for the huge growth nationwide of Roman Catholic convent secondary schools in the last decades of the nineteenth century'.[31]

Alexandra College had an ambitious programme running in 1873; although the college was in severe financial difficulties, the curriculum included mathematics in all its branches, arithmetic, algebra, trigonometry, as well as natural philosophy, Hebrew, Greek, Latin, German, geology and biology.[32] This was a step on the way to broaden the curriculum in girls' schools and was a pointer to the way forward for other schools. As O Céirín noted above, it was a challenging change from the 'accomplishments' curriculum of the existing convent schools. The religious who managed the Catholic secondary schools were spurred on by the pioneering Protestant ladies, especially Anne Jellicoe and her colleagues in

Alexandra College, who had such a broad vision and worked diligently for the educational advancement of women in the 1860s. The success particularly of Alexandra College, Dublin, undoubtedly had a significant influence on the thinking of the Dominican nuns in Sion Hill, in particular, in the development of their new foundation in Eccles Street, Dublin in 1882. In the climate of the time, Catholic bishops were very fearful of young Catholic girls attending Protestant schools, and it was believed that if the Catholic schools did not update their curriculum and bring it into line with the needs of the time, pupils might be enticed from the Catholic schools to Alexandra or other non-Catholic schools. It was sincerely believed that in attending a non-Catholic school or college Catholic boys and girls would be in grave danger of losing their faith. The legacy of the Penal Laws and the experience and fear of active prosyletism, which was common even in the mid-nineteenth century, died hard with the hierarchy. The ideals which inspired Anne Jellicoe to provide classes for ' "respectable" young girls of limited means' in the Queen's Institute in Dublin doubtless was instrumental particularly in leading Mother Antonina Hanley to open Our Lady of Sion Orphanage in Eccles Street.[33]

CATHOLIC LAY WOMEN

The absence of Catholic lay women from among the group of prominent activists for women's education has already been mentioned. Luddy claims that,

> from the early years of the nineteenth century Catholic women's con-
> tribution to charity work became vested in religious congregations. ... This
> obviously had important consequences for the extent to which lay women
> became involved in voluntary effort and it also defined the structure and
> limits of the societies they organised.[34]

It was not by accident that the foundresses of the eighteenth- and nineteenth-century Irish religious congregations of women, alone or with some like-minded ladies, were very often involved in charitable works before they set up, or were advised to set up, a religious congregation: Nano Nagle (1718–84), Catherine McAuley (1781–1841) and Margaret Aylward (1810–89) are noted examples of this. Nagle's congregation, established in 1769 as the Sisters of the Charitable Institution in Cork, took simple vows which allowed them a certain amount of freedom of movement, to go outside their own house to work for the poor.[35] The structured and regulated life-style provided continuity and stability for their work. In a post-Emancipation Church the Catholic hierarchy became more authoritative and exercised control in a wider sphere than had previously been the case. Most of the congregations were under the diocesan bishops' control. Their Protestant counterparts were free to support publicly the groups which were campaigning for change in the provision of educational opportunities for women. It called for courage and a certain self-confidence for Catholic women, especially women religious, to act independently of the church authorities.

As time passed and the number of Congregations increased in Ireland, many Catholic women who would, in a previous generation, have been drawn to charitable works, now entered one of the new or existing congregations or, if they did not choose religious life, they subscribed financially or with their own voluntary work to the institutions which the religious now managed. Anna Maria Ball (1785–1871) and Ellen Woodlock (1811–84) are two examples of such women. Anna was the wife of John O'Brien, a wealthy Catholic, and she was instrumental in setting up an orphanage for girls which she gave over to the care of the Poor Clare nuns in Harold's Cross Dublin; she also started a House of Refuge which later was transferred from the Coombe, in the Liberties of Dublin, to Stanhope Street, north of the Liffey, and which in 1814 was given into the care of the Irish Sisters of Charity.[36]

Eleanor Woodlock, born into the Mahony family of Cork, was educated in France and married Thomas Woodlock of Monkstown, Dublin. She was widowed before the birth of her son. She then 'tried her vocation' as a St Louis nun in France – placing her son in school with the Sisters of St Louis – but decided religious life was not for her. She returned to Ireland and during a life-time of charitable work she was the leader among a group who set up Temple Street Children's Hospital Dublin in 1872. Woodlock was responsible for bringing the St Louis Order to Monaghan. She was friendly with the Dominicans in Sion Hill and donated money and furniture to them when the nuns were setting up the Eccles Street convent in 1882.[37] Woodlock probably realized, during the four years which she spent with the St Louis nuns, that the very rule of life of a religious precluded women religious from engaging in any form of political or quasi-political activity. Such a 'political' life-style was necessary to further the causes of their charitable ministries; this did not, of course, prevent some religious from using their contacts and from having the views of religious made known through third parties. This remote contact would not have had the same impact as having a direct input in public debate or making suggestions in the political forum.

It was not until the religious had their secondary schools well developed and had had some experience of advancing the cause of higher education, that women who had been to Catholic schools and colleges emerged to take their part in the public debates of the day about women's issues. Hanna Sheehy Skeffington, Mary Hayden, Nora Meade, Mary Macken and others are notable examples. Later in the chapter the contribution of Dominican College, Eccles Street, one of the colleges where some of these women were educated, will be discussed.

CONVENT BOARDING AND DAY SCHOOLS PRE-1878

Anne O'Connor makes the point that the French religious who came to Ireland in the nineteenth century did not have to alter their educational system to any great extent prior to 1880 in order to fit in with the prevailing educational system in Ireland at the time.[38] In two of her publications, 'Influences Affecting Girls' Secondary Education in Ireland 1860–1910' and 'The Revolution in Girls' Secondary Education in Ireland 1860–1910', O'Connor contends that, prior to the introduction of the Intermediate Act of 1878, most convent schools had very similar curricula.[39] This statement, and its implications for the education offered in early and mid-nineteenth-century Dominican schools, deserves to be tested before proceeding with the Dominicans' response to the 1878 Intermediate Act. While the model of the French boarding school came to Ireland with the Ursulines in 1771 and the Society of the Sacred Heart, Sisters of St Louis and other religious orders in the mid-nineteenth century, the model of Dominican education for young girls had been set in early eighteenth-century Ireland and was well typified by the Dominican schools in Galway, Drogheda and Channel Row, the forerunners of Dominican Convent Cabra.

New models of education

Three schools of French origin, the Ursulines in Sligo, Society of the Sacred Heart, Mount Anville, Dublin, and the Sisters of St Louis in Monaghan, are chosen for comparison with Dominican schools. The orders chosen came from a French cultural background, all three had boarding schools in Ireland and catered for children from a social class similar to those in the Dominican schools. The occupation of the father of the family gives some indication of the social status of those families. Dominican Convent, Taylor's Hill, Galway, is the only school which includes the record of the fathers' occupations. The fathers' occupations for the Sion Hill and Mount Anville pupils were obtained from research on the home addresses of pupils while *Thom's Directory* gave the occupations of the householders at those addresses (see Figure 2).[40] The years researched covered the period 1850–1902. The occupations varied alphabetically from accountant to watchmaker. The resulting over-all image of the family background of the pupils in any one of the three schools was of the professional, farming or merchant class. The farming class from which the pupils came was commonly known in Ireland as 'strong farmers', a term used to describe well-to-do tenant farmers, or land-owning farmers. In her study of four English Congregations of nuns, Barbara Walsh found that many of the Irish recruits to the religious congregations in the nineteenth century in England, 'emanated from the strata of "strong farmer" communities in the rich cattle and dairy counties of Munster and south-east Leinster'.[41] Numerous pupils in the boarding schools in Ireland, including Dominican schools, came from that same rural and farming background and some would have chosen to join the order with whom they were educated.

Figure 2. Occupations of fathers of pupils in three secondary schools

---

**Sacred Heart Convent, Mount Anville, Dublin,
Dominican Convent, Taylor's Hill, Galway,
Dominican Convent, Sion Hill, Dublin.**

1850–1912

Accountant	Hairdresser
Army Officer	Hotelier
Barrister	Magistrate
Building Contractor	Member of Parliament
Caretaker	Merchant
Cattle Dealer	Pawnbroker
Chemist	Policeman
Civil Servant	Professor of French
Distiller	Solicitor
Doctor	Surgeon
Farmer	Teacher
Gardener	Veterinary Surgeon
Grocer	Warehouseman
Haberdasher	Watchmaker

Ursuline schools

The Ursuline Order was the first to come to Ireland from France in 1771; the nuns were brought to Cork by Nano Nagle. Later other Ursuline foundations were made in Thurles, Waterford and Sligo. In their prospectus, the Sligo Ursulines offered '[to pay] the strictest attention to the morals, health, and manners of the children'. Habits of industry, order, and economy were inculcated, and the overall system of education included 'all those attainments which are necessary, useful and ornamental in society'.[42] The Ursulines had very definite written instructions about the system of reports which was used as a means of 'exciting Virtuous Emulation'. Other incentives to good behaviour in the school were: daily marks for conduct, manners and studies; public accounts of conduct; distinction of places; particular and general examinations, and concerts.[43] Religion of course, was the bedrock of the Ursulines' educational ministry. Their curriculum or 'course of instruction' is that given for 1840, and included English, French and Italian languages, writing, arithmetic, history, geography, astronomy and use of globes. The unusual subjects were: conchology – the study of shells and shell-fish; mineralogy, inlaying, heraldry and japanning – the Japanese method of varnishing. The accomplishments were catered for with music, dancing and painting.[44] The Ursulines nuns were one of the first teaching orders to accommodate their school curriculum to the Intermediate examination system and were to the forefront in their school in Cork in the campaign for the university education of women in Ireland.

Schools of the Society of Sacred Heart

The nuns of the Society of the Sacred Heart came to Thurles, Co. Tipperary, in 1842, and to Glasnevin in Dublin in 1853; after a short time, they moved from Glasnevin to Mount Anville in Dundrum, Co. Dublin. The nuns set up a boarding school which was very much in the tradition of their schools in France. Like the Ursulines, the community brought handbooks with them: *Les Règlements des Pensionnats*, 'Regulations for Boarding Schools' and *Plan d'Etudes*, 'Plan of Studies'.[45] These two handbooks set out the Society's ideas about education, the running of the schools and the course of studies. The senior pupils' curriculum included the elements of Christian philosophy, while the study of ethics was introduced 'to strengthen their sense of human responsibility … an ability to think for oneself, and [to acquire] a breadth of view, strength of judgement and fineness of perception'.[46] These subjects were unusual in girls' schools at the time. History and literature were taught on broad lines and above all, faith and religion were to be the foundation of education. The Sacred Heart schools all followed a disciplinary code which was demanding, orderly and planned in detail and was set out in *Disciplines et Usages du Pensionnat*, 'Customs and Code of Discipline of the Boarding School'.[47] In the senior classes, the exercise of judgement was cultivated by exercises in literary criticism and research. The sciences were not neglected and included mathematics. Needlework was recommended as a remedy for idleness and 'its disastrous consequences'.

Discipline in a Sacred Heart school was strengthened by regular reports held at various levels: once a week, once a term and annually. At the term and annual reports, the whole school assembled formally, gloves were worn, and curtsies were made to the superior of the convent, who presided at the function. The pupils were placed in rank order according to their individual success in the examinations. This formal regime in the Sacred Heart schools was softened by the atmosphere of the school, which was one of 'mutual affection, respect, trustful give and take, and of joy'. The children learned the value of happiness of life 'when it unfolds before the eyes of God, along the lines of duty, and in a spirit of friendliness'.[48] A past pupil of a Sacred Heart school in England bears out the truth of these statements in her reminiscences:

> [t]here was always laughter; there was discipline, of course, but there was always fairness. … There was a great deal of encouragement. We had rewards like the *Ruban Rouge* and the *Ruban Bleu* and they were what you aimed for. You feel that you are important, that you're being allowed to

develop. ... Their teaching was very good, ... they taught you how to learn and ... you can bet your boots if I don't know something I know how to find it out.[49]

The Sacred Heart nuns retained the French style of boarding school in Ireland and seem not to have been unduly influenced by the educational developments introduced by the Intermediate Education Act. Not until 1931 did the first pupils from Mount Anville enter for the intermediate examinations; this was fifty-three years after the introduction of the state system.

St Louis Convent School, Monaghan

The Sisters of St Louis came to Monaghan in 1859, just six years after the Society of the Sacred Heart settled in Dublin. From the St Louis' records, it is evident that the nuns of this new order were, as were the Ursulines and the Society of the Sacred Heart, faithful to their French inheritance. French language was introduced as the language of the Monaghan school, including prayers; curtsying and 'mannerly forms of bearing and social expressions' were encouraged. There were *soirées* once a month for the nuns and pupils at which the pupils recited and sang.[50] Even so, the St Louis nuns, like the Ursulines, quickly adopted the educational system prevailing in Ireland, and soon after the introduction of the Intermediate Education Act in 1878 entered pupils for the examinations in the early 1880s. The most striking step taken in St Louis Convent, Monaghan, was the adoption of the 'Celtic' language and a strong commitment to the Gaelic League ideals.[51] An entry in 'Reflections', a retrospective account of life in the boarding school in St Louis Convent, notes that a pupil, 'Mary Cleary and companions, were the only girl candidates in the country to take Irish as an Intermediate subject in 1895'.[52] In time, Irish replaced French as the language of the school, and by 1901 a writer in *The Western People* of the time rebuked the Irish convents in general for aping English education, and praised the nuns of the Order of St Louis for their splendid work for the Irish language at the Intermediate examinations in Monaghan, Carrickmacross [Co. Monaghan], and Kiltimagh [Co. Mayo].[53]

Though the St Louis nuns thus adapted well to Irish culture and language and to the ideals of the Gaelic revival, there is no doubt that these three French orders brought a strong sense of their own identity and some sense of French culture to their pupils. To their work in the schools they introduced a very well-regulated code of conduct, and in each case this code was set out in directories or handbooks. In summary, in the nineteenth century some French convent schools developed a ritualized assembly; pupils' progress in school work was publicly reported; marks were allocated and pupils were placed in rank order of merit. The assembly, which was common to all three orders, was presided over by the superior of the community: all pupils were required to curtsy to her when their names were called for their report. This ceremony must have been a great ordeal and test of nerve for the pupils, especially for the more timid among them. In particular, the St Louis nuns used the *soirée* and school concerts to good effect as a method of 'exciting virtuous emulation', a phrase used also by the Ursulines.[54]

Sr Dominic Kelly in *The Sligo Ursulines* lists the texts studied by the novices in preparation for their teaching: ancient and modern history and geography with astronomy were taught, while literature included 'elegant extracts' from the classics. The Society of the Sacred Heart also had a very definite style and well-documented plan of studies, calculated to develop the intellectual formation of the pupils. Phrases such as 'an ability to think for oneself', an intellect with 'a breadth of view', the studies are 'serious and strong', give an idea of a curriculum which aimed to develop more than 'the accomplishments necessary for the education of a young lady'.

DOMINICAN CONVENT SCHOOLS

The Dominican school in Taylor's Hill in Galway has a history dating back to the seventeenth century. Historically the present school in Taylor's Hill is the successor of the first Dominican girls' school in Ireland and its educational legacy has been inherited by later generations of Dominican women in Ireland.[55] Most Dominican schools now centre around the east coast, particularly in the Dublin area. Map 3 indicates the approximate site of each of the Dublin schools.

The Galway Dominicans had experienced exile and separation in Spanish Dominican convents (1652–86) where they taught in the convent schools in Bilbao, Zamora, Toledo and Valladolid.[56] Two nuns, Juliana Nolan (c.1612–1701) and Mary Lynch (born c.1626), returned to Galway in 1686 to re-found the Galway convent and in time opened another school in Kirwan's Lane. The school closed shortly after 1817 for lack of numbers, the unsuitable location in the centre of Galway city and the condition of the house in which they lived. No other Dominican school was opened in Galway until the nuns moved to Taylor's Hill, on the west side of the city in 1859. This, then, was the legacy which later generations of Dominican women in Ireland inherited. It is not surprising, given the history and background of the Dominican nuns, that the education provided in their schools, even in the later foundations from Cabra, tended to concentrate on what was acceptable to the upper and middle classes of the day.

Cabra's nineteenth-century daughter houses in Sion Hill, Kingstown and Belfast, while being autonomous convents, held in respect the traditions which they in turn indirectly inherited through the Channel Row convent. Dominican Convent Wicklow was founded from the Kingstown Dominican convent, but it had a strong association with Cabra through the Maher and Moran families. These older eighteenth-century and early nineteenth-century schools of the order catered totally for the daughters of the landed gentry and the wealthy merchant classes of their time; in many cases the nuns were educating their own nieces and the daughters of family friends. The pupils in Siena Convent Drogheda were

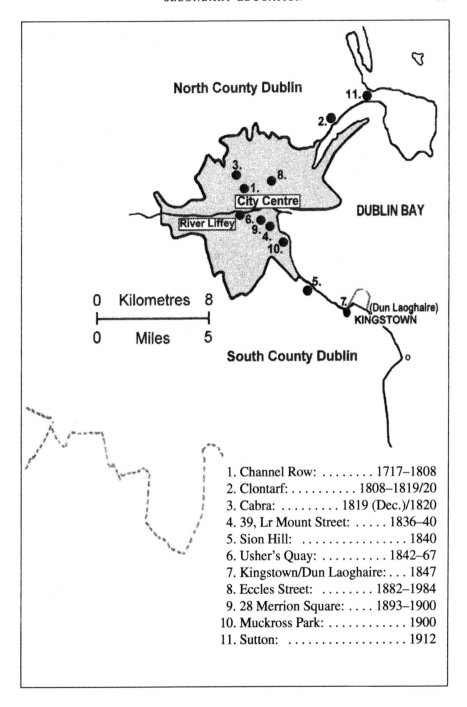

North County Dublin

11.

2.

3.

8.

1.

City Centre

River Liffey

6.

9.

4.

10.

DUBLIN BAY

5.

7.

(Dun Laoghaire)
KINGSTOWN

South County Dublin

0   Kilometres   8

0   Miles   5

1. Channel Row: 1717–1808
2. Clontarf: 1808–1819/20
3. Cabra: . . . . 1819 (Dec.)/1820
4. 39, Lr Mount Street: 1836–40
5. Sion Hill: 1840
6. Usher's Quay: 1842–67
7. Kingstown/Dun Laoghaire: . . . 1847
8. Eccles Street: 1882–1984
9. 28 Merrion Square: 1893–1900
10. Muckross Park: 1900
11. Sutton: 1912

Map 3. Foundations and schools in the City and County of Dublin

described in the school's prospectus as 'children from the best families in the adjacent counties'.[57] Surnames such as Bellew, Wyse, Weever, Plunkett, Esmond, de Burgo, Browne and Netterville in the roll books bear out these family ties and the social milieu which was their everyday life.

Accepting the stereotype

Alison Jordan, in her biography of Margaret Byers, neatly sums up what was considered a fashionable education: 'the sort of "flimsy" education which prepared girls to speak a little French, sing and play the piano a little, do a little painting on satin and velvet and look pretty at a concert or a ball'.[58] The first prospectus of the boarding school in Cabra is worth studying. In the light of the definition of a fashionable education it gives the reader an insight into the mind-set of its author(s) and it leaves no doubt about the kind of regime which was promised in Cabra for the education of its pupils. The prospectus makes it quite clear that the nuns, while dedicated to the temporal and eternal welfare of the pupils,

> will not in any manner sanction the imprudence of parents, who attaching undue importance to what is called a fashionable education, waste time and money in having their children taught, to the exclusion of useful and necessary knowledge, accomplishments for which they have neither taste, capacity, nor use.[59]

The prospectus stated that the girls should be made aware of their position in life and that should they 'rise in society', their Cabra education would permit them to take their place 'with propriety, ease and dignity'. In the meantime, imitation of 'elegant demeanour' was not to be sought after: the nuns' expectation was that the girls should leave the school with 'the solid information that qualifies for the due management of the domestic circle'. There is a certain ambiguity in the attitude of the nuns as set out in the prospectus: parents who wished to have social skills taught in the school were criticized, while at the same time dancing, music and painting were taught in the school. Extra fees were charged for the service. It is fair to assume also that the Cabra school, perhaps with slight variations, was the appropriate model for Dominican education in the pre-1878 era. The Dominicans taught what was called at the time 'the usual branches' of English education: grammar, history, geography, the use of the globes, writing and arithmetic; French, Italian, and in some schools, German. Almost every convent school had on the prospectus, 'every species of Plain and Ornamental needlework and the accomplishments necessary to complete the education of a Young Lady'. The Dominican education portrayed by the Cabra prospectus would definitely have had the approval of Cardinal Cullen and Bishop Nulty.

Some comparisons can now be made between the Dominican schools and the style and content of the education offered by some of the French orders, which

4. Boarders' orchestra, Cabra

came to Ireland in the late eighteenth and mid-nineteenth centuries. For one thing, the Dominicans have a tendency towards informality and a less regimented way of life for the pupils. Nevertheless a certain degree of 'virtuous emulation', as with the Ursulines and St Louis schools, was encouraged at the annual Parents' Day in Cabra. A concert was produced for the parents, at which the pupils could perform their music, singing, drama and recitations: prize-giving followed. In Dominican Convent, Wicklow there was a custom of having monthly 'reports', much on the pattern of that in Mount Anville; white gloves were worn, the prioress presided, curtsies were made to her and the pupils were given a placing in class, according to the marks awarded in the monthly tests. There is a strong similarity with the French boarding school customs here which may, perhaps, be explained by the fact that some of the Dominican nuns had been educated in France before they entered the Dominican convents and introduced some of these customs to the Dominican schools. Certainly, Sr Hyacinth in Taylor's Hill, educated by the Ursulines in Boulogne-sur-Mer, used note-books in her teaching which she had kept from her own school days and which are still in the archives in Taylor's Hill.[60] In Sion Hill and Eccles Street, an annual prize-giving took place also, but it was conducted more informally than that of Wicklow or Mount Anville. White gloves were not worn, children were not put in rank order of results and there was no curtsying.

CONVENT BOARDING SCHOOLS: PAST-PUPILS' VIEWS

In the decade of the 1870s, convent boarding schools in general, both in England and in Ireland, were subject to criticism. Two articles appeared in 1874 in *Fraser's Magazine*, an English publication: 'Convent Boarding Schools for Young Ladies' and 'A Word for the Convent Boarding Schools', the first written anonymously, the other under the *nom-de-plume* 'An Old Convent-Girl'. The author of the first contested the statement that 'the highest perfection of education is claimed for the conventual system'. Numerous faults were found with convent education in Ireland: the curriculum was defective; the fees were high. The author held that there was an *entente cordiale* between the convents with no competition between them; and 'the only solid knowledge which will remain [with the girls] after years of expensive instruction is that which they took with them from the national schools'. Spelling and reading were poorly taught; in fact the general teaching methods of convent schools were severely criticized. If that is true, it is some indictment. The author gave Alexandra School and College as an example of an institution which offered a much better education for lower fees. Latin, Greek and mathematics were taught at Alexandra, while 'the humbler branches of education are not neglected'. The opening of Alexandra School and College proved that Irish women valued really solid instruction, proven by the numbers attending that school.[61] The reply to 'An Old Convent Girl'came in another issue of *Frazer's Magazine*. One might think that the defence of Catholic convent education would have been vigorous and positive, yet while disputing the generalizations made in the first article, the author of 'A Word for the Convent Boarding Schools' admitted that the education given in these schools left much to be desired. However, she argued that the number of nuns who taught in the convent schools, '[made] all the difference in the world'. Each nun understood her subject; some were educated on the Continent and imparted their knowledge of languages very well. 'Each of these ladies is interested in her *specialité*, and any of her pupils who have special aptitude may pick up a good deal from her, and often do.'[62] This still leaves the question of incompetent teachers and of those who lacked the qualities necessary to control a class, as Katherine Tynan points out in her reminiscences.

SIENA DOMINICAN CONVENT, DROGHEDA

Katherine Tynan, poet and novelist, spent two years at school in Siena Dominican Convent Drogheda around 1872–74. Life as a boarder she thought was very old-fashioned; the girls were not allowed newspapers or magazines and while the curriculum was 'very simple', the nuns' human defects and weaknesses were obvious to the pupils. Nevertheless, Tynan believed they were,

> excellent musicians and linguists. They taught the ordinary subjects with ordinary success I imagine. But the progress of the world had stopped for them some ten or twenty or thirty or forty years before. Their [library] books were old-fashioned.[63]

Tynan attributed the refinement of Irish girls 'of the shop-keeping and farming classes' to their convent training: '[w]hatever of ladyhood is in a girl, the convent school fosters and brings it to perfection'.[64] Katherine Tynan was a boarder in Siena convent during the years preceding the introduction of the Intermediate Education Act. Her recollection of her years as a boarder is surely true to life in the school in her time; her memory of the school is a realistic appraisal of her education by the nineteenth-century Dominicans in Drogheda. Nevertheless, Tynan showed her affection and appreciation of the nuns and the system, in spite of their 'very simple curriculum'. She saw also the need for a more active and outgoing ministry to the poor; but, owing to their enclosed way of life, the Dominican nuns in Drogheda were unable to provide such a ministry. Tynan wrote,

> [b]eyond the convent walls there are the cabins of the poor. The poor Irish House-mother cannot cook, cannot sew, cannot wash, cannot clean. She has not an idea of simple domestic remedies. She would accept teaching at the hands of the nuns as she would not at the hands of the laity. What a waste of energy! ... Alas the nuns are enclosed as they were in the Middle Ages when enclosure was necessary, and the poor go untaught. We want a new Catherine of Siena, a new Teresa, to set the helper free to come to the aid of the one who needs help.[65]

Had Tynan the power of foretelling the future, she might have added, 'we need a Pope John XXIII to open the windows and allow the nuns to look out at the real world'.

In response to 'An Old Convent-Girl' it must be agreed that the curriculum was defective, and the fees were high. The convent competed for pupils but the competition was low-key and was done quietly. By the 1870s, the convents were well-established; numerous families who had nun-relatives in various orders throughout the country sent young nieces to the aunts' convent boarding schools. In country towns, where there was no secondary school, those who could afford to do so sent their daughters to boarding-schools in Cork, Galway, Dublin or one of the provincial towns, and it was not uncommon for groups of girls from the same locality to enrol in a particular school. The advertisements in *The Catholic Directory* gave some small indication of the work carried out in the various schools, but it is doubtful if the laity in great numbers read that publication.

Clerical friends of families were another source of information for parents making decisions about their daughters' education. Changing the way of life of the Dominican teaching nuns was to come, but it was a slow process and not as rapid as Tynan might have wished. In 1913, the date of publication of her book, that day was still some decades away. It required the directives for religious of the Second Vatican Council in the 1960s to bring the changes where enclosure was no longer a barrier nor an excuse for restricting nuns, even 'medieval nuns', from working outside the cloister for the poor or other necessitous groups.

'Convent Boarding Schools for Young Ladies' and 'A Word for the Convent Boarding School' were written in 1874. By that time, Margaret Byers had established her Ladies' Collegiate School in Belfast (1866), Haslam and Jellicoe had campaigned and founded the Irish Society for the Training and Employment of Educated Women (the Queen's Institute, 1861) in Dublin, and Isabella Tod's efforts on behalf of secondary and higher education for women were well known in Ireland and England. Their influence sparked off an interest in the subject of girls' education and articles such as those quoted above were beginning to criticize the *status quo*. Jordan writes:

> [t]he history of Victoria College was contemporaneous with the rise and evolution of women's higher education, for it had become accepted by the last quarter of the nineteenth century, that, ... one of the great rights was to have a girl's mind cultivated to the highest pitch.[66]

Keenan's work in the early years of the 1870s brought the debate on education in general on to the national stage and as a result of that, Hicks-Beach's plan secured the approval of the hierarchy. Fortunately, the provision of secondary education for girls was included in the terms of the Act bearing out Patricia Branca's assertion that,

> [b]y the second half of the nineteenth century national governments became more active in the control of education. They were spurred by the general desire to educate the citizenry and were roused by critics of the education most women received.[67]

The difference between Dominican schools and schools of other orders may have been intangible, manifested in the day-to-day interaction of pupils and nuns and in what might today be termed the ethos and general atmosphere of the school. Each religious congregation or order claims to have a special charism or *cachet* based on the Founder's ideals and understanding of a particular vocation. Each order or congregation would claim to bring some quality of its founder's/foundress's vision of the Christian life to its pupils. The Dominican ideal has been set out briefly in the introduction: in summary, a Dominican school aims to give its pupils a love of truth in all its manifestations; being upright, being true to oneself, seeking to find the truth of God's revelation through the life and teaching of Jesus Christ. This presupposes a respect for others and, in schools, a progressive training in the use of liberty. The task of a Dominican teacher is to lead the students to a realization of God's view of human life and to help them to shape their lives accordingly.

EXTERNAL EXAMINATIONS – FORE-RUNNERS OF THE IRISH SYSTEM

Prior to the introduction of the Intermediate Education Act of 1878, schools which wished to enter their students for public examinations had the opportunity to do so to a limited extent, but very often they had to look outside Ireland for accreditation. The Oxford Local Examinations and the Cambridge Local Examinations were introduced in 1857 and 1858 respectively and provided just such a form of validation. The two bodies amalgamated and from 1870 they were known as the Oxford and Cambridge Schools' Examination Board. The function of the Board was to act as an examining body to those schools which sent large numbers of boys to university. In later decades of the century, the matriculation examination of London University was also used as a leaving certificate by many pupils who had no intention of proceeding to university. Many Irish schools, both for boys and girls, availed themselves of these examinations.[68] A further specialist form of appraisal in science, art and design was made available through the South Kensington system of examinations. This institution was the result of recommendations by a select committee of the House of Commons, whose members had in 1836 enquired into the best methods of encouraging the fine arts. The committee recommended the establishment of a Normal School of Design and £1,500 was voted for the school. From this fund a Department of Practical Art was formed in 1852. This was followed by a Science Division, and the name of the institute was changed to the Department of Science and Art, having its headquarters in South Kensington. From that time forward, the institute's examinations were familiarly known as the South Kensington Art and Science exams. The remuneration of the teachers of science depended on the number of pupils who passed the special examination set by the Science and Art Department, and additional fees could be claimed if the pupils obtained prizes.[69] Many schools in Ireland, including the Dominican schools, presented their pupils for the South Kensington Science and Art Department examinations and some also entered pupils for those of the Oxford and Cambridge Schools Examination Board.

INTERMEDIATE ACT [IRELAND] 1878: THE CATALYST

The introduction of the Intermediate Act [Ireland] 1878, however, changed the pattern of education in many secondary schools, including some of the girls' boarding schools. The Oxford and Cambridge and South Kensington Science and Art examinations were phased out, since the Irish students now had their own local examinations which were more suited to their needs in the changing society which was emerging in late nineteenth-century Ireland. A new era indeed dawned for all secondary schools, both boys' and girls', because of the passing of this Act. A board of seven commissioners was appointed, and instituted and administered a system of public examinations in secular subjects. The schools became known as intermediate schools; new curricula were put in place, and the pupils would now sit for examinations which were set in Ireland by a Board of Examiners from within the country. Public examinations enabled the pupils to win prizes, exhibitions and certificates, and advance their subsequent careers. Fees were paid to school managers.[70] In the early stages, the boys had the choice of proceeding to university. In the later decades of the nineteenth century, exclusion of women from university education gave way to university education for all who could afford it, men and women, provided they were matriculated students.

Earlier in this chapter it was noted that the religious who managed the Catholic girls' secondary schools in Ireland were spurred on by the pioneering Protestant ladies, especially Anne Jellicoe and her colleagues in Alexandra College, who had such a broad vision and worked diligently for the educational advancement of women in the 1860s. The ideals which inspired Anne Jellicoe to provide classes for girls of limited means in the Queen's Institute in Dublin, and the success particularly of Alexandra College, Dublin, undoubtedly had a significant influence on the thinking of the Dominican nuns in Sion Hill. In their Introduction to the history of Alexandra College and School, O'Connor and Parkes claim that,

> [b]y its very existence Alexandra College was living proof that girls were capable of benefiting from such an education, and should therefore be admitted to the advantages of the Intermediate Education Act.[71]

This is a legitimate claim. A further reason for the Dominicans' interest in Alexandra College stemmed from the bishops' (and indeed the nuns') ever-present fear that Catholic girls might attend non-Catholic schools. In the climate of the time, Catholic bishops were very jealous of young Catholic girls attending Protestant schools, and it was believed or feared that if the Catholic schools did not update their curriculum and bring it into line with the needs of the time, pupils might be enticed from the Catholic schools to Alexandra or other non-Catholic schools. Alexandra College and the Queen's Institute unwittingly challenged the Catholic educationalists of Dublin; Mother Antonina Hanley met this challenge when she opened Our Lady of Sion Orphanage in Eccles Street in 1882.

FOUNDATION OF SION HILL, 1840

For Dominicans, the major educational breakthrough came as the indirect result of the transfer of jurisdiction of the Cabra Dominican nuns from that of the

Table 4 Secondary schools and colleges under Dominican management

Location of School	Girls' Secondary Boarding School	Girls' Secondary Day School	Commercial College	Third Level University (U) and Teacher Training (TT)
Taylor's Hill, Galway	1858	1859		
Cabra, Dublin	1835	c.1933		
Siena, Drogheda, Co. Louth	c.1725	Date uncertain		
88 Lr Mount St, Dublin	1838	1836		
Sion Hill Blackrock Dublin	1840	1841		St Catherine's College of Domestic Economy 1930
34, Usher's Quay, Dublin	1843–67	1843–67		
Kingstown/Dun Laoghaire	1847	1847		
Wicklow	1870	1870		
Falls Road, Belfast	1870	1870		St Mary's Training College 1900
19 Eccles St., Dublin	1882	1882	1930	St Mary's University College 1885–93 and 1903–1910 St Dominic's Training College, 1909–13
28 Merrion Sq., Dublin		1893		St Mary's University College, 1893–1900
Muckross Park, Dublin	1900	1900		St Mary's University College 1900–1903
Sutton, Dublin	1912	1912		
Portstewart, Co. Derry	1917	1917		
Scoil Chaitriona, Eccles St, Dublin	1928	1928		
Fortwilliam Park, Belfast	1930	1930		

Master of the Order to the Archbishop of Dublin; this has been treated of in Chapter 1. In May 1831 the papal approval for the transfer came into operation. The transfer was a very big step to take as the move caused soul-searching and distress within the community. In 1836, a group of Dominican nuns left the Cabra community and opened a 'House for Education' at 39 Lower Mount Street, Dublin.[72] The *Cabra Annals* [1836], states, '[a] good day-school was soon working [in Mount Street], some boarders were received, and postulants admitted'.[73] Mount Street Convent lasted only three years until, in 1840, the community moved to the parish of Booterstown on the south-east coast of Dublin, where they bought a property which was part of the Pembroke Estate and already named Sion Hill. The admission of postulants to the Mount Street Convent underlines the complete break between St Mary's Dominican Convent Cabra and the new foundation. It meant that the Mount Street convent would henceforth be independent of the Cabra community and could elect its own prioress and house council.

The Mount Street community's move to Sion Hill, Blackrock was made six years after the building of the first railway from Dublin to Kingstown.[74] This development of public transport meant that there was a movement of well-to-do business people to Booterstown, Blackrock and Kingstown, who commuted to the city every day by train; the day school in Sion Hill catered for the education of the girls from some of these families. The railway may even have been one of the contributory factors in the Dominican nuns' choice of Sion Hill as their new home. When they settled in Sion Hill in 1840 the nuns opened a boarding and day school, but soon found that the fees they expected to charge in the new school were beyond the means of their clientele. As noted in Chapter 1, the nuns had made a decision to charge a fee of £50 per annum. The school was not viable at this fee and it was proposed to reduce it; this became a source of disagreement within the community. As previously cited in Chapter 1, the Annals recorded,

> on leaving Mount Street the Foundresses ... opened the School at Sion Hill for the children of the upper classes at a pension of £50 per annum, all extras included. For some time this succeeded ... though we never had a large school. At length we found that our efforts to keep our school so extremely select by excluding children of the middle class, offended and estranged many of our friends and we did not receive sufficient support from the upper classes to enable us to continue this system.[75]

The Foundresses, however, were not disposed to change their views and so the school gradually declined. At this stage, the Dominican nuns continued to cater for the upper classes as distinct from the middle classes. The numbers in the school continued to fall until a new prioress, Mother Gertrude O'Kelly, was elected in December 1845. Mother Gertrude determined to receive children of the middle classes and reduced the annual fee from £50 to £30 per pupil in January 1846. The Annals again record, 'the good result of these measures was soon apparent by the influx of pupils, while the school still retained its character for being select'.[76] Market forces came into play here; the decision to reduce fees and cater for the middle class reflected the pressure of economic considerations. In this instance, the nuns' adaptation to the needs of the time was an intimation of things to come, for economic considerations are of course very important in the lives of most families. A rising demand for schooling on the part of 'middle-class' parents with not unlimited means (clerks, shopkeepers, civil servants, teachers), drove fees down in a keenly competitive market. From that time, the nuns were obliged to take account of the needs of pupils with new expectations and the outstanding demand from many would, in the decades ahead, be for an education which would enable the girls to earn their livings. The willingness to adapt to the needs of the times and of the pupils whom they were teaching, which the nuns had shown in 1846, was a significant factor in enabling the Sion Hill community to be willing to adapt once again in the decades ahead. They followed with keen interest the negotiations which led to the passing of the Intermediate Education Act in 1878; they appreciated the importance of a broader curriculum for girls and the opportunities it might offer in terms of qualifications for employment for them.

The work of Anne Jellicoe has been mentioned above as having a strong, positive influence on the Dominican nuns in Sion Hill. That community was the first Dominican group to take up the cause of women's education and to press the Archbishop of Dublin for permission to participate in the state examinations which followed on the Intermediate Education (Ireland) Act 1878. The passing of the Act 'created great excitement' in Sion Hill.[77] It would appear that the nuns had hoped to enter some pupils for the new examinations. It has been claimed, earlier in the chapter, that all the Dominican schools which existed prior to the introduction of the Intermediate Education (Ireland) Act 1878 ran on very similar lines: their curricula were almost identical; their clientele was similar; the nuns in the various convents were educated to much the same level.[78] What made 1878 a watershed in education for Sion Hill, while the other Dominican schools held back for a longer time from participating in the new Intermediate system? I hold that the experience of moving from Cabra to Mount Street and again from Mount Street to Sion Hill had given these Dominicans a more flexible attitude towards the running of a school. Change was not new to them. To use a biblical phrase, 'they read the signs of the times'.[79]

GIRLS' EDUCATION: BREAKING THROUGH THE BARRIERS

The *Sion Hill Annals* record in the month of October 1878:

> [t]he School numbered seventy-seven boarders, about twenty-four were refused admission owing to want of accommodation.
> The Intermediate Education Bill for Girls was passed, it created great excitement, but Dr McCabe informed us that neither he nor the Cardinal [Cullen] approved of public examinations for Girls.[80]

The nuns' excitement at the passing of the Intermediate Act was obviously dampened by the disapproval of the two eminent bishops, but their enthusiasm was undimmed by ecclesiastical frowns and they pressed ahead, but not immediately. In 1883, Cardinal McCabe sent letters to the secondary schools in the archdiocese requesting information about the numbers in the school and the number of any pupils who had been entered for the intermediate examinations.[81] Mother Clare Elliott, the prioress of Sion Hill, reported to the archbishop:

> during these years about six of the parents objected to their daughters *not* going in for the Intermediate examination, but we only lost two pupils in consequence ... the great majority of parents express strong objections to the system and many stipulate that their girl shall not go in for the examination'.[82]

In Dominican Convent, Cabra, the same sentiments were expressed as late as 1900:

> There had always been amongst the members of the Community a strong feeling against allowing their pupils to enter the arena of public examinations. ... It was believed by the Community that the educational standards of the Examining Boards did not attain the ideal which the Sisters set before them in the teaching and training of young girls.[83]

Dominican Convent Kingstown's reply in 1883 was, 'none of our Boarders ever went in for the Intermediate'.[84] The attitude underlying this thinking was not uncommon in the Ireland of the time. Many convent schools and many parents were unsure of the merits of the intermediate system for the education of girls. In the final report of the Intermediate Commission of 1899, James Macken, representing thirteen convent schools, reported that in the opinion of some school principals,

> if they [the girls] entered into the competition they would not be trained in subjects and accomplishments which they regard as more fitted to form part of the education of girls. Others refused to allow their girls to go in for the examination, and that the strain would be too severe.[85]

The Dominican nuns, on the whole, were not enthusiasts for the new intermediate system. Sion Hill's 'great excitement' seems to have been dampened not only by the McCabe's and Cullen's disapproval but also by the pressure brought to bear on them from parents. Clare Elliot's report to the archbishop is witness to that pressure: 'the great majority of parents express strong objections to the system'.[86] In the light of the above entry, it is ironic that within four years, in 1882, Sion Hill established the school in Eccles Street, Dublin, with the approbation of Dr McCabe, now archbishop and cardinal (1878–85). He succeeded Cardinal Cullen who died unexpectedly on 24 October 1878. A revolutionary change was coming about in Irish society in the late nineteenth century: while parents were reluctant to allow their daughters to enter for public examinations, a new generation of women were claiming their places

5. Domestic Science class, Sion Hill

as independent individuals who were not content to be economically reliant on their parents or husbands. Mary Cullen and Maria Luddy in their introduction to *Women, Power and Consciousness in Nineteenth Century Ireland*, referring to the women whose life stories are included in their book, write:

> [n]ot all the women here explicitly espoused 'women's rights'. Not all may have even implicitly supported such claims. But each, by her life and work, challenged and contributed to change in accepted nineteenth-century gender roles.[87]

Due to the nuns' way of life, it was not possible for them to campaign publicly for women's educational rights, but those who worked tirelessly for women's right to university education contributed to the change. The question of women's rights relating to university education in Ireland will be dealt with in Chapter 3. In following the history of the Dominican intermediate schools in the nineteenth century, we are made aware of a growing consciousness in the minds of the nuns, particularly in Sion Hill, of the need for change in curricula together with the acceptance of a competitive examination system. The system, though far from perfect, was the best on offer and would help their pupils to develop their gifts and talents to the full. Dominican women who adapted their ideology to the changing times were entirely in harmony with the traditional ethos of the Order. Not until the publication of the *Constitutions of the Congregation of Irish Dominican Sisters* in 1947 were the guiding principles set out which were carried out in practice by the Sion Hill community in the 1880s.

> [w]hile the secular part of the education conducted by the Sisters is secondary in importance to the religious, they must not suppose that it need not be as thorough in its kind. It is indeed an obligation of justice to the child (and to those who entrust her to the Sisters' charge) ... to prepare her adequately for the place she is to occupy in life.[88]

The question undoubtedly is: what is meant by 'the place she is to occupy in life'? In the context of Sion Hill's foundation, it can safely be assumed that the nuns were no longer thinking in the mind-set of the 'good wife and mother' whose exclusive care was to be the home-maker. Here we see in practice that they were indeed willing to learn new disciplines, adopt new approaches and expand the boundaries of systems no longer viable in this new era of publicly-funded education.

The Sion Hill nuns were well-informed about matters pertaining to education; they had access to the daily newspapers and would have had discussions and exchanges of views with clergy and laymen and women who had an interest in education. The Holy Ghost priests from the neighbouring Blackrock 'French College' were chaplains and frequent visitors to the convent in Sion Hill. These priests entered their pupils for the Intermediate examinations with great benefit to their school, and there must certainly have been conversations with the Sion Hill nuns about Anna Maria Haslam's campaign for the improvement of standards in women's education in Ireland and England, not least discussion about the part Haslam played in having girls included in the provisions of the Intermediate Education Act. More immediate to the future well-being of Sion Hill was Anne Jellicoe's successful work in Alexendra College in Earlsfort Terrace, Dublin. Apart from their awareness of current educational trends there was another dimension to be considered by the nuns. How would ambitious young girls and their parents react if Catholic schools were *not* prepared to update their curriculum and enter for the state examinations? There was a strong possibility that such families might defy the wrath of the bishops and transfer their children to the Protestant schools which entered pupils for the Intermediate examination. Alexandra College and School was an attractive alternative to Sion Hill and other Catholic schools which did not adopt the new system. Such must have been the thoughts not only of the prioress, Mother Clare Elliott, but also of her community who, when an opportunity arose, circumvented the objections of the archbishop and others who were cautious about the modernization of education for girls. This opportunity came their way when the foundation of a new school in Eccles Street was suggested.

DOMINICAN COLLEGE, ECCLES STREET, 1882–1984

There was one group of young women who fell between two stools; their families were neither poor enough to accept only a national school education for the girls in the family, nor rich enough to afford further education in a boarding school or fee-paying day school. These were the daughters in families who had lost their financial security through misfortune in business, illness or the death of the father. In the language of the nineteenth century these were 'the respectable families' from middle-class backgrounds, whose parents would not have been satisfied to see their daughters joining the ranks of the domestic servants or female factory workers on low wages in Dublin. Two of the Dominican nuns in Sion Hill community had great sympathy for such families: Antonina Hanley and Gonzales O'Connor. The O'Connors were a County Dublin merchant family with a business in Camden Street.[89] Gonzales is mentioned in the Sion Hill annals as being 'mainly responsible' for establishing the orphanage. The Hanleys were land owners and sustained heavy losses in the land agitation. Antonina had great sympathy with other families in a similar situation:

> [Hanley] desired very earnestly to found an Institution for the children of the upper and middle classes left destitute by the death of parents and reverse of fortune and whom for obvious reasons, it would not be suitable to place in the orphanages for the very poor.[90]

The story of Sion Hill's new establishment in Eccles Street is a story worth recording. It began as an orphanage situated close to the centre of Dublin; from this initial short-lived phase as an orphanage it developed into a very successful boarding and day school in 18 and 19 Eccles Street. Later in 1884 the Dominican nuns opened a centre for university studies for women there. This was the first Catholic college for women's university education opened in Dublin.

Transition from orphanage to boarding school

The central characters in the story make it difficult to determine who precisely suggested such a venture, though some of those involved were not of one mind about the exact nature of the proposed school. One thing is certain: the Dominican Orphanage of Our Lady of Sion, however short its existence, was never intended to be an orphanage in the accepted sense of the word, that is, a school in which the children of poor destitute parents would get a primary school education together with some training for domestic or industrial work. There is no doubt that from the beginning Mother Hanley and Sister O'Connor had a secondary school in mind, a school where some orphans would receive a secondary education which under normal circumstances they could not have obtained. The first prospectus, 'Institution for Free Catholic Education for the

6. Sr Gonzales O'Connor, 1844–85, Sion Hill

Orphan Girls of the Upper and Middle Classes', issued for the benefit of future benefactors states:

> [i]n the upper and middle classes, amongst our friends and intimates, which of us has not known cases where a Father and Mother dying, and leaving their little ones unprovided for, had to look forward to the time when those children ... would have to depend on the charity of strangers and perhaps be placed in Orphanages destined only for the lower classes, and thus lose that position in society to which birth entitled them.[91]

Those associated with the new foundation were Mother Clare Elliott, prioress of Sion Hill, and members of her community, particularly Mother Antonina Hanley and Sr Gonzales O'Connor. Two priests of the archdiocese of Dublin were involved: Canon Farrell, the parish priest of Booterstown, in which Sion Hill was located, and Canon MacMahon who urged the nuns to buy the Eccles Street properties and to open a day school there. Christopher Ryder, a Poor Law Guardian in Dublin City, generously subscribed to the new foundation, as did a Miss Short, 4 Harcourt Street, of whom no other record survives.[92] Mrs Eleanor Woodlock, a lady of means, was actively involved in the work. Cardinal McCabe, 'who [gave] it his blessing and warm approval', was cited as patron of the institute.

The Sion Hill nuns, who were ultimately responsible for the day-to-day running and development of the school, had had years of experience in their very successful boarding and day schools both in Mount Street and in Sion Hill itself. The records of the initial stages of the new foundation may not be as full as one would wish; nevertheless, there is enough evidence to show that at the time, the venture was unique in Dominican educational history in eighteenth- and nineteenth-century Ireland. Unique it may have been, but it is not surprising. In the light of the Sion Hill community's history of readiness to adapt to the educational needs of a growing Catholic middle-class from the 1840s, the Eccles Street foundation again shows how this group of Dominicans had a pragmatic attitude to the needs of another generation of girls; the 'distressed' and orphan daughters of parents who had 'seen better days' and who therefore left their children with no provision for their future. To my knowledge, there is no letter extant which gives authorization for the foundation, but there was constant communication between the diocesan authorities and the convents. In the case of the Dublin Dominican convents there were fairly frequent visits, formal and informal, by successive archbishops and their vicars general, to the communities. Matters of moment were often discussed at these visits and in some cases decisions were made without any written records surviving.

Ambivalence about Eccles Street school

There must undoubtedly have been discussions about the foundation in Eccles Street between the prioress of Sion Hill, Mother Clare Elliott, Canon Farrell, the parish priest, and the Cardinal or Canon MacMahon acting for the Cardinal. An entry in the *Sion Hill Annals*, in August 1882, relates that,

> Canon MacMahon, P.P. of North Anne Street, Dublin, called here urging us to buy 18 and 19, Eccles Street, in order to establish a Day School. He called on Cardinal McCabe. The Cardinal came here and got the houses reduced to £1,500 – £2,000 had been asked. Mr Ryder offered £300 towards their purchase. Mother Clare, Mother Martina, and Sister Bernard went to see the houses. They liked them and the Sisters were unanimous in agreeing to purchase them.[93]

Apart from a mention in the *Sion Hill Annals* of Canon MacMahon's visit to the convent, there is no detailed account of conversations or discussions about the nature of the 'Day School'. The prospectus and this quotation from the Sion Hill Annals constitute the official evidence of Cardinal McCabe's approval and

7. Dominican College, Eccles Street, Dublin

encouragement of the new foundation. Christopher Ryder, the Poor Law
Guardian already mentioned, was a Dublin gentleman who had close philan-
thropic connections with the archdiocese; his name is engraved on the trowel
used in the formal opening of a new wing in 1888; in fact he is named as the
founder.[94] Not only did Christopher Ryder donate £300 outright but he also lent
the nuns £1,000 towards the purchase of the houses in Eccles Street. In
November of the same year, 1882, Ryder converted the loan into an outright gift.

Canon MacMahon was not at all in favour of the Dominicans opening an
orphanage. In a letter he wrote to Mother Antonina in April 1883, four months
after the nuns took up residence in Eccles Street, the Canon set out his strong
feelings on the matter. He was by now a vicar general, with the title of archdeacon,
and so was a person of considerable authority and influence in the diocese.[95] He was
at that time parish priest of St Michan's, Halston Street. Archdeacon MacMahon's
argument was that the orphanage in Eccles Street would interfere with other
institutions in the neighbourhood, especially St Joseph's orphanage in Mountjoy
Street which was run by the Irish Sisters of Charity, who were at this time caring
for about ninety orphans. The Archdeacon wrote:

> I am sure you never intended nor would wish to interfere with any other
> Community or Institution. But indirectly I fear you will – a great number
> of the class you contemplate are the very class which make up St Joseph's
> – and if you take them for what that Institution asks and strives to get, ...

don't you think that the friends of the applicant would naturally strive to get them into what they consider the more respectable school? And thus St Joseph's would be deprived of that support which would help and enable them to admit others, [who] tho' deserving could pay nothing.There are so many orphanages already in the Parish that I really tremble at the idea of another. Be wise, be prudent, let your day school take root.[96]

Canon MacMahon's concern about St Joseph's was not unreasonable; there were two other orphanages in the vicinity of Eccles Street, one in Stanhope Street also conducted by the Irish Sisters of Charity, the other in George's Hill by the Presentation Sisters. The latter was also in Archdeacon MacMahon's parish of St Michan's.[97] Stanhope Street is less than two miles from Eccles Street and the entry in the *Catholic Directory* for the Stanhope Street orphanage shows that the Irish Sisters of Charity had in mind a similar clientele to that which Mother Antonina Hanley intended for her orphanage. The Stanhope Street entry read 'this Institution is for the children of respectable parents, or orphans, who are unprotected, or whose guardians wish to have them trained to industry'.[98] Mother Antonina had a more specific clientele in mind. In a second prospectus the wording was very specific: 'daughters of parents of the mercantile, professional, or private gentlemen class'.[99]

There is a definite note of class distinction in these advertisements: clearly the Archdeacon feared rivalry and competition between the two institutions. In the light of Archdeacon MacMahon's letter to Mother Antonina, drawing her attention to the number of similar institutions in the area of St Joseph's parish, Berkeley Road, the Dominicans could not but have been aware of this element of competition. There is, however, no record of Mother Antonina's response to the strong plea of the archdeacon. The answer was in the deed: the Orphanage of Our Lady of Sion went ahead, though the title was dropped after some years. Perhaps the Archdeacon's opposition may explain why the Dominicans dropped the title 'orphanage' from their letter-heads and eventually took his advice: 'be wise, be prudent, let your day school take root'.[100]

Aspirations to better education of women

In undertaking the work of the orphanage, short-lived though it was, the Dominicans of Sion Hill, and, in particular, Mother Antonina saw the new school in Eccles Street as an opportunity for the nuns once again to adapt to the social needs of the time. They were aware of the Intermediate Act of 1878 and the openings which the new system would offer to girls for an education which was previously denied to them. Thus we note the transition from the wording of the earlier advertisements with the emphasis on an education rendering the girls 'trustworthy guardians of the rising generation' and educated in 'all the accomplishments included in a young lady's education', to a new style of curriculum which would give the girls 'an education similar to that of the higher educational establishments, and, besides that, to give a thorough and special training for the important duties of governesses, together with provision for training for industrial and civil posts open to females'. Here then, we have an acknowledgement by the nuns that in the years to come, the pupils of this school in Eccles Street would be taking their places in the business and professional world of the time, and that their education should reflect that fact. In this respect, the Dominican nuns' objective was similar to that of Anne Jellicoe in founding Alexandra College.

Echoes of Channel Row

The notice for Our Lady of Sion Orphanage begins with a list of the patrons, headed by His Eminence Cardinal McCabe, Archbishop of Dublin. The names of the lady patrons are of more than passing interest to Irish Dominicans:

> The Marchioness of Londonderry
> The Countess of Granard
> The Lady O'Hagan
> The Lady French
> The Lady Nugent, Ballinlough Castle
> The Lady de Vere
> The Lady Netterville
> The Lady O'Donnell
> The Hon. Mrs O'Hagan

There is an echo here from the Channel Row days; the names French, Nugent, Netterville, Esmond were on the account books of Channel Row and Siena Convent Drogheda in the eighteenth century. These ladies would have had an interest in a school which would provide an education for girls who might, as the notices of the time repeated constantly, 'have seen better days and were by reverse of fortune, left without the means of maintaining themselves or providing for their education'.[101] The idea that the Countess of Granard, Lady French or Lady de Vere might fall on hard times and become economically embarrassed is not in fact as fanciful as one might think. It was just such families as these who in the last quarter of the eighteenth century lost their money through bank failures and other economic circumstances beyond their control; circumstances which adversely affected the nuns in the Dominican community in Channel Row who depended on the patronage of these families. The nuns there were forced to close their school for lack of pupils when the families were in financial distress.[102]

Link with the O'Brien Institute

The circular, 'Institution for the Free Catholic Education for the Orphan Girls of the Upper and Middle Classes' has additional information which is very important in establishing the type of orphanage which the Archbishop and the nuns had in mind. This longer notice states that at the time of foundation, 'no such Institution exists in Ireland', that is, for girls, and the text continues:

[t]he Christian Brothers, and now the O'Brien Foundation, have done much to supply this want as regards Boys; it is needless to refer to the numerous advantages which the Protestant minority enjoys in this respect, for Catholic Orphan Girls of the class above named *nothing* has yet been done. ... The project has been laid before the Cardinal Archbishop, who has given it his blessing and warm approval, declaring it much needed, especially as a counterpoise to the numerous Free Protestant Institutions now existing.[103]

The O'Brien Institute in Marino, close to Clontarf in Dublin, was an orphanage for boys of the same social class as that of the girls who were to benefit from the Eccles Street foundation. The O'Brien Institute was founded by two wealthy sisters whose father, Michael O'Brien, left his daughters an estate valued at £115,000. Two of his daughters who were twins, Mary and Bridget, never married. Bridget was the last to die, in 1876: in her will she directed that the remainder of her property, which was valued at £80,000, should be given to the Archbishop of Dublin and his vicar-general and their successors,

for the purpose of founding, forming, and endowing a respectable and becoming dwelling-house, establishment, school or seminary in or contiguous to the City of Dublin, for the support, and comfortable lodging, dieting, clothing, and educating, from time to time, for ever, of a certain number of poor children (male or female or both) professing the Catholic Faith.[104]

The Christian Brothers took possession of the O'Brien Institute in 1878, as was proposed by the Archbishop of Dublin. It was placed under the management of the Christian Brothers, but it remained an archdiocesan institute, directly under the Archbishop of Dublin.

This then, was the model which was proposed for the Dominican nuns in Eccles Street. One difference between the two schools was that the Dominicans from the beginning, in keeping with the tradition of the Order, and the independent character of the nuns, were the owners and managers of the school. The Dominican Orphanage of Our Lady of Sion developed into a conventional boarding and day school. Throughout its history until its transfer to 204 Griffith Avenue in 1984, the school was popularly known as 'Eccles Street'. The custom of helping families who could not afford full fees was always preserved, as indeed it was in most convent schools in Ireland, whether Dominican or otherwise. It must be emphasized that Archbishop McCabe and his successors were ever supportive of the nuns and their school, and in later years Dr McCabe's successor, Dr William Walsh (1885–1921), encouraged them in their efforts to develop Dominican College, Eccles Street, as a centre for women's university education. Besides his frequent attendance at dramatic and musical productions in the school, a very practical example of Archbishop Walsh's help and interest was shown by his sponsoring 'A Bazaar and Grand Drawing of Prizes' in aid of the school in 1887.[105]

There are unanswered questions about the foundation of the orphanage in Eccles Street; tantalising, because there are no records to show why Sr Gonzales O'Connor, a relatively young nun, should have had such a strong voice in the foundation of Eccles Street. The *Sion Hill Annals* have entries for November 1883 which read:

> [b]y the intervention of Sister Gonzales O'Connor and Miss Short, Mr Ryder [later Count Ryder] was induced to hand over the houses 18 and 19 Eccles Street, entirely to the Nuns releasing them from paying off interest for the purchase money – £1,400.[106]

It is legitimate to speculate that perhaps Sr Gonzales had donated money to Sion Hill with a proviso that the money should be spent to provide for orphans. She died in July 1885 when she had been professed less than five years. *Sion Hill Annals* record that,

> conscious of affectionate obligations to her family, but influenced by a holier desire of her obligations to God, she ... resolutely cast aside all worldly considerations and determined to consecrate her life ... in the cloister. ... It may be mentioned that she was mainly instrumental in establishing the valuable Orphanage in the Convent of Our Lady of Sion, 18 & 19 Eccles Street.[107]

We have evidence that Count Ryder, a man of property, was also a very generous benefactor not only to the Dominicans but to other worthy causes. His obituary in the *Freeman's Journal* of October 1898 reported that he was:

> a liberal benefactor to many religious and charitable institutions not alone in Dublin but in various parts of the Catholic world. The Dominican Convent Eccles Street, High Park Convent [Drumcondra], Stradbally Convent, the Pro-Cathedral in Dublin and the new church of St Patrick in Rome are among those which have benefitted by his liberal charity. His many beneficent acts moved the Sovereign Pontiff to create him a Count of the Holy Roman Empire.[108]

Count Ryder, who died aged 94 years, was noted in *Thom's Directory* as 'gentleman'.[109] Another benefactor, Eleanor Woodlock of Bray, Co. Wicklow (1811–84) has been already mentioned; Woodlock was a well-known philanthropist who championed the care of children.[110] In relation to the new foundation of Dominican nuns in Eccles Street, she ordained that 'any orphan girl trained and educated by the Dominicans in Eccles Street, needing a temporary home, or any way in want of shelter for a short time, was to receive from the Nuns of 18 & 19 Eccles Street, Dublin, *a hearty welcome*'.[111]

The move from Sion Hill

Six Sisters from Sion Hill moved into the new convent in Eccles Street, four in late December 1882 and two in early January 1883. They were, Mother Antonina Hanley (prioress), Sisters Patrick Sheil, Rose Dillon-Brady, Gonzales O'Connor, Veronica, and Francis Harris. These were the pioneers who set the school up and received the first day pupils and boarders, and the first orphans who presented themselves. Three of these pioneering nuns, Mother Antonina and Srs Rose and Gonzales, were to die within six years of the date of the foundation. On 10 January 1883 about fifteen day pupils were received. In April the orphanage was opened: 'Emma Russell, Mr Ryder's friend, being the first orphan received, soon followed by the three Fogartys and others'.[112] Sion Hill community sent in a lay member of its own staff, Fraulein Freckmann, as German governess and language teacher. In June 1884, their second academic year in the school, 'three pupils "went in privately" for the Intermediate examinations and were most successful, [all] passing with honours'.[113] Regular study for the Intermediate examinations began in September 1884. Eccles Street was off to a good start, and the foundation for future success was laid by those first pupils.

Mother Antonina Hanley

Mother Antonina Hanley, the first prioress of the convent of Our Lady of Sion, Eccles Street, was educated for a time in one of the lay-run boarding schools in the city and came to Sion Hill when she was about 15 years of age. After the death of her mother she entered in Sion Hill in 1869 or 1870. According to the records, Mother Antonina was a woman of remarkable good sense and sound judgement and of a cheerful and bright disposition. Many of her family sustained heavy losses as a result of the agricultural depression of the late 1870s and early 1880s and she had great sympathy with all in similar circumstances.[114] Hoppen sets out some of the immediate causes of the Land War of 1879–82 which affected landlords and tenant farmers in Ireland, some of whom seemingly, were relatives of Mother Antonina:

> [the] world-wide depression, coinciding as it did with a series of disastrous seasons in Ireland, triggered a crash which abruptly snatched back from farmers their very recent return to the comparative prosperity of the mid-1850s. ... The decline in cattle prices hit those small farmers of the West. ... Elsewhere a significantly reduced tillage output caused by bad weather was no longer being matched by a rise in prices, for these now responded as much to North American as to domestic levels of production.[115]

The 'new departure', a term used to describe the political movement which combined revolutionary and constitutional nationalism in Ireland, became the driving force which eventually achieved land reform through the various Land Acts in the 1880s and early 1900s.[116] These were factors with which Mother

8. Mother Antonina Hanley, 1841–88, Eccles Street

Antonina Hanley was very familiar, and which made her sympathetic to the plight of those who were financially affected by the fall in income of some of the more affluent farmers and landlords. She too, like Sr Gonzales, desired very much to found an institute for the education of children whose parents unexpectedly experienced financial hardship. Mother Antonina exerted all her influence to secure supporters and to raise funds for the school. During the early months of the summer of 1888 she began a new wing to provide more suitable accommodation for the school. In September she was in frail health and developed 'acute rheumatism in her limbs [but] she retained consciousness until the first chimney of the new building was erected; she could see it from her room, and on its completion she sent the usual gratuity to the men'.[117] Mother Antonina Hanley died in December 1888 aged 47 years. Obituary notices appeared in the Irish newspapers and in *The Tablet. The Freeman's Journal* said of her that 'she lived almost in advance of her age'.[118] Afterwards, when the school had developed its university classes, the name Convent of Our Lady of Sion, Eccles Street, was changed to Dominican College, Eccles Street and became known familiarly as 'Eccles Street'.

THE INTERMEDIATE EXAMINATION SYSTEM: PUBLIC INTEREST

Each year the Intermediate Board published comprehensive reports in the national and provincial newspapers. The names of all schools were given in which the managers were paid 'results fees'. This was a capitation grant system paid according to the number of pupils who were successful in the Intermediate Examinations. The three entrants from Eccles Street in 1884 were the first Dominican pupils to participate in the examinations; from 1886 Eccles Street was officially listed in the annual reports published by the Intermediate Board. Sion Hill and Dominican Convent Belfast were listed for the first time in the official report of 1894. By 1899, these three Dominican schools were regularly listed, together with another new Dominican foundation, St Mary's University College and High School, Merrion Square, Dublin. The Dominican schools in Galway, Cabra, Drogheda, Kingstown [Dún Laoghaire] and Wicklow eventually joined in the state Intermediate System.

A comparison might be made with the policy of the Institute of the Blessed Virgin Mary [Loreto], which, collectively and at an earlier date, were more willing to enter their pupils for the state examinations. Prior to 1886, the Loreto convents in St Stephen's Green and in Enniscorthy, Gorey, Kilkenny, Navan, Omagh and Wexford all had candidates for the Intermediate examinations. In 1888 a new Loreto Mother General, Mother Michael Corcoran, was elected and her educational policy brought about a change in attitudes within the Institute. Her anonymous biographer recorded:

> [t]he Intermediate examinations had started in 1879 and our convents, or at least some of them had been very successful from 1880–1883 winning many distinctions, gold medals, exhibitions and prizes but for various reasons they had stopped sending in their students for these examinations. One reason was that some of [the] nuns ... considered the girls were better without them. However, Mother Michael's views were modern and sensible and she urged all the houses to take up the Intermediate System again.[119]

The phrase '[the] nuns ... considered the girls were better without them', has the same kind of ring of disapproval of the system, as that of the Cabra and Kingstown Dominicans' response to Cardinal McCabe's query in 1883 – 'none of our boarders ever went in for the Intermediate'. The difference between Loreto's collective response and that of the Dominicans' more individualistic approach to participation in the intermediate examination system, may be explained by the structure of the two orders. The Loreto Sisters belonged to a unified institute under the central authority of a superior general and council, while the Dominican convents were, at the time, single autonomous communities, each one determining its own policy in these matters. The Ursulines in Cork, Thurles, Waterford and Sligo had regular examination entries from their schools from at least 1894 onwards.

From 1884 Victoria College Belfast 'held premier position among girls' schools in ... the Intermediate Examinations'.[120] Alexandra College in 1878, though financially stressed, 'faced the additional burden of preparing for the Intermediate Examinations'.[121] These two women's colleges in particular had been earnestly seeking equality for women in the educational field. Margaret Byers did not agree with the argument that examinations were harmful to girls: parents who allowed their daughters to shirk the examinations did so, according to Byers, 'through an unwise tenderness'.[122] As time passed, an increasing number of convent schools throughout the country availed themselves of the new opportunities for girls' educational advancement. By 1899 religious congregations from Europe had made foundations in Ireland – the Sisters of St Louis, Congregation of the Faithful Companions of Jesus, Sisters of the Sacred Heart of Mary and Sisters of St Joseph of Cluny, together with the native Irish Congregations of Sisters of Mercy, Presentation and Brigidines – were all participants in the Intermediate System.

THE PALLES COMMISSION REPORT

A commission known as The Palles Commission, from the name of its chairman, Baron Christopher Palles (1831–1920), was set up by the government in 1888 to survey 'the working of the Intermediate Education Scheme' which had been in operation since 1878.[123] The Commission issued a report in 1899 criticizing the narrow examination programme and the heavy burden placed on the staffs and pupils of the schools by the system of payment by results. A recommendation was made that the grants to schools should be paid as a block capitation payment rather than on an individual basis. Changes in the curriculum were suggested to encourage the teaching of what the Commission termed 'modern subjects', particularly mathematics and the sciences. Special grants were given for the provision of equipment for science teaching

> [the Commission] held that the examination system as it was operated in Ireland, has a tendency to hamper a good teacher in his choice of educational methods and instruments, to lead teachers to concentrate their attention on the pupils sent in for examination to the comparative neglect of others and to interrupt the regular school work by preparing for periodical examination.[124]

Objections were also made by parents that the pupils were over-pressurized and the danger for girls of over-work engendered by 'the too keen competition caused by the exams' were singled out for criticism.

Palles sent out queries to the schools about the examination system and numerous schools replied. Mother Joseph Keighron, Sr Peter McGrath and Sr Patrick Sheil of the Sion Hill, Eccles Street and St Mary's University and High

9. Chemistry class, Sion Hill

School, Merrion Square, respectively replied on their own behalf.[125] On the practical working of the system, they made the following comments, which though extended, are worth quoting in full:

[a]fter consultation with the members of the teaching staff of Sion Hill Convent, Blackrock Dublin, Dominican Convent, Eccles Street and St Mary's University College, Merrion Square, we desire to submit the following observations:

Compared with other educational systems in the country, the intermediate appears to be eminently impartial and satisfactory in its results, therefore any proposal to substitute examination by inspection for the present written examination, could not have our approval. Our experience of girls and their teachers leads us to believe that examinations by inspectors would fail in its object, as in practice it would not afford a genuine test of the work during the year. Young children, especially, would be easily intimidated by the latter method. Though, no doubt, susceptible of much improvement the Intermediate system has done incalculable service to the schools of the country, and one cannot but feel that not a little of the credit for this is due to the vigilance, and zeal, and efficiency of the present Assistant Commissioners. We heartily approve of the existing arrangement whereby the prizes and exhibitions are allotted to girls *apart*; and we consider that any alteration involving competition of girls and boys, for prizes, would be fatal to many of the smaller girls' schools, and highly injurious to the majority of the larger schools.[126]

One cannot fail to notice the fulsome praise given to the Assistant Commissioners, but the nuns had practical proposals to put in answering the detailed questions relating to the various subjects of the curriculum. *A propos* remodelling the English programme, they had some criticism to make of the selection of texts: they observed, '[i]t is hard to see why Shakespeare should be stereotyped as a stock subject to such an extent as to exclude other great authors'.[127] About the study of history they had this to say:

> [t]he knowledge of ancient history should not be confined to students who pursue a course of Ancient Classics.; and under the heading of each of the Modern Languages, or of English, or of a separate subject, should be included some knowledge of the history of European countries.[128]

There was no doubt that the Intermediate system could lend itself to cramming for examinations and in some cases this was a justifiable criticism. McElligott in his chapter on the work of the Intermediate Education Commission writes,

> economic reasons made it difficult for schools to preserve their independence and the principle that the money did matter and that the reward of work was a money prize ... pervaded the whole country and cannot have failed to influence the minds of the people. As one writer not unfairly put it: 'The formation of character, the cultivation of taste, the disinterested love of learning not being capable of being tested by examinations, were disregarded in this sordid race for results fees'.

However, the report continued, 'the commission was to hear little but praise of the system from the people who, after all, mattered most – the headmistresses'.[129]

COMPETITIVE SYSTEM OF EXAMINATIONS

Writing in 1890, Archbishop Walsh, Catholic Archbishop of Dublin (1885–1921), said, 'the great radical defect of the system is that, instead of helping on the work of *education*, it encourages a system merely of successful *preparation for competitive examinations*. ... In such a system the constant effort of the teacher must be ... to prepare his pupils for the ordeal of an examination.'[130] Regarding the comment of the author quoted by McElligott, about the 'formation of character, the cultivation of taste and a disinterested love of learning', many convent schools certainly cultivated these very important aspects of education. The records of the Loreto, Ursuline, St Louis and other Orders, show that a much broader education than mere preparation for examinations was of prime importance to the nuns in the education of their pupils during that era. In the case of the Dominican schools, the convent archives dating from those years have numerous copies of programmes of dramatic presentations and concerts which included orchestral items, choral singing, dancing and elocution. Lectures on the arts, sometimes illustrated with lantern-slide shows, were a common feature of school life in Eccles Street. In Taylor's Hill, Cabra, Sion Hill, Eccles Street, Wicklow and Falls Road the entertainments were enhanced by the performances of the school orchestras. While the examinations loomed large for pupils and teachers, the formation of character and the cultivation of taste were not forgotten.

There certainly was keen competition between schools, fuelled by the publication of results in the national and local newspapers of the time. Each school took a great pride in the number of prizes, exhibitions and scholarships awarded to its pupils and some schools, including Dominican schools, used lists of successes in the advertisements which the schools placed in the public press each year to notify parents and pupils of the re-opening dates of the schools every September. *The Freeman's Journal*, as a national newspaper, devoted whole pages to recording the results from all the Intermediate Examinations in schools throughout the country. The names of those students who gained the highest marks in the various subjects were listed under the title of 'The Leaders'; the actual number of marks they attained were also published. One could buy from the Government Publications Office in Dublin the complete lists of all candidates with their schools named, and the rank placing of each school in the country. In 1930, there were seven Dominican schools listed: Dominican College, Eccles Street, Scoil Chaitríona, Cabra, Taylor's Hill Galway, Sion Hill, Wicklow and Muckross Park. Altogether in that list there were seventy-six girls' schools named.

The time of the publication of results must have been a very stressful week for many students and their teachers, and the system cannot have been encouraging for the less able pupils. Muckross Park College, which was founded in 1900, issued a press notice in September 1902 which triumphantly proclaimed its successes:

Number of honours	131
First Class Scholarships	3
Second Class Scholarships	1
Dr Hutchinson Stewart Scholarship in Arts	2
First Class Exhibitions	8
Second Class Exhibitions	27
Studentship in Modern Literature	1
Junior Fellowships	2

This was an accumulation of results over a two year period, which included university awards; the notice was headed 'Grand Total of Distinctions Already Gained'. The previous year the notice for Muckross Park in *The Freeman's Journal* was much more modest:

> pupils are prepared for the Examinations of the Intermediate Board. The successful candidates have won several Exhibitions in all grades and many minor distinctions including gold medals and composition prizes.[131]

THE DALE AND STEPHENS REPORT 1905

In 1902 the government invited two inspectors of the English Board of Education, Messrs Dale and Stephens, to conduct a survey of Irish intermediate schools.[132] The inspectors' report was published in 1905. Dale and Stephens recommended the abolition of payment by results and the substitution of block capitation grants and inspectors' reports as a means of assessing the competence of the schools. The report also recommended that a registration council for teachers should be established to improve the standard and conditions of secondary teachers. The report was a perceptive analysis of the major problems of Irish secondary education and it was to influence educational policy in the following years. Ó Buachalla regards the Dale and Stephens' report as trenchantly exposing the weaknesses of both primary and secondary education at the beginning of the twentieth century. Especially noted was the depressed role of assistant teachers within the system.[133] The large number of religious who taught in the schools left little room for lay teachers, and of the relatively small number of laity who were engaged by the religious, some had no academic qualifications for teaching.

In time, practically all secondary schools in the country accepted the Intermediate System and its examinations as the norm; two examinations, Intermediate and Leaving Certificate, were taken by the majority of pupils. It was not unusual for girls who wished to pursue a business career in the civil service, the local authorities or in private commercial firms, to study for the Intermediate Certificate and then proceed to a Commercial College to study the necessary business subjects. Eccles Street Convent opened such a commercial college in 1930. In general, girls who wished to take up careers in nursing, teaching and in professions which required university education, continued for a further two years to complete the Leaving Certificate and/or Matriculation. The system of education which was inherited from the British administration in Ireland prior to the foundation of the State in 1922 was not subjected to any great change with the transfer of power to the new government of the Irish Free State. One of the issues which came to the forefront in the years before the establishment of the Free State in 1922 was the place and status of the Irish language. The influence of the Gaelic League was widespread among those prominent in political and cultural circles: Pádraig Pearse (1879–1916), Douglas Hyde (1860–1949), Eoin MacNeill (1867–1945) and Patrick J. Hogan (1891–1936) were among the founders of the League widely known for their interest in the restoration of the language.

SCOIL CHAITRÍONA, ECCLES STREET 1928

Diarmaid Ferriter, in *The Transformation of Ireland*, writes that the significance of the Gaelic League was perhaps:

> its ability to become central to educational and cultural questions in the first decade of the century, rather than saving the language. It did manage to place pride in the cultural legacy of Irish, ensuring those not proficient could at least speak a little and perhaps read.[134]

This 'pride in the cultural legacy of Irish' was to play a significant part in the foundation of Scoil Chaitríona in Eccles Street Dublin in 1928. The school was another pointer to the willingness, when requested, of the Dominicans to undertake a new initiative in the educational field. Another event momentous in the lives of Irish Dominican nuns took place in that same year, 1928: the amalgamation of the Dominican convents, Cabra, Sion Hill, Dún Laoghaire (Kingstown), Wicklow, Belfast, Eccles Street, Muckross Park, Sutton and Portstewart. This merging of convents under one central government had far-reaching effects on the development of the existing Dominican schools and colleges. The resulting Congregation of Irish Dominican Sisters was headed by a Prioress General and Council who were responsible for the over-all government of the newly formed Congregation, called the Congregation of Irish Domincan Sisters.[135] The convents were no longer subject to the direct authority of the local bishops, but were governed by the Congregation for Religious in Rome. Scoil Chaitríona was the first school opened under the government of the new Prioress General, Mother Colmcille Flynn, in September 1928. This is an Irish medium school, a school in which all subjects are taught through the medium of the Irish language: business transactions and social conversations within the school are, as far as possible, conducted in Irish. As the final seal of approval was given to the school by the new central government of the Congregation in Cabra, legally Scoil Chaitríona was the first school that could be termed 'of the Congregation'.

The newly established Irish Free State took over responsibility for all government departments and the civil servants who administered them. The Department of Education was located in Marlborough Street, Dublin, and two Irish-medium national schools for boys and girls, named respectively Scoil Cholmcille and Scoil Mhuire, were established in 1927. The foundation of these schools was influenced largely by Risteárd Ó Maolcatha (Richard Mulcahy).

Minister for Local Government in William T. Cosgrave's government.[136] The pupils in these national schools required follow-on secondary schools for their education through the medium of Irish. Máirín Ní Dhomhnalláin, one of the first pupils of Scoil Chaitríona, whose father, Pádraig Ó Domhnalláin, was a member of the Gaelic League, recalled that a delegation went to the prioress of Dominican College, Eccles Street, Mother Reginald Lyons, requesting that the nuns set up an Irish-medium school. This request was in tune with the political ground-swell of approval for the revival of the language.

RESTORATION OF THE IRISH LANGUAGE – POLITICAL POLICIES

The government of the day was under the presidency of William T. Cosgrave (1880–1965), leader of the political party Cumann na nGaedheal. R.F. Foster holds that 'the dominant preoccupation of the regime was self-definition against Britain – cultural and political'.[137] Cosgrave was not one of those who vigorously promoted the Irish language; neither was he antagonistic towards it. In his position as head of the government he was politically conscious of Éamonn de Valera's newly formed Fianna Fáil party who were in the opposition. Many of de Valera's followers would, like their leader, be ardent and highly motivated advocates of the restoration of Irish to everyday social and political life as quickly as possible. The Cumann na nGaedheal government in the 1920s, laid 'heavy emphasis on the Gaelic nature of the new state ... [and] the prosecution of the Irish language became the necessary bench-mark of an independent ethos'.[138] One must go back further than the new Irish Free State, to the foundation of the Gaelic League, to understand the enthusiasm which had grown for the revival of the Irish language. In 1893 in Dublin, the organization was founded by Dr Douglas Hyde (1860–1949) and Eoin MacNeill (1867–1945). Both men were Gaelic scholars and enthusiasts who were anxious for the revival of the Irish language. Hyde, who was a Protestant, hoped that 'a non-political and non-sectarian organization would offer common ground on which all sections of Irish political and religious opinion could meet for a cultural purpose'.[139]

Influence of the Gaelic League

The Gaelic League had branches throughout the country; it sponsored Gaelic festivals – called feiseanna – engaged travelling teachers who conducted classes in the Irish language for children and adults, encouraged the revival of Irish step-dancing, and established the first college for training teachers of Irish in Ballingeary Co. Cork in 1905. As a result, the cause of the Irish language became popular and fashionable in some circles; some families adopted it as the everyday language of the home. The Gaelic League was the forum in which many of the leaders of the Easter Rising learned Irish and with the other agencies, such as the Irish Volunteers and Cumann na mBan – the women's supporting group for the Irish Volunteers – it was one of the contributory factors in the national movement towards independence from British rule in Ireland.[140]

The more immediate political and national circumstances surrounding the foundation of Scoil Chaitríona, Eccles Street, was that it first opened its doors to pupils just twelve years after the Easter Rising. The Dáil was in session under the presidency of William T. Cosgrave of the Cumann na nGaedheal party, whose members were supporters of the Anglo-Irish Treaty of 1921. The Irish Free State had been established on 6 December 1922 and the aspirations of many at the time were for a new beginning for Ireland in which the country would be not only free but Gaelic as well. One of the means of achieving this Gaelic state was through the schools. By 1924, new secondary examinations had been set up and Irish became an essential subject in the Intermediate and Leaving Certificate examinations.

Parental aspirations

The parents of the pupils of Scoil Mhuire Marlborough Street, Dublin, were anxious to have a secondary school for their daughters where they could continue their education through Irish. John Marcus O'Sullivan was minister for education in the newly formed Irish government. McCartney says O'Sullivan was one of the 'generation who had grown out of a period of struggle to win a university for Catholics'.[141] He was professor of history in University College Dublin and would be sympathetic towards the new school. At the very least, he did not object to it and allowed the civil servants in his department to negotiate with the nuns in Eccles Street for their support and help. There was an appreciable number of civil servants whose children attended the new Scoil Mhuire; these were some of the first pupils in Scoil Chaitríona. Pádraig Ó Brolcháin and Micheál Breathnach were two of the higher civil servants 'instrumental in persuading the nuns to establish the new school for the girls'.[142] Ó Brolcháin had been appointed the administrative head of national education in 1922. His entry in *Beathaisnéis a hAon* (a research biographical dictionary), says of him,

> from the first day he took charge at Tyrone House [the head office, of the Department of Education], his predominant ideal was to Gaelicize the schools and through the schools to restore Irish as a living tongue. To this he dedicated his official life.[143]

Those who were members of the Gaelic League were not alone in their aspirations to have the Irish language restored. While the daughters of some civil servants, teachers and members of the Gaelic League were among the first pupils of the school, there were other parents who for unknown reasons also sent their daughters to the school. These did not necessarily aspire to have Irish as the spoken language of the home. John Hutchinson writes, the sympathy for things Gaelic was not confined to a political elite, for, as the rebels succeeded from 1918 onwards in mobilising the support of the Catholic community, so the struggle for Gaelic authenticity and political freedom became equated. The Gaelic League now under the Presidency of Eoin MacNeill soared to unprecedented heights of popularity as a symbol of political and cultural resistance. After independence moreover, all the major political parties vied to attest their support for the Gaelic ideal and Irish parents tolerated the increasing concentration on Irish in the schools at the expense of more obviously 'practical' training.[144]

DOMINICAN INVOLVEMENT IN THE FOUNDATION
OF SCOIL CHAITRÍONA

The internal evidence points to O Brolcháin and Breathnach as being the persons most likely to have approached the nuns in Eccles Street to open Scoil Chaitríona in 1928. The Christian Brothers later began a similar secondary school for boys, Coláiste Mhuire in Parnell Square in 1931, thus catering for the needs of the young boys in Scoil Cholmcille, Marlborough Street. Negotiations about the foundation of Scoil Chaitríona were well advanced prior to the amalgamation of the convents. Were the nuns to provide the school premises and the staff, the Department of Education would sanction the school, provided it was of the required standard and fulfilled the regulations pertaining to all secondary schools in the state. Dublin Corporation awarded competitive scholarships to pupils of academic ability from primary schools, which financed their school fees. The prioress of Dominican College, Mother Reginald Lyons, delegated the conduct of the negotiations with the relevant officials of the Department of Education in Dublin to Sr Teresa Flanagan (later better known as Máthair Treasa Ní Fhlanagáin). Unfortunately, written record of the negotiations between the Department of Education and the community in Eccles Street, if any exist in the archives of that Department, are not available for research and to date, no record has been found in the Dominican archives.The year 1928 is still within the living memory of some of the Sisters and of lay people who were pupils of Scoil Chaitríona at its foundation or soon afterwards.[145] Sr Cajetan Lyons taught in the school from the 1930s until her retirement in the 1970s. Sr Aquinas Nic Chárthaigh, OP, Sr Catherine Whelan, a Daughter of Charity, Ms Máirín Ní Dhomhnalláin and Ms Máire Ní Muireadhaidh were among the first pupils in the school; their recollections form the basis of research of its history.[146] From the nuns'point of view, the philosophy which formed the *raison d'être* of the school was grounded in the idealism of the newly formed Irish state.

Scoil Chaitríona opened in September 1928; eighty pupils enrolled, among them five girls from Scoil Mhuire who won Dublin Corporation scholarships and availed themselves of the opportunity to continue their education in Scoil Chaitríona. There was a certain hesitancy among some of the Eccles Street community about the proposed school; it was feared that Scoil Chaitríona might damage the existing school, Dominican College. Some pupils and some members of staff were recruited from Dominican College to give a good start to Scoil Chaitríona; at the time this recruitment of staff and pupils did not help relationships between the existing school and Scoil Chaitríona. Happily, these initial difficulties were overcome in time and both schools flourished side by side.

Sr Cajetan, a past pupil of Dominican College Eccles Street, recalls that prior to the foundation of Scoil Chaitríona, in the early 1920s, there was a great impetus towards learning Irish and this love of the language was fostered in Dominican College and outside school hours by attendance at Coláiste Laighin, in Parnell Square. Coláiste Laighin was a centre for cultural activities founded by Toireallach Ó Rafartaigh, who later became Secretary of the Department of Education. Sr Cajetan also remembered that the pupils of Dominican College were encouraged to enter the competitions of *Feis Átha Cliath*, the Dublin Feis, a competitive festival of music, song, drama and dance, with a strong emphasis on Irish culture in all its aspects. They were also encouraged to enter for the oral Irish tests, conducted by the Gaelic League; successful entrants were awarded an emblem called the Fáinne (a small circular silver or gold badge), which was worn as a sign that the wearer was capable of speaking, and willing to converse in, Irish. Dominican College, Eccles Street therefore was well known in Gaelic circles for its efforts to foster and revive the Irish language, before any approach had been made to the nuns to found Scoil Chaitríona.

The parents of many of the first pupils in the new school came from a background of the relatively recent events of the Easter Rising of 1916. Some indeed may have been participants in the Rising or in the war of independence which followed in 1919–22; some were members of the Gaelic League; others were civil servants or teachers. Some were involved in all those fields. Parents who were actively involved in any or all of these movements were enthused by the idea of political independence, living in a new state with its own government and which would, they hoped, revive the native language and give Irish its proper place as the first language of the land. The slogan, 'Ireland not only free, but Gaelic as well' was a strongly held aspiration for many people who were influenced by the writings of Patrick Pearse and Douglas Hyde. The Gaelic Athletic Association (GAA), founded in mid-1884, also had a strong influence in 'awakening interest in the traditions and values of the ordinary people ... [and it] may be seen as an expression of that remarkable crusading spirit, to be found in the Gaelic League as well, which sought by active means, to save the nation from anglicization'.[147] While the GAA was concerned mainly with athletics, its founder, Michael Cusack, was an enthusiast for the Irish language. David Greene, in his essay, 'The Founding of the Gaelic League', writes:

> the vision of an Irish-speaking Ireland was far more dynamic and inspiring than anything which had yet been offered to the Irish people and they responded to it with enthusiasm.[148]

An Mháthair Treasa Ní Fhlanagáin

Micheál Breathnach, prominent in the Gaelic League, also had links with the Irish Colleges which had been founded by the Gaelic League in Gaeltacht areas, that is areas in Connemara, Cork, Donegal, Waterford and Kerry, where Irish was the day-to-day language of the people. The Irish Colleges were established to train teachers who were beginners in learning Irish or who were not proficient in the language. In September 1910, a new Irish college was opened by Eoin MacNeill in Spiddal, Connemara. Among the teachers first appointed to Spiddal College was Eilís Ní Fhlanagáin (Elizabeth Flanagan). Eilís was one of the women who graduated from the Royal University with a B.A. degree, having taken her lectures through Dominican College Eccles Street, 1906–1909.[149] Eilís was from Doolin, Co. Clare, and as a member of the Gaelic League, her enthusiasm for the language was outstanding. She entered the Dominican novitiate in Sion Hill in 1917, was received into the Order and given the name in religion of Sister Teresa. After her profession in 1919, Sr Teresa was sent to the community in Dominican College, Eccles Street, where she took up a teaching position in the school. She was appointed mistress of studies in Dominican College in 1928. This post was equivalent to that of a modern school principal.

The members of the school staff in the first few years were: An Mháthair Treasa, Sr Enda Purcell (1900–84), the Misses Molly Cotter, Eibhlín Ní Dhubhaill, a Miss Warde, and Miss O'Neill – later Sr Colman OP – all of whom transferred to the new school while retaining some teaching hours in Dominican College. Miss May Pigott – Mairéad Piogóid – who had such an immense influence in the development of music and language teaching in the school, gave up her position in another Dublin school to return to her *alma mater* in Eccles Street. It must be recorded that Mairéad was not a fluent Irish speaker at that time, but she took tuition and mastered the language in order to take up the new post in Scoil Chaitríona.

Sr Teresa Flanagan (An Mháthair Treasa), was appointed manager of the new school while retaining her position as mistress of studies in Dominican College. Catherine of Siena (1347–80), the Italian Dominican saint, was chosen as patron of the new school for two reasons. First, Catherine was a woman of strong faith who did not hesitate to confront the Pope himself when she was convinced that he was not acting according to right norms and justice: the Dominican motto 'truth' and love of the Church were her guiding principles. Secondly, Catherine by her writings in her own Tuscan dialect, is credited with raising that dialect to the status of a literary language.[150] Catherine of Siena was thought to be, therefore, a fitting patron for a school which set itself clear Dominican, linguistic and cultural goals.

The choice of An Mháthair Treasa as manager was probably obvious at the time, but her appointment proved to be inspirational. For almost fifty years, An Máthair Treasa played a leading role in directing the school with vision and foresight, a broad outlook on education, and a love of all things both Gaelic and Dominican. Her regime in the school was always benign and calm and she

10. An Mháthair Treasa Ní Fhlanagáin, 1888–1975

sought at all times to have a curriculum which embraced all aspects of education, the arts and sciences. While the promotion of the Irish language was Mother Teresa's primary aim, the culture of other countries, their languages, music, drama and choral singing were encouraged in Scoil Chaitríona; nothing cultural was alien to her. Her great friend, Monsignor Pádraig de Brún (1889–1960), professor of mathematics in Maynooth College, a brilliant linguist, translated into Irish many songs, *lieder*, and operatic arias for school concert performances. A very memorable performance was Euripides' tragedy *Iphigenia* translated from Greek; the play was produced in the school concert hall by the pupils. It was also performed in Loreto Hall, St Stephen's Green and in the Drishane Convent, Millstreet Street Co. Cork, convents which also benefitted from Dr Browne's friendship.[151]

One of An Mháthair Treasa's first pupils wrote of her experience of being a pupil in the early days of the school:

> [n]o one can remember Scoil Chaitríona without thinking of Máthair Treasa. She had within herself, the will, the energy, the capability, the spirit, the sympathy, and every other accomplishment necessary to guide and extend the school and to promote its special ethos.[152]

An Máthair Treasa became prioress of the convent in Eccles Street in the mid-1940s, but she never, until her death in 1975, lost her abiding interest in Scoil Chaitríona. Patricia Herbert, a past pupil of the 1940s, wrote a letter to a national newspaper in which she summed up the atmosphere prevailing in the school during her own years as a pupil:

> in secondary school where, … all subjects were taught through Irish under the guidance of the liberal Dominican sisters and the remarkable Mairéad Pigóid, I came to realise that the pursuit of European culture and the cultivation of our native language were not incompatible. There, in the school-choirs, in addition to the Irish songs, I came to know and sing in Irish the works of Schubert and Mendelssohn, the choruses of Wagner and the music of Humperdinck – all translated for us from the original German.The vision of Ireland which people like Mairéad Piogóid has, was clearly one in which the assimilation of the best of European culture would go hand in hand with the cultivation and promotion of the Irish language and its traditions. From such an enriched culture a Bartok, Falla or Sibelius might have emerged.[153]

These last two quotations are fitting tributes to An Mháthair Treasa and to the vision and dedication of all who have been associated with Scoil Chaitríona since 1928.

DOMINICAN COLLEGE, FORTWILLIAM PARK, BELFAST

Education for the world of commerce

In 1930 two new establishments were opened to cater for girls who wished to have a career in the public services or in the business world. One of these was the Commercial College in Eccles Street, the other was Dominican College, Fortwilliam Park, Belfast. The final section of this chapter records the Fortwilliam Park foundation. In the nineteenth century most Dominican schools evolved from the traditional boarding school model to schools which had come to terms with the demand for change. All Dominican schools entered for the Intermediate examinations, although hesitantly in some cases. The twentieth century brought change of another kind: a commercial education for girls who did not wish to go to university and who were anxious to get employment in the offices of the civil service, industrial and commercial firms. Dominican College, Fortwilliam Park, in north Belfast was founded with that specific need in mind. This was another new area of education for the Dominican nuns, undertaken at a time of great change, which affected each of the members of the communities at a personal level. All the Dominican convents in Ireland, which directly or indirectly sprang from the Cabra foundation, had agreed to amalgamate and form a congregation under the jurisdiction of the Sacred Congregation for Religious in Rome. This took place in 1928, just two years prior to the foundation in Fortwilliam Park.

The implications for the nuns included the acceptance of a centralized authority within the group; each convent had been autonomous until 1928. In the educational sphere, all decisions which involved opening new schools would henceforth be made by the general council of the congregation, and the religious staff of each school was assigned to a convent by the council.

Decline of industry in Belfast

Between the two world wars, the traditional Belfast industries of shipbuilding and engineering declined. Not alone did the heavy industries suffer an economic down-turn but the textile industry experienced a decline in demand for its products, especially in the demand for linen goods. The economic historian Black writes:

> [a]fter the war ... linen and shipbuilding suffered a substantial decline, and engineering a major set-back. The impact on the city was severe and unemployment was tragically high. ... Things could have been much worse had it not been for the growth of the service industries during the period. In 1926 the number of people employed in these industries – whole-sale and retail distribution, professional services, education, Government etc. – was about 80,000, by 1937 this had risen to over 100,000.[154]

Unemployment, particularly among men in Belfast had increased; in many families women were the sole bread-winners and with the growth in the service industries employment for women increased. Office work became a popular career for girls who did not wish, nor had the financial means, to take up teacher training or continue on to university. There was an increase in the number of commercial colleges in Belfast which catered for girls who wished to take up secretarial positions in commercial offices or in the expanding Northern Ireland civil service. These commercial colleges were 'secular', and did not include religious instruction in their curriculum.

Commercial training for Catholic girls

The increase in the number of secular commercial colleges in Belfast was a cause of anxiety for the bishop of Down and Connor, Dr Daniel Mageean. He approached the Dominicans in Falls Road convent with a request to open a new school in north Belfast which would cater for the commercial training of young Catholic girls. A house was purchased in Fortwilliam Park and the nuns from the newly amalgamated convents, now known as the Congregation of Irish Dominican Sisters, took charge of it. The *Irish News*, a Belfast daily newspaper, announced the opening on 15 September 1930. The new school would have two sections, a commercial college and a preparatory day school for girls and young boys. In the commercial college the girls would be 'prepared for all branches of

Business, for Civil Service and other examinations'.[155] The school prospectus stated that the school was organized on modern lines together with an all-round secretarial education, in a religious atmosphere. Mathematics, general science, Latin, French, Irish and German were taught, commercial subjects were well served by the inclusion of shorthand and typewriting, commercial law and accountancy. The *Times Educational Supplement* added, 'all who know anything of the Dominican work in education will be glad to see them entering these new fields'.[156]

CONCLUSION

Dominican Convent Eccles Street with its two schools, Dominican College and Scoil Chaitríona, has been given more attention in this chapter than any of the other Dominican schools. On the whole Dominicans, while embodying their own ethos, ran their boarding and day schools in the nineteenth century much as the other religious orders ran theirs. What was different about the Dominicans in the Eccles Street complex was their readiness to change, not the schools' ethos, but the approach to the education of girls, in the last decades of the nineteenth century. Scoil Chaitríona was another example of this awareness of the needs of the time, the awareness of the needs of a growing population of Irish-speakers or of those who espoused the cause of the revival of the Irish language and who wished to have their daughters taught through that medium. The opening of the commercial schools in Eccles Street and Fortwilliam Park in Belfast was another sign that addressing the obvious needs of twentieth-century girls was still part of the Dominican ministry in education. It will be seen in Chapter 3 how Dominican College Eccles Street developed a section for the higher education of women at the end of the 1880s.

NOTES

1. For the context of the political history of secondary education in Ireland see, T.J. McElligott, *Secondary Education in Ireland 1870–1921* (Dublin: Irish Academic Press, 1981), referred to henceforth as McElligott, *Secondary Education*.
2. P. MacSuibhne, *Paul Cullen and His Contemporaries* (Naas: Leinster Leader, 1972), Vol. V, pp.249–50.
3. McElligott, *Secondary Education*, p.5.
4. E. Howley, *The Universities and Secondary Schools of Ireland with Proposals for their Improvement* (Dublin: Evening Post, 1871).
5. V. Hicks-Beach, *Life of Sir Michael Hicks-Beach (1857–1916)* (London: Macmillan & Co., 1952), Vol. 1, p.54.
6. McElligott, *Secondary Education*, p.16.
7. Hicks-Beach, *Life of Sir Michael Hicks-Beach*, p.55.
8. Cited in McElligott, *Secondary Education*, p.20.
9. Ibid., p.23.
10. MacSuibhne, *Paul Cullen and His Contemporaries*, Vol. V., pp.249–50.
11. McElligott, *Secondary Education*, comments of Cardinal Cullen on Hicks-Beach's Memorandum cited, p.25.

12. British Parliamentary Papers (BPP), Intermediate Education (Ireland) Act, 1878 (41 & 42 Vic., c.66).
13. P.J. Dowling, *A History of Irish Education: A Study in Conflicting Loyalties* (Cork: Mercier Press, paperback edition, 1971), p.134.
14. J. Burstyn, *Victorian Education and the Ideal of Womanhood* (New Jersey: Rutgers University Press, 1984), p.33.
15. Among the continental orders which came to Ireland in the nineteenth century were: Society of the Sacred Heart (1842); Faithful Companions of Jesus (1844); Daughters of Charity, St Vincent de Paul (1855); Sisters of St Louis (1859); Sisters of St Joseph of Cluny (1859); Sisters of La Sainte-Union des Sacrés Cœurs (1862); Sisters of Sacred Heart of Mary (1870); Marist Sisters (1873); Sisters of the Cross and Passion (1880s).
16. D. Kerr, 'Dublin's Forgotten Archbishop: Daniel Murray, 1768–1852', in J. Kelly and D. Keogh (eds), *History of the Catholic Archdiocese of Dublin* (Dublin: Four Courts Press, 2000), p.248.
17. D. Keogh, *Edmund Rice, 1762–1844* (Dublin: Four Courts Press, 1996), p.56.
18. Kerr, 'Dublin's Forgotten Archbishop', p.250.
19. M. Cullen, 'Anna Maria Haslam (1829–1922)', in M. Cullen and M. Luddy (eds), *Women, Power and Consciousness in Nineteenth-Century Ireland* (Dublin: Attic Press, 1995), p.168. Referred to henceforth as Cullen and Luddy, *Women, Power and Consciousness*.
20. C. Clear, *Nuns in Nineteenth-Century Ireland* (Dublin: Gill & Macmillan, Dublin, 1987), p.123.
21. J.J. O'Sullivan, *The Complete Catholic Registry, Directory and Almanck, 1836–1900* (Dublin: Mullany, 1873), pp.40–7.
22. A. Jordan, *Margaret Byers, Pioneer of Women's Education* (Belfast: Institute of Irish Studies, n.d.), p.4.
23. Cullen and Luddy, *Women, Power and Consciousness*, pp.168 and 201.
24. Jordan, *Margaret Byers, Pioneer of Women's Education*, p.3.
25. Anne V. O'Connor and Susan M. Parkes, *Gladly Learn and Gladly Teach. A History of Alexandra College and School, Dublin, 1866–1966* (Dublin: Blackwater Press, n.d.), p.6. Cited henceforth as O'Connor and Parkes, *Gladly Learn and Gladly Teach.*
26. Cullen, 'Anna Maria Haslam (1829–1922)', in Cullen and Luddy, *Women, Power and Consciousness*, p.167.
27. M. Luddy, 'Isabella M.S. Tod (1836–1896)' in Cullen and Luddy, *Women, Power and Consciousness,* p.200.
28. N. Armour, 'Isabella Tod and Liberal Unionism in Ulster, 1886–96', in A. Hayes and D. Urquhart (eds), *Irish Women's History* (Dublin: Irish Academic Press, 2004), p.84.
29. I.M.S. Tod, 'Girls in National Schools in Ireland', *Englishwoman's Review,* Vol.20 (Sept. 1889), pp.394–7, (p.395).
30. A.V. O'Connor, 'Influences Affecting Girls' Secondary Education in Ireland 1860–1910', *Archivium Hibernicum,* 41 (1986) (Maynooth: Catholic Record Society of Ireland), pp.83–98 (p.84).
31. K. and C. O Céirín, *Women of Ireland, A Biographical Dictionary* (Galway: Kinvara, Tír Eolas, 1996), p.114.
32. O'Connor and Parkes, *Gladly Learn and Gladly Teach*, p.28.
33. O'Connor, 'Influences Affecting Girls' Secondary Education in Ireland', p.94.
34. M. Luddy, *Women and Philanthropy in Nineteenth Century Ireland* (Cambridge: Cambridge University Press, 1995), p.21.
35. M. Luddy, 'Presentation Convents in County Tipperary', *Tipperary Historical Journal,* (published once a year. The 1992 edition is Volume 5, pp.84–5).

36. Luddy, *Women and Philanthropy in Nineteenth-Century Ireland,* pp.36–7.
37. LHCM, Information, courtesy Srs Margaret and Mona, from unattributed cutting, 'Children's Hospital, Temple Street, Dublin, 1872'. OPSH, *Sion Hill Annals,* p.133.
38. O'Connor, 'Influences Affecting Girls' Secondary Education in Ireland, p.89.
39. Ibid and O'Connor, 'The Revolution in Girls' Secondary Education in Ireland, 1860–1910' in Mary Cullen (ed.), *Girls Don't Do Honours: Irish Women in Education in the 19th and 20th Centuries* (Dublin: WEB, 1987), pp.31–54.
40. *Thom's Official Directory of the U.K. and Ireland* 1850–1902, (Dublin: Alex Thom, published annually).
41. B. Walsh, *Roman Catholic Nuns in England and Wales, 1800–1937* (Dublin: Irish Academic Press, 2002), p.145.
42. Sr D. Kelly, *The Sligo Ursulines, The First Fifty Years, 1826–1876* (Sligo: Ursuline Sisters, n.d.), p.208.
43. Ibid.
44. Ibid., p.62.
45. MAA, *Règlements des Pensionnats et Plan d'Etudes de la Société du Sacré Cœur* (Orléans: Alex Jacob, 1852). Boarding School Regulations and Plan of Studies of the Society of the Sacred Heart.
46. MAA, Anonymous pamphlet, No. 496, *Life at the Sacred Heart, Past and Present* (London: Convent of Sacred Heart, Roehampton, n.d.).
47. MAA, Discipline et Usages du Pensionat (*Customs and Code of Discipline of the Boarding School*).
48. MAA, 'Life at the Sacred Heart', Pamphlet 496.
49. K. Boyle, 'Katie Boyle', transcript of interview in Jackie Bennet and Rosemary Forgan (eds), *Convent Girls* (London: Virago Press, 2003), pp.50–1.
50. SLA, Anonymous, 'Eirighe an Chlochair', in *Réalt na Mara,* School Year-Book, 1918/1919, p.6.
51. S. O Buachalla, *Education Policy in Twentieth Century Ireland* (Dublin: Wolfhound Press, 1988) p.342. The Gaelic League was founded in 1893 by Douglas Hyde, Eoin MacNeill and others. It accorded a priority to education reform, its aim being to secure that Irish history, cultural traditions, and the Irish language would be 'cherished, taught and esteemed'.
52. SLA, *Reflections,* Clochar Louis, Muineachán (Dublin: Folens, n.d.) 1859-1972, p.15.
53. SLA, 'Notes on Gaelic Movement', newspaper cutting from *The Western People,* c.1901.
54. SSHA, *Plan d'Etudes, passim.*
55. Rose O'Neill, *A Rich Inheritance, Galway Dominican Nuns, 1664–1994* (Galway: Dominican Sisters, 1994), pp.9–17.
56. Ibid., p.12.
57. D. Forristal, *The Siena Story, 1722–1997* (Drogheda: Siena Convent, 1999), p.21.
58. Jordan, *Margaret Byers,* p.9.
59. OPC, *Cabra Annals,* pp.101–3.
60. OPT, Sr Hyacinth McAuliffe's Notebooks.
61. Anonymous, 'Convent Boarding Schools for Young Ladies', *Fraser's Magazine for Town and Country,* 9 (1874), pp.778–86 (pp.778–9).
62. An Old Convent Girl 'A Word for the Convent Boarding-Schools', *Fraser's Magazine for Town and Country,* 10 (1874), pp.473–83.
63. Katherine Tynan, *Twenty-Five Years; Reminiscences* (London: Smith, Elder & Co, 1913), p.49.
64. Ibid., pp.50–1.
65. Ibid., p.56.
66. Jordan, *Margaret Byers,* p.68.
67. P. Branca, *Women in Europe since 1750* (London: Croom Helm, 1978), p.173.
68. D.M. Turner, *History of Science Teaching in England* (London: Chapman & Hall, 1927), p.100.

69. Turner, *History of Science Teaching in England*, p.74.
70. J. Coolahan, *Irish Education, History and Structure* (Dublin: Institute of Public Administration, 1981), p.62.
71. O'Connor and Parkes, *Gladly Learn and Gladly Teach*, p.1.
72. OPSH, *Sion Hill Annals*, p.1.
73. OPC, *Cabra Annals*, p.105.
74. E.E. O'Donnell, *The Annals of Dublin* (Dublin: Wolfhound Press, 1987), p.143.
75. OPSH, *Sion Hill Annals*, pp.1–12, and Chapter 1 p.41 of this book.
76. Ibid., p.12.
77. Ibid., p.36.
78. Ibid, p.96.
79. New Testament, Gospel of St Matthew: 16. 3.
80. OPSH, *Sion Hill Annals*, p.96.
81. DDA., 360/1/111 McCabe Papers 1883.
82. Ibid.
83. OPC, *Cabra Annals*, p.147.
84. DDA., McCabe Papers, unsigned, undated correspondence.
85. Excerpt from *Report of Commissioners of Education* 1899, cited in McElligott, *Secondary Education*, p.72.
86. DDA, 360/1/111 McCabe Papers, 1883.
87. Cullen and Luddy, *Women, Power and Consciousness*, p.14.
88. OPC, *Constitutions of the Irish Dominican Sisters*, Cabra Congregation (Dublin: Cabra, 1947), Constitution 220, p.78.
89. *Thom's Directory*, 1882.
90. OPSH, *Sion Hill Annals*, pp.171–2.
91. OPE, Prospectus 1, Appendix 2, pp.199–200 for full text of prospectus.
92. *The Freeman's Journal*, 18 and 19 October 1898, obituary notice of Count Christopher Ryder, 'a frequent contributor to Catholic charities in the city [of Dublin]'.
93. OPSH, *Sion Hill Annals*, August 1882, pp.130–1.
94. OPE, The trowel is held in the archives of Dominican Convent, 204 Griffith Avenue, Dublin.
95. MacMahon had meanwhile become parish priest of St Michan's, Halston Street, which was sub-divided and a new parish of St Joseph's Berkeley Road was formed. Eccles Street then became part of this new parish.
96. OPE, Letter from Archdeacon MacMahon to Mother Antonina Hanley, Eccles Street, 26 April 1883. Appendix 4, pp.202–3 and for text of letter.
97. OPC, *Catholic Registry* 1895 (Dublin: Duffy, 1895), pp.110 and 112.
98. Ibid., entry for Stanhope Street Convent, p.112.
99. OPE, Prospectus 2, Appendix 3, p.201.
100. OPE, Letter from Archdeacon MacMahon to Mother Antonina Hanley; Appendix 4, pp.311–14.
101. OPE, Circular, 'Dominican Orphanage of Our Lady of Sion, 18 & 19 Eccles Street Dublin'.
102. M.M. Kealy, 'The Dominican Nuns of Channel Row, 1717–1820' (Unpublished MA Dissertation, Lancaster University, 1998), pp.73–81.
103. OPE, Eccles Street Papers.
104. DDA. Anon, 'O'Brien Institute, Clontarf (1878–1932),' in *The Christian Brothers Educational Record* (Published privately, n.d.).
105. OPE, Copy of an original raffle ticket.
106. OPSH, *Sion Hill Annals*, p.143.
107. Ibid., p.149.
108. *The Freeman's Journal*, 21 October 1898.
109. *Thom's Directory*, Index of citizens of Dublin, various years in the 1880s and 1890s (Dublin: Alex Thom, published annually).

110. Luddy, *Women and Philanthropy in Nineteenth-century Ireland*, p.37.
111. OPSH, *Sion Hill Annals*, p.133.
112. Ibid., p.143.
113. Ibid., p.144.
114. Ibid., pp.171–2.
115. K.T. Hoppen, *Ireland Since 1800* (London: Longman, 1989), pp.94–5.
116. Ibid., pp.110–18.
117. OPSH, *Sion Hill Annals*, p.170.
118. *The Freeman's Journal*, 5 December 1888.
119. LSG., Anon., 'Résumé of M. Michael Corcoran's Life, 1888–1918. Fourth Superior General'.
120. Jordan, *Margaret Byers*, p.83.
121. O'Connor and Parkes, *Gladly Learn and Gladly Teach*, p.38.
122. Jordan, *Margaret Byers*, p.24.
123. BPP, Intermediate Education (Ireland) Commission, 1898. First Report referred to as Palles Report.
124. BPP, Palles Report, p.13.
125. St Mary's University and High School Mount Street (one establishment), was founded in 1893 from Sion Hill.
126. BPP, Palles Report, Appendix XI p.208, Answers to Queries.
127. Ibid., p.209.
128. Ibid.
129. McElligott, *Secondary Education in Ireland*, pp.65, 66 and 72.
130. William Walsh, *Statement of Chief Grievances of Irish Catholics in the Matter of Education* (Dublin: Browne & Nolan, 1890), p.223.
131. OPE, Newspaper cuttings, *The Freeman's Journal*, 1 September 1901.
132. BPP, *Report of Messrs F.H. Dale and T.A. Stephens, on Intermediate Education in Ireland*. H.c. 1905, XXVIII.
133. Ó Buachalla, *Education Policy in Twentieth Century Ireland*, p.51.
134. D. Ferriter, *The Transformation of Ireland, 1900–2000* (London: Profile Books, 2004), p.100.
135. OPG, Archives of the Congregation of Dominican Sisters, Cabra, Dublin, Boxes dated 1927–28.
136. D.J. Hickey and J.E. Doherty, *A New Dictionary of Irish History from 1800* (Dublin: Gill & Macmillan, paperback edition, 2005), p.176.
137. R.F. Foster, *Modern Ireland, 1600–1972* (London: Penguin Books, 1989), p.516.
138. Ibid., p.518.
139. Hickey and Doherty, *A New Dictionary of Irish History from 1800*, p.162.
140. Ibid., pp.98, 242.
141. D. McCartney, *UCD, A National Idea* (Dublin: Gill & MacMillan, 1999), p.225.
142. M. Ní Dhomhnalláin, oral reminiscences recorded in December 1995.
143. T.J. O'Connell, '100 Years of the INTO', in D. Breathnach and M. Ní Mhurchú (eds), *Beathaisnéis a hAon* (Baile Atha Cliath: Clóchomhar Tta, 1986).
144. J. Hutchinson, *The Dynamics of Cultural Nationalism. The Gaelic Revival and the Creation of the Irish Nation State* (London: Allen & Unwin, 1987), p.305.
145. I am indebted to the following people who gave oral recollections of the founding of Scoil Chaitríona: Srs Cajetan Lyons OP and Aquinas McCarthy OP, Sr Catherine Whelan, DC, Máire Ní Mhuireadhaidh. Sadly, Sr Catherine, Máire Ní Muireadhaidh, Máirín Ní Dhomhnalláin and Sr Cajetan have died since recording their stories.
146. These interviews took place at various times, those with Srs Cajetan Lyons and Aquinas McCarthy c. 1988; the others more recently, between 1995–2000.

147. Kevin B. Nowlan, 'The Gaelic League and Other National Movements', in Seán Ó
     Tuama (ed.), *The Gaelic League Idea,* Thomas Davis Lecture Series (Cork: Mercier
     Press, 1969), pp.42–3.
148. David Greene, 'The Founding of the Gaelic League', in Ó Tuama (ed.), *The Gaelic
     League Idea,* p.19.
149. Chapter 3 deals with women's higher education.
150. OPE, *Annals of Dominican Convent Eccles Street,* September 1928, p.118.
151. M. Cruise O'Brien, *The Same Age as the State* (Dublin: O'Brien Press, 2003), p.99.
152. M. Ní Mhuireadhaidh, 'Scoil Chaitríona', *Iona News* (Dublin: Parish Magazine,
     St Columba's, May 1978), p.4, Translated from Irish.
153. P. Herbert, *The Irish Times,* 24 September 1990. Letter to the editor. Mairéad Piogóid
     was a noted musician, linguist, radio broadcaster, and teacher in Scoil Chaitríona.
154. W. Black, 'Industrial Change in the Twentieth Century', in J.C. Beckett and R.E.
     Glassock (eds), *Belfast, Origin and Growth of an Industrial City* (Belfast: British
     Broadcasting Corporation, 1967), p.163.
155. OPFW, *The Irish News,* proof copy of the advertisement.
156. *Times Educational Supplement,* 29 September 1930.

3

Women's higher education

The university question was the general term given during the years 1845–1909 to the efforts of the Irish Catholic Church and of various political administrations to have a state-funded university acceptable to Catholics and Protestants alike. The movement towards higher education for women in Ireland in the late nineteenth and early twentieth centuries cannot be separated from the wider 'university question', as it is called by Irish historians. From its foundation in 1592, the insistence on attendance at the Anglican services in the college chapel, and the anti-papal oath which was demanded of all who aspired to take degrees debarred practising Catholics from attending Trinity College, the only university in the country. Not until the Catholic Relief Act of 1793 were Catholic students permitted to take degrees there without compromising their faith. However, the ethos and atmosphere of the college remained Protestant, and though attendance at chapel and oaths of allegiance were no longer required, Trinity College continued to be seen by the majority of Catholics as a bastion of English domination. McCartney cites Judge Webb, a distinguished graduate of Trinity College, who declared in 1891 that it 'was founded by Protestants, for Protestants and in the Protestant interest ... and Protestant might it ever remain'.[1]

In 1845 the foundation of the Queen's Colleges by the British government under Sir Robert Peel, in Belfast, Cork and Galway, was an attempt to give Catholics an equal opportunity for higher education, but because these colleges were nondenominational and had no public funding for theological teaching, the Catholic bishops regarded them as irreligious and 'godless'. Nevertheless, a considerable number of Catholics attended the Queen's Colleges. The bishops in 1850 adopted a recommendation of the Synod of Thurles, as proposed by Pope Pius IX, to establish an Irish Catholic University on the model of the Catholic University of Louvain which, besides humanities, also had chairs of medicine and science.

A Catholic University Committee was therefore set up and chaired by Archbishop Cullen in 1850. Initially Cullen formally invited John Henry, later Cardinal, Newman (1801–1900), to advise on the appointment of staff and to 'give us a few lectures on education'. Newman became a member of a sub-committee of three who were to make preliminary plans for the new college.[2] The proposed institution fitted well into Newman's idea set out in discourses later published as *The Idea of a University*.[3] Newman's ideal university would aim at giving a liberal university education, where there would be a broad sweep of disciplines and interaction between students of varying faculties. He contended that a university should not only have a multiplicity of faculties, but that it could not claim to engage in the pursuit of universal knowledge unless it had a faculty of theology. The primary duty of a university in Newman's opinion was neither to inculcate virtue nor to prepare for a vocation; restrictions of any kind were inconsistent with the very name of university. His ideal was a university that taught all subjects, in fact, a university which taught universal knowledge.[4]

In July 1850, Cullen proposed that Newman should be the first rector of the Catholic University in Dublin, a proposal that became a reality when the university was opened in 1854. Gwynn holds that it was Cullen's personal idea to invite Newman; other Irish bishops, especially Archbishop McHale of Tuam, were not in favour of Newman and some were luke-warm towards the very idea of establishing a Catholic University. According to Gwynn, 'the rest of the hierarchy were profoundly sceptical as to [the university's] success and were by no means sympathetic to the idea of having an Englishman – still less a recent English convert – as its Rector.'[5] Newman had ambitiously hoped that the Catholic University in Dublin would be 'the intellectual headquarters for Catholics of the English-speaking world'.[6] He also held that special attention should be paid to Celtic studies. A Celtic revival was also one of the aims of the Young Irelanders, a political movement led by Thomas Davis (1814–45) and Sir Charles Gavan Duffy (1816–1903); the Young Irelanders were also pledged to economic reform. Cullen, who was strongly conservative, was totally opposed to the Irish cultural revival and was not at all supportive of the ideals of the Young Irelanders who, as late as 1848, had led a failed rebellion in Ireland. On the other hand as Gwynn writes,

> Newman was very soon attracted by the sincerity and the idealism of the younger men. They were just the type of active and generous minds whom he desired to attract to the University. ... Their devotion to the revival of Celtic studies and national tradition had created ... the atmosphere in which he had hoped to conduct his faculty of Celtic research.[7]

To attract students from England and other English-speaking countries Newman, in 1854, appointed eminent Catholics to professorships. Among them were: Eugene O'Curry (1796–1862), appointed to the chair of archaeology and Irish history (his book, *Manuscript Materials of Ancient Irish History*, was highly regarded by scholars); Aubrey de Vere (1814–1902), a prolific writer and poet of some renown, appointed professor of political and social science; Denis Florence McCarthy (1817–1882), a barrister, poet and journalist, a contributor of political verse to the *The Nation* newspaper, appointed professor of poetry. McCartney holds that the appointees were 'more akin to what would now be described as honorary or research professors'.[8] One might assume that the choice of Newman as first rector was inspired: he seemed eminently suited to open and supervise a new university in which he had scope to carry out his ideals for higher education as set out in *The Idea of a University*, but that was not to be.

Given the hostility of some of the hierarchy and Cullen's suspicions of Newman's proposals, it soon became obvious that they were not sustainable in the circumstances under which he had to operate in the Ireland of the 1850s. His stay in Dublin was short-lived. In spite of his best endeavours, by 1858 he felt that he had to withdraw and he returned to England, a disillusioned and disappointed man. The immediate cause of Newman's withdrawal from Dublin was a total break-down in relationships between Newman and the Irish hierarchy, in particular, between himself and two of the archbishops, Cardinal Cullen and John McHale, Archbishop of Tuam. According to McCartney, Cardinal Cullen was, 'by temperament, tradition, and training, very different from the English convert whom he had invited to be rector'.[9] Newman, on his own behalf, complained, 'these bishops are so accustomed to be absolute that they usurp the rights of others and ride roughshod over their wishes and their plans, quite innocently without meaning it'.[10] His rectorship lasted just four years.

The Catholic University survived from 1854–79, to be superseded by the Royal University of Ireland, which was established as an examining body only, under Disraeli's government, when the University Education (Ireland) Bill 1879 passed through parliament. McCartney explains:

> [t]he Royal University incorporated by charter in 1880, was a non-teaching, degree-awarding institution on the model of the University of London. Students of any of the existing colleges or indeed by private study could take its examinations. Fellows were appointed to set the courses for degrees and act as examiners, and this system allowed the state to endow indirectly the Catholic University, since half of all the fellows appointed were to be drawn from its staff. ... The Catholic University was re-organised in 1882, when a number of seminaries and other educational establishments under religious orders were added to the Medical School and the St Stephen's Green institution as constituent colleges. The St Stephen's Green institution [the Catholic University] was renamed University College. Its management was transferred to the Jesuits in 1883; and it was soon thereafter revitalised.[11]

The first Jesuit president of University College was Fr William Delany (1835–1924), whose term of office ran from 1883–88. Delany was an influential and prominent figure in educational circles in Ireland in the last three decades of the nineteenth century. Before his appointment to University College, he had been headmaster of a Jesuit school in Tullabeg, Co. Carlow, and was a leading figure in the negotiations which brought about the introduction of the

Intermediate Act of 1878. Delany also had influence with people in government circles, for example, with Sir Michael Hicks-Beach, the Chief Secretary, Randolph Churchill and Patrick Keenan, the Commissioner for Education. Delany was very well-informed about the politics of education in Ireland and was a founder-member and first president of the Catholic Headmasters' Association, which was formed in 1878 in order to counteract the possible over-riding influence of the Protestant Headmasters' Association. In Delany's opinion, the Catholic Headmasters' Association was necessary if the new Intermediate education scheme was not, in Delany's words, 'to be shaped from the very start so as to suit the Protestant schools'.[12]

During the years between the establishment of the Royal University of Ireland in 1879 and 1908, several attempts were made to bring the university question to a conclusion which would satisfy the needs of all interested parties. Between 1879 and 1908, in fact, four proposals were made to solve the problem. Each proposal in turn was set aside because agreement could not be reached between the University of Dublin, the Catholic hierarchy, the Church of Ireland bishops, and others. In 1901 a Royal Commission was set up which took its name from its chairman, Lord Robertson; this was followed by another commission under the chairmanship of Sir Edward Fry in 1906. The Fry Commission was to advise on the means which might be taken to increase the 'usefulness to the country' of Trinity College.[13] The number of enquiries about the future of the universities – Dublin University, the Royal University and the Queen's Colleges – form a tangled web, with proposals, counter-proposals, agreement and disagreement.[14] The sequence of events, with the proposals and the reaction of the protagonists in the debate, are set out in Figure 3, p.126; it is based on Morrissey's account of the events leading up to the passing of the Irish Universities Act in 1908.[15]

DEBATE ON HIGHER EDUCATION FOR WOMEN

In Chapter 2 above, in the section headed 'Influence of Protestant women educators', the names of Anna Maria Haslam, Margaret Byers and Isabella Tod were prominent. These same women come to the fore again in the literature connected with the struggle to gain access for women to university education. Anne Jellicoe, while she did not write publicly on the subject, was actively concerned that Alexandra College should provide courses for girls who wished to become governesses or teachers and who might have had ambitions to proceed to university. Jellicoe set up the Association for Promoting the Higher Education of Ladies as Teachers.

Logan explains how this body acted as an 'appointments bureau, a funder of scholarships, and as a pressure group with the aim of having university examinations available for women candidates from Alexandra College.'[16] In October 1881, Margaret Byers read a paper in the Education Department in

Figure 3. University structures

Date	Structure of university	Proposed by	Favourable or unfavourable reactions [F/UF]
1873	Dublin University to comprise within it Trinity College; the Catholic University; the Queen's Colleges in Belfast and Cork.	Gladstone	[F] Archbishop Walsh *if* Catholic University were financially endowed. [UF] Other Catholic Colleges; Trinity; Queen's Colleges
1879	Royal University of Ireland (1879–1901) established as Examining Body. Existing Queen's University abolished but constituent Colleges, Cork, Galway, Belfast continued under the name Queen's Colleges.	Disraeli's Government	Trinity College to keep its autonomy. All others, including the nuns' colleges, to work within the framework of the Royal University, until the passing of National University Act.
1899	Three teaching universities: University of Dublin (Trinity College); two new universities – one for Catholics in Dublin and one for Protestants in Belfast.	R.B. Haldane, a Liberal, with the approval of Balfour	Catholic bishops had no cohesive plan, did not respond strongly. [UF] Outcry in England. Saw this as Endowment of Catholic priest-ridden university.
1901/02	Reorganization of the Royal as a teaching university. Retain the Queen's Colleges in Cork, Galway, Belfast. Open a new college for Catholics in Dublin. All these to be constituent colleges of the reorganized Royal University.	Robertson Commission and Report	[F] Attractive to number of Catholics. [UF] Walsh; did not consider Royal to have a sufficiently high standard.
1904	University of Dublin to include: Trinity College; Queen's College Belfast; a Roman Catholic university in Dublin; Maynooth College and Queen's Colleges in Galway and Cork to be downgraded.	Lord Dunraven, a resident, improving, landlord; convert to Catholicism	[F] Walsh and O'Conor Don, an influential Catholic. [UF] Trinity College.
1908	Leave University of Dublin with Trinity College as it stands. Queen's Colleges in Cork and Galway to join a new University College in Dublin as constituent Colleges of National University of Ireland. Cork and Galway to be named University College, Cork and University College, Galway, respectively. Belfast College to become Queen's University, Belfast. All to be non-denominational. Maynooth College to be a university in its own right.	Birrell, Chief Secretary	On 1 August 1908 the Irish University Act was signed into law. This was the final solution to the 'universities question' until the 1960s.
1967	New debate about structures when government proposed reorganization of universities.	Donogh O'Malley, Minister for Education	That debate does not lie within the scope of this study.

Source: T. Morrissey, *William J. Walsh, Archbishop of Dublin, 1841–1921*, pp.210–31.

Dublin, 'The Better Education of Women', in which she pointed out some of the obstacles which retarded the spread of liberal education among women of the middle class in Ireland. In the 1880s there was little public awareness of the importance of women's higher education and of the necessary means to further the cause. To hasten the process, Byers advocated some practical measures including conferences for teachers and the general public, in order to awaken the minds of the public to the importance of education in general for girls. Byers also called for reform of education, educational research and the implementation of best practice in teaching. Further, the help of parents as fund-raisers was suggested so that girls' schools should be self-supporting. In areas of small population, boys and girls should be taught together. Most important perhaps was Byers' insistence on the importance of teacher training.[17] Byers' assumption was that teaching is the highest service which women can give to the next generation, and she saw the lack of training for [secondary] teachers as crucial to the whole question of higher education for women. Some of the audience contributed to the discussion. Most of those present agreed with Isabella Tod when she deplored the lack of endowment for middle-class schools for girls and advocated mixed schools in small towns where the population could not carry both boys' and girls' schools. A dissenting voice came from Professor O'Ryan of Queen's University, Cork, who held the view that 'girls should be content with good training in the so-called intermediate schools', a view which was challenged by the Provost of Trinity, the Rev. John Hewitt Jellett (1817–88).[18]

The views expressed by Byers, Tod and others in the 1880s were carried forward into the next two decades by others who had benefitted from their own educational experience in preparing for the examinations of the Royal University. The new generation of women was aware of the moves to have a university which would be acceptable to all interested bodies and which would be inclusive of women students, giving them equal status with men. This equality of treatment for men and women was to include common lectures for men and women together in the same lecture halls. However, there were dissenting voices; a minority favoured women's endowed colleges, separate from the men. The *New Ireland Review* of January 1897 carried an article by Alice Oldham, one of the first women graduates of the Royal University and a teacher in Alexandra College.[19] Oldham feared that the university question would be considered by the government from the point of view of the male students, and more especially Catholic male students. Her article was focused on 'another class labouring under disabilities as great, if not greater – Irishwomen, Catholic or Protestant'. The establishment of the Royal University in 1879 afforded those who could not attend Trinity College or the Queen's Colleges an opportunity to study for the Royal University examinations in other institutions. Colleges such as Blackrock, under the management of the Holy Ghost Fathers, Tullabeg College, under the management of the Jesuit Fathers, and some of the diocesan colleges, entered boys for these examinations up to degree level. Colleges under the management of nuns – Loreto and Dominican in Dublin and Ursuline in

Cork – took up the challenge and also prepared girls for degree courses. These women's colleges were not endowed and bore the expense of tuition, staffing and accommodation themselves. The cost was partially financed by the fees of the students and subsidized by the secondary boarding and day schools along-side the colleges. Oldham recognized the contribution of the women's colleges and acknowledged that they 'provided real instruction and mental discipline' for the girls in their preparation for the Royal University examinations. The debate gained momentum and was brought into the public forum in the early years of the twentieth century.

THE CASE FOR AND AGAINST SEPARATE COLLEGES FOR WOMEN

Other articles on the subject of separate women's colleges appeared in the *New Ireland Review* and the *Irish Educational Review*. Lilian Daly, writing in *New Ireland Review*, contended that the means which make for the education of men need not necessarily suit women. Her argument rested on the philosophical notion of men and women having distinct roles in creation – the biblical ideal of woman as a 'help-meet' (*sic*) for man.[20] Another advocate of women's colleges was Nora Meade, who had strong objections to mixed education, but would favour occasional lectures in the university which might be open to all; in general, however, according to Meade, men should teach men and women teach women in both cases, in separate colleges. Meade based her objections on what she claimed was the difference in the mode of thought in men and women: 'I always consider that boys make up their work by main force, girls by a kind of intuition and clear perception of what exactly is important and what is not'.[21] Meade held that 'highly cultured, refined and self-reliant women' were 'produced only in separate women's colleges', and this was because 'the mere physical superiority of the man would induce a sense of inferiority in the woman': the men would over-shadow the women's subtle discursive powers by their solid facts and reasoning. Meade's argument was, in essence, for a well-organized, endowed women's college where there would be no competition between men and women and each sex would benefit to the fullest from that system of university education.

On the other side of the argument, formidable forces were aligned: the Association of Women Graduates and two very able lady-graduates, one a Junior Fellow of the Royal University, Mary Hayden, and the other, Hanna Sheehy Skeffington, the renowned champion of women's rights. The Women Graduates' Association submitted a statement to the Robertson Commission in 1902, of which, for the purposes of this book, the most important petitions were numbers three and four:

> 3. attendance at recognized lectures to be a necessary preliminary to graduation

4. that the lectures of the Fellows and Professors in the general colleges
   only and not lectures delivered in colleges exclusively for women be
   recognized.[22]

This was a clear statement of the Association of Women Graduates' stance on
the question of special colleges for women. However, the Association made a
plea for some endowment for halls of residence for women, 'where they may enjoy
the full advantages of collegiate life'. A forcefully worded memorial was also sent
to the Chancellor and Senators of the National University urging on them

> as strongly as it can be the undesirability of weakening the forces of the
> university at its outset by recognizing any course of lectures for women
> students for the Arts Degrees other than those delivered in the Lecture
> Halls of the Colleges named in the Charter of the National University.[23]

The Association of Women Graduates gave as their reason for their petition that
recognition of women's colleges would not be in the best interests of women
students nor of the National University.

The Hayden/Sheehy Skeffington joint response to Meade's argument for a
women's college was that her objections to mixed classes relied on theory
unsupported by facts or experience: her argument about the modes of thought of
men and women was unproven. Experienced teachers of Cambridge University
disagreed with the argument that women would suffer disadvantage in mixed
classes. On practical grounds, separate women's colleges would be very costly
to the state; staffing and facilities would have to be duplicated or triplicated,
depending on the number of women's colleges allocated to Dublin and/or other
centres. Meade had in fact not thought through the consequences of special
women's colleges. Hayden and Sheehy Skeffington held the view very firmly
that, 'unless these were fully provided for each, either the male or the female
students would be unfairly handicapped and deprived of the full benefits of the
University'.[24] The most desirable outcome for women would be, in the opinion
of Hayden and Sheehy Skeffington, full and equal access to the university, with
lectures attended by both sexes, and equal rights for men and women to have full
access to all aspects of university life.[25] The fact that there were existing colleges
catering solely for women, for example, St Mary's University College under the
head-ship of Mother Patrick Sheil in Eccles Street, introduced another element
into the argument.

Mother Patrick (Mary Jane) Sheil

One of the existing women's colleges was begun by a remarkable Dominican
nun, Mother Patrick Sheil. In Chapter 2 it was shown that Mother Patrick, of
Dominican College, Eccles Street, had ambitious plans for the furtherance of the
education of the girls in her secondary school. The matriculation of two of her

pupils, Katherine Murphy and Katie Brady, in 1884, opened the way for Mother Patrick to begin university classes on the premises in Eccles Street. The Royal University of Ireland, as we have seen, was an examining body with power to confer degrees on all candidates, men and women, who passed the examinations set by the university. Teaching and lectures could be organized by any group who had the personnel and facilities necessary. It was this structure which allowed the Dominicans to begin their university lectures in Dominican College, Eccles Street in September 1885.[26] The gradual change in the nuns' perception of a suitable curriculum for the girls in their schools, with the introduction of the Intermediate examinations, has been noted in Chapter 2. The communities in the Sion Hill and Eccles Street convents were the first Dominican schools to enter for the examinations of the Intermediate Board, and it was these communities who also interested themselves in organizing university courses for their pupils. Cabra had its first matriculated class in 1899; thereafter Cabra also prepared its 'advanced students' for degrees through the Royal University of Ireland (RUI).[27]

The Royal University of Ireland was the first university in the country to confer degrees 'upon every person, male or female', who qualified according to its regulations; women were admitted as of right, not on sufferance.[28] The part played by Dominican College, Eccles Street, as the first establishment in Ireland to make university education possible for Catholic women, was acknowledged by Akenson when he wrote:

> [t]he first institution specifically intended for the [higher] education of Catholic women [in Ireland] was the Dominican convent founded in Eccles Street, Dublin during 1882. Candidates were prepared by visiting lecturers for the examinations of both the Intermediate Board and the Royal University.[29]

The Dominicans in Eccles Street in 1884, Sion Hill in 1886, and in Cabra in 1899 were not the only women's colleges to take advantage of this opportunity: Loreto College in St Stephen's Green (and many other Loreto schools), Alexandra College, Earlsfort Terrace, Dublin, the Ursulines in Cork and Sligo and Victoria College in Belfast, to name some other schools, all had university degree classes in their respective establishments, and all were acutely aware that their students' achievements were published annually in the national press. The examinations were competitive, in that exhibitions and scholarships were keenly contested and were awarded on results. Whatever the shortcomings of the Royal University system, this was the only pathway open to Mother Patrick and the nuns in Dominican College, Eccles Street.

The Dominicans were fortunate in having a person of the calibre of Mother Patrick as headmistress in Eccles Street at that particular time in the history of the school. As Mary Jane Sheil, Mother Patrick came from an old Dublin Family and had been sent as a boarder to Dominican Convent, Sion Hill, when she was seven years old. Her father, James Sheil, was a barrister listed in *The Dublin*

Almanac of 1843 as having been called to the bar in 1811.[30] James Sheil either lived, or had his offices, in 58 Upper Dorset Street, Dublin, which is only a short walk from Eccles Street where his daughter, Mary Jane, was later to champion the cause of higher education for women.[31] Mary Jane Sheil, in religion known as Mother Patrick, possessed, according to Sr Benvenuta MacCurtain,

> a brilliant mind and was an ambitious student. To an astonishing degree, she manifested in later middle-life an all-round culture which was evidenced in such diverse ways as lecturing at college level in French language and literature, producing Shakespeare with distinction, and directing an orchestral society good enough to give public recitals to a critical audience.[32]

In community, Mother Patrick held the office of sub-prioress, which assumed she also played a leadership role within the group. Her talents and foresight as a teacher were shown by the broad curriculum she drew up for the school. Another tribute to her speaks of her 'great teaching ability'; she also had tireless energy and undaunted courage. Mother Patrick pushed on where others feared to go; she drew forth from others real work and service and her work was blessed.[33]

Mother Patrick was not alone in her endeavours; the mother-house in Sion Hill still had to be convinced of the value of her educational aims and ambitions to allow her the freedom to develop them in her own way. Pivotal to this support were the prioress of Sion Hill, Mother Clare Elliott and her council. Other members of the community, Srs Joseph Keighron, Gonzales O'Connor, Augustine Clinchy and Stanislaus McCarthy, were actively supportive of the enterprise in Eccles Street. It was also fortunate that Sr Clare Elliott was in a position of authority and influence in the community for forty years. The system of governance in Irish Dominican convents in the nineteenth century could indeed leave the same individual or group within a community 'in power' for protracted periods: the family of Mahers in Cabra, as well as Clare Elliott in Sion Hill, are examples of nuns who held office for several terms.[34] Elliott's position was unusual: between 1864 and 1903 she was prioress of Sion Hill eight times. On two occasions, permission from the Sacred Congregation for Religious in Rome was sought and obtained for her re-election. In addition, she was sub-prioress once and served a term as mistress of novices and another as prioress of the Eccles Street convent for three years. Yet Clare Elliott's dynamism and innovative qualities were not always appreciated. As in all societies – and religious communites are no exception – the leader is not always acceptable to every member. In July 1895 an anonymous letter-writer from the Sion Hill community pleaded with Archbishop Walsh not to allow Sr Clare Elliott's re-election, on an allegation that it would be 'disastrous'. One cannot speculate on the strength of this opposition, but in fact Clare Elliott was re-elected and was continuously in very influential positions. Whatever her strengths and weaknesses, Elliott made it possible not only for Mother Patrick

Sheil in Dominican College, Eccles Street, to prosper but also presided over the school's transformation into St Mary's University College, Merrion Square under Mother Patrick's guidance.

ST MARY'S UNIVERSITY COLLEGE

The curriculum of the secondary school in Eccles Street, with its emphasis on modern languages and Latin, paved the way towards a university education. Obviously, the pupils could with ease, if they so wished, continue their studies for arts degrees. In 1884 four students were presented for matriculation and in the following year they sat their first university examinations. Although the nuns sought to give the university department its own identity, as distinct from Dominican College, which was the intermediate school, success brought its own problems as numbers increased. Furthermore, the university section was perceived by outsiders as an appendage to the intermediate school, because all students, both intermediate and university, were housed under the same roof; it was obvious that new premises would be needed.

The names of the first four graduates from Eccles Street have been recorded and handed down to posterity; recognition that these four young women made educational history in Ireland. They were Gertrude Cahill, Mary Jo McGrath, Agnes O'Sullivan and Katherine Roche. Mary Jo McGrath entered the Sion Hill novitiate after graduation and she, too, very soon played a distinguished role as a teacher and principal in Dominican College, Eccles Street, under the religious name of Sr Peter McGrath. When Mother Patrick went to St Mary's College, Merrion Square, in the autumn term of 1893, Mother Peter McGrath continued the tradition of an academic education for the pupils in Dominican College, Eccles Street.

Throughout all that period, Archbishop Walsh of Dublin took a keen interest in the university classes in Eccles Street. He presided over the prize-days in the school and college, and was in frequent contact with the nuns both in Sion Hill and Eccles Street. As a member of the hierarchy, he had vast experience in educational matters: his book, *Statement of the Chief Grievances of Irish Catholics*, published in 1890, set out at length and in detail the objections and difficulties which Catholics had with the educational system in Ireland in the nineteenth century. Walsh was a prolific writer, contributing to many journals, including the *Contemporary Review*, the *Fortnightly Review*, and the *Dublin Review*. His biographer, Morrissey, comments: '[a]lthough the range of subjects in Walsh's writings was unusually wide, the main emphasis was on education. … [He] became commissioner of Charitable Donations and Bequests in 1893, a role linked to educational establishments. He was a member of the Intermediate Board of Education from 1892 to 1909 and a commissioner of National Education from 1895 to 1901.'[35] Walsh had himself been an undergraduate in Newman's university; in 1878, while he was vice-president of Maynooth, together with Fr Delany SJ and Fr Reffé, of Blackrock College, he founded the Catholic Headmasters' Association. Morrissey adds that 'his major influence was felt in the quest for a solution of the university question'.[36] It is, therefore, not surprising that during his unusually long term as Archbishop of Dublin, from 1885 to 1921, he should have taken such an interest in the cause of women's higher education, to the extent that one of the nuns in Eccles Street could state in a letter, 'the archbishop is our best friend, and does all in his power to help us in any way'.[37]

In 1893 a decision was taken, at the suggestion of the archbishop and certainly with his approval, that a house totally separate and away from Eccles Street should be rented for the university students' classes: that change, it was hoped, would establish that the new institution named St Mary's College was not just an appendage to an intermediate school, but a place of higher education for Catholic women. Mother Clare in Sion Hill wrote to Mother Patrick on May 10; she reported that the archbishop had visited Sion Hill 'and wound up approving of the house of studies at the south side, if we saw our way'. A written authorization was given by the archbishop in August 1893:

> I authorise you to make known that the important work which, in the earnestness of your zeal in the cause of Catholic Education, you are now taking in hand upon so large a scale, has my blessing. ... Eminently praiseworthy and successful as has been the work done by the Dominican sisters – more especially in Eccles Street – and by our other teaching communities in Dublin and its neighbourhood, we have nevertheless to recognise that a gap yet remains to be filled, and that it can be filled only by the establishment of a well-equipped college, set apart, as this new college of yours will be, exclusively for the work of higher education.[38]

The archbishop's approval of the new house in Merrion Square for the Dominicans' university college unfortunately caused some anxiety to Mother Michael Corcoran in Loreto Abbey, Rathfarnham. Her unease was legitimate. Mother Michael feared the move to the south side of the city would give the Dominicans an unfair advantage over the Loreto College in St Stephen's Green, which is close to Merrion Square, and she was of the opinion that Archbishop Walsh was 'taking an active part in their [Dominicans'] work'. She set out her views with courage and candour.[39] It is gratifying to note that both the Loreto and Dominican university classes continued until 1909, when the Royal University of Ireland was brought to an end and University College Dublin replaced it.

As matters developed, the house in Merrion Square was opened and St Mary's University College moved from Eccles Street. A high school was also opened, this was necessary if the new venture were to be financially viable, because the fees from the university students were not sufficient to cover all the costs of staffing and maintaining St Mary's. In 1924 an obituary notice of the death of Mother Clare Elliott recorded that 'the late Archbishop of Dublin [Dr Walsh] ... in furtherance of his design for the organisation of a University College for Women, appealed to Mother Clare ... in Sion Hill. [She] was not one to hesitate. The work was undertaken without delay and St Mary's College, Merrion Square, formed yet another branch of the parent stem.'[40]

Archbishop Walsh's interest in St Mary's did not end when the new Dominican house was set up as a college. At a meeting in Sion Hill on 8 August 1893, Walsh drew up a list of the council of the college, a kind of board of management, for St Mary's. The list was lengthy: twenty-one men, not including Dr Walsh himself, who was to be the president of the council. No woman was included, not even Mother Patrick. In later years when there was a question of a similar council for the Dominican Hall of Residence in 49 St Stephen's Green, Archbishop Walsh dismissed the suggestion, saying that the council in St Mary's Merrion Square was not very effective. One cannot help wondering if the absence of women on the council was a great mistake. The objective of the college was set out in the prospectus: 'St Mary's University College and High School has been founded for the purpose of affording Catholic Ladies facilities for Higher Education in all its branches.' Included in the curriculum was an advanced course of religious instruction, obviously regarded as a very important part of the programme of studies. The college council directed the general course of studies, and a tutorial committee, which was composed of the principal members of the teaching staff, advised on details of the teaching work of the college.[41]

As if to provide proof of the status of the college, the *Book of Annals* records the successes of the year:

> [t]his Catholic Girls' College places seven Graduates on the Register of the Royal, secures five Distinctions at the Degree Examination, and a First-Class Scholarship as the result of the autumn contests. ... In the summary of the results, St Mary's is third on the list, and first of all the Women's Colleges in Ireland.
> 1 Queen's College, Belfast.
> 2 University College, Dublin.
> 3 St Mary's University, Dublin.
> 4 Alexandra College, Dublin.
> 5 Magee College, Derry
> 6 Victoria College, Belfast, etc., etc.[42]

The use of the word 'contests' emphasizes the perception of what the examinations really signified for both staff and students of the time. McCartney makes this comment about publicizing results:

> [o]n this policy of advertising success in examinations Archbishop Walsh and Father Delany [the Jesuit Rector of University College] were at one. The archbishop emphasised the successes of the Catholic colleges

generally, and more especially those of Blackrock College and the Medical School (of whose board he was chairman). The whole point behind this kind of propaganda was to make the case that Catholics, under great handicaps, financial and other, deserved a university worthy of their achievements.[43]

The publicity surrounding St Mary's University College was aimed at establishing the college as a fully recognized institute for higher education. This caused some disagreement between the community in Eccles Street and Mother Patrick, who had been transferred to the new college in Merrion Square. An undated letter from Mother Imelda Harris, the then prioress of Eccles Street, to Archbishop Walsh shows how concerned the Eccles Street nuns were that the excellent reputation of Dominican College should not be over-shadowed by the new St Mary's. The letter reads,

[w]e understand that Mother Patrick is again urging that the name of this convent should not appear at all in the Intermediate Results of this year. At your last visit here I thought you decided that this convent *should appear* in results coupled with St Mary's. I have consulted with the Sisters here and they are unanimous in refusing their consent to give up the name and credit of Eccles Street. Your Grace will I know excuse the trouble I am giving in bringing this matter under your notice, but I am certain you wish to see justice done.[44]

The matter was settled amicably and both schools published their results. Mother Patrick Sheil, while herself applauding examination success, did not measure success on results alone; she aimed, *The Lanthorn* recalled, 'at all-round culture and took care to open up every available source other than study proper'.[45] Thus Mother Patrick founded St Mary's Literary Society at an early date, and used it as a forum in which the students presented papers on literary subjects and their fellow-students discussed the papers in open debate. Eminent literary figures were invited to attend the meetings and address the students. Rosa Mulholland, novelist and poet (1841–1921), and Katherine Tynan, a past pupil of Siena Convent, Drogheda, author, poet and journalist (1861–1931), were guests on more than one occasion. Tynan was vice-president of the society.

St Mary's was not a residential university college; the nuns rented a house a short distance from Merrion Square, at No. 17 Upper Mount Street, for students who wished to board there. It was supervised by a 'Lady Superintendent', a Mrs Gray. Five members of the Eccles Street community moved into Merrion Square: Mother Augustine Clinchy, prioress, Mother Patrick Sheil, Prefect of Studies, Sr Aloysius Keighron, Sr Reginald Mulcahy and Sr Martha Roche. Mother Stanislaus McCarthy from Sion Hill joined the group and was appointed sub-prioress. The list of professors and lecturers is impressive. Fr Delany proved generous with his time and gifts, and helped Mother Patrick to select those best suited for the posts.[46]

MUCKROSS PARK COLLEGE

Five years after the move to Merrion Square, there was a serious lack of accommodation and space for the growing number of students who applied to St Mary's. On 30 August 1898 Mother Augustine Clinchy, then prioress of Sion Hill, wrote to Archbishop Walsh about a property on Marlborough Road, Donnybrook, which had come on the market:

> [t]he name is Muckross Park; there are four acres, a very fine house, a lease forever, but the price is £6000 with a yearly rent of £20 – we have nothing. It is even difficult for us to meet the expense of rent and taxes for the house in Merrion Square and Sion Hill which is over £600 per annum. The community in the Square are anxious I should ask your permission to borrow this money.[47]

The Muckross Park property was purchased for £4,000 and the move from Merrion Square to the new foundation was made in September 1900. The *Book of Annals* of Sion Hill has a long entry about the relocation of the college. Having rehearsed the achievements of St Mary's students over the six years in Merrion Square, the annalist was not shy in quoting – without attribution – a long passage, probably from a newspaper of the time, in praise of the college and enumerating its successes. The annalist wrote that 'a busy thoroughfare was not the ideal site to choose to realise the idea of Newman' and once again St Mary's University moved house, this time to Muckross Park, Donnybrook.[48] In contrast to the busy thoroughfare of Merrion Square, Muckross Park was situated in spacious grounds and conveniently within a few minutes' walking distance of the tramway system into the city. Two houses of residence were purchased close to Muckross Park and classes and lectures were resumed immediately.

ST MARY'S RETURN TO ECCLES STREET

Unfortunately, Muckross Park as a centre for university studies for women did not prove satisfactory. The numbers attending university lectures quickly diminished following this move. The site was not convenient for students who lived on the north side of Dublin, nor was it sufficiently close to St Stephen's Green, which was the centre of university life in the city. Some students transferred to Loreto College, Stephen's Green, and some went to Alexandra College, Earlsfort Terrace, both situated at the heart of academic life. As a result

Eccles Street, 17, 23 & 24.

Muckross Park

28 Merrion Square

11. The three locations of St Mary's Dominican University College: Eccles Street, 28 Merrion Square and Muckross Park

of this setback, once more the nuns moved their university sector, this time back to Eccles Street. The Muckross Park annals record that the Sion Hill house council decided that the move be made; in the intervening years between 1894 and 1903, the Eccles Street community had purchased numbers 23 and 24 Eccles Street. This allowed more accommodation for classrooms and living quarters for the returning students. Mother Patrick Sheil, Sr Margaret Mary and Mother Gonzales Stone returned to Eccles Street with the students, while Muckross Park continued with their intermediate boarding, day and junior schools. Eleanor Butler, who became a renowned geographer after graduation, paid tribute a quarter of a century later to the nuns who founded the school in 1900. She recalled:

> I was one of the first pupils at Muckross in the foundation year, and was witness of the great courage and earnestness with which the founders faced their task. I profited from the chance which they opened for the higher education of women at a time when women's chances of higher education in Ireland were almost nil.[49]

Once again the element of competition motivated, in large part, the move of St Mary's University College from Muckross Park back to Eccles Street. It was obvious that some students who would have enrolled in St Mary's had it remained in Merrion Square were now more attracted to either Alexandra College, Earlsfort Terrace, or to Loreto College, St Stephen's Green. Competition had also a large part to play in the final stages of the Dominicans' direct involvement in women's university education – the issue of special women's colleges or a university which would cater for men and women in a mixed educational environment, with lectures and all facilities open to both sexes on an equal footing. Though the wheel had come full circle, the move back to Eccles Street did not signal a final answer to problems for Mother Patrick and her staff. The Royal Commission on University Education in Ireland (known as the Robertson Commission after its chairman, Lord Robertson), was appointed in 1901. The larger issue of the future of the whole university question had not yet been solved and in its solution St Mary's University College and the other women's colleges were to struggle bravely for their place in the new dispensation.

ROBERTSON COMMISSION ON UNIVERSITY EDUCATION IN IRELAND 1901–03

The Robertson Commission was appointed to inquire into the present condition of the higher, general and technical education available in Ireland outside Trinity College, Dublin, and to report on what reforms, if any, were desirable in order to render that education adequate to the needs of the Irish people.[50] As McCartney notes, the great issue of the day was 'the requirements of the

Catholic population generally as regards university education'.[51] To recapitulate: the Commission advised in its Report (1903) that the Royal University be converted into a federal teaching university, its constituent colleges being Queen's Colleges in Belfast, Cork and Galway, together with a new college for Catholics, to be sited in Dublin.[52] One of the positive outcomes of Robertson was that it afforded an opportunity to all interested parties to make submissions to the Commission, an opening widely availed of by various women's groups – those in favour of endowed women's colleges and others strongly supporting mixed education in a university which would give equality to men and women in all aspects of university life.

The groups and individuals who favoured women's colleges were: the Central Association of Schoolmistresses represented by Alice Oldham, a lecturer in Alexandra College; Miss H.M. White, Lady Principal of Alexandra College who represented her college; and the Loreto Sisters, St Stephen's Green, represented by James Macken, a lecturer in St Patrick's Training College, Drumcondra. Collectively, their argument was very similar: women's colleges which had gained such success without state endowment should now be endowed, have their lectures recognized and be allowed to continue their work as constituent colleges of the university. Macken, for the Loreto Sisters, stated that the quality of higher education of Catholic women 'is essentially a part of the general provision for the higher education of the general Catholic body'.[53] If the Loreto College were given financial assistance and recognition, their own nuns could have further higher education and be better fitted for teaching. It should also be noted that those who favoured women's colleges were closely associated with these colleges. Hayden and Sheehy Skeffington, in their reply to Meade's article in *The Irish Educational Review*, pointed out that the Association of Schoolmistresses was hardly an impartial body of women:

> [W]e must remember that practically all the members of the small Association [of Schoolmistresses] mentioned ... were all past students of one women's college, and the great majority of them teachers, while the two lady-witnesses were themselves heads of important women's colleges; thus in the case of each, vested interests were involved.[54]

Another group closely involved with a women's college, though not yet pressing its claim at the Robertson Commission for full recognition, was Mother Patrick Sheil and her Dominican colleagues. Mother Patrick seems to have gone through some years of uncertainty regarding the preferred status for St Mary's. Should St Mary's opt out of university teaching and give its blessing to a new type of university which gave full recognition to women students, or should the authorities of St Mary's and the Dominican community lobby for financial assistance from the state and remain a 'Women's College' recognized by the university? It was a dilemma which was to cause much trouble and worry to Mother Patrick. Mary Hayden, who had an educational background in both

Alexandra College and St Mary's and who was on the staff of St Mary's, was a trusted friend of Mother Patrick's. In February 1896 Hayden wrote the following entry in her diary: 'went out with Miss Kathleen Murphy at Mother Patrick's request to canvas for signatures to a petition to the Chief Secretary, [Gerald Balfour], to get an endowment for women's higher education.'[55] Hayden found canvassing 'a baleful job', which seemed not to yield results, but it is an indication that Mother Patrick in 1896 was prepared to canvas for financial endowment for a Women's College at that time. The memorial 'earnestly asks that in any legislation to meet the claims of certain sections of the Irish people ... the needs of Irishwomen may not be overlooked'. The closing sentence refers to 'the just and long-neglected claims of women' to a share in the endowments.[56] The memorial was signed by 378 people, among them some Fellows of Trinity College, and RUI. Many women well-known in educational circles put their names to the memorial, including Mary Hayden herself, Margaret Byers, Isabella Tod and H.M. White, of Alexandra College, with several of her staff. At that time, 1896, nothing came of the effort made by the women to gain endowments for the Women's Colleges. The banding together of the Dominicans, Mary Hayden, Margaret Byers, Isabella Tod and Henrietta White points to what was unusual in 1896 – an ecumenical grouping in the cause of women's higher education.

Seeking endowments was not quite the same as canvassing for full recognition of St Mary's as a women's college. A fully recognized women's college would require more spacious accommodation for laboratories, libraries and other facilities as well as the recognition of their lecturers by the university. That question became more relevant for St Mary's College after the Robertson Commission, which sat and reported in 1901–03. During the taking of evidence by Robertson, Mary Hayden went along to represent the Dominican nuns. Armed with a comprehensive brief from Mother Patrick, Hayden stressed the importance of higher education for women especially, but not only for those who would have to earn a livelihood. There followed a statement which can only indicate that the Dominicans had changed their minds and were not then in favour of a women's college in 1902/03:

> [The Dominicans] express their conviction that the scheme which has been suggested of erecting a Women's College where women study apart, and where they would obtain degrees in competition with one another *would not meet the necessities of the case.*[57]

Hayden went on to outline the reasons for this conviction: a very large endowment would be necessary for the women's college or efficient teaching could not be given: laboratories and libraries could not be provided; the university would not wish to duplicate expense and that would result in unfair treatment for the women. In general, the Dominicans felt that women's colleges would not work out in practice. They believed that public opinion would be against them and that there would be a lack of confidence in the value of the women's degrees; in turn this would lead to loss of good employment: '[e]ven in Ireland, the best posts would go to English and Scotch women graduates'. In their evidence to the Robertson Commission the authorities in St Mary's also 'explained' that their interpretation of co-education meant 'merely the *teaching* of men and women students together' and they drew the attention of the Commission to the statement made by Mr W.B. Harris, the United States Minister of Education.[58] Harris, replying to a query from the Central Association of Irish Schoolmistresses on the subject, assured the Association that 'all reports [in the United States] are entirely favourable to the policy of co-education in our schools and higher institutions'.[59] This conviction of the value of co-education was confirmed by eighteen professors of Cambridge University – all of whom without exception 'declared themselves in its favour'.[60] Following the rejection of the Robertson Commission's suggestion of the reorganization of the Royal University as a teaching university, the position of the women's colleges was uncertain and St Mary's continued as it had been – a teaching facility for women who took their degrees from the Royal University.

THE STRUGGLE FOR RECOGNITION OF WOMEN'S COLLEGES

In 1896, Mother Patrick and the Dominicans would have welcomed an endowment, but it was not granted. Robertson followed in 1901–03: its final proposals to reorganize the Royal University were not acceptable to Archbishop Walsh, who considered the Royal University's academic standards insufficiently high. Mother Patrick had made her preference known to the Commission that, as far as the Dominicans were concerned, a Women's College 'would not meet the case' for reasons explained at the hearing of evidence. The next significant proposal came from Chief Secretary James Bryce in 1906 – a radical proposal which allowed for the enlargement of the University of Dublin to include the other universities of Dublin, Galway, Cork and Belfast. Bryce's proposal, which was rejected, would have destroyed the unique quality and status of Trinity College as a 'stand-alone' university with complete autonomy.[61] It was left to Bryce's successor, Augustine Birrell, Chief Secretary (1907–16), to bring about a lasting solution. Birrell, who came to Dublin mentally well prepared to grasp the nettle of the university question, wrote in his memoirs:

> I had for some years nursed the hope that if the time ever arrived for establishing in Ireland a teaching university to which the Catholics of Ireland could flock with pride and pleasure, I might be allowed to play a part in the settlement ... I had made up my mind to succeed quickly or go.[62]

Birrell's ambition was achieved. Two new universities were established in 1908 – Queen's in Belfast and the National University, with three constituent colleges in Dublin, Cork and Galway. Maynooth College was affiliated to the new National University. Men and women would now have access to lectures, laboratories and all facilities of University College, Dublin on an equal footing. Sr Margaret (Benvenuta) MacCurtain, in her impressive article 'St Mary's University College' writes, 'the solution offered by the University Bill made co-education, which had seemed so remote a possibility at the Robertson Commission, an actuality.'[63]

ESTABLISHMENT OF THE NATIONAL UNIVERSITY OF IRELAND

Acceptance of co-education

The years between 1903–10 were a period of uncertainty for the women's colleges; after the passing of Birrell's Irish University Act in 1908, intensive lobbying was carried out on behalf of St Mary's College and Loreto College in Dublin. It was during these years that Mother Patrick evaluated the position of St Mary's. There was, she knew, no hope of St Mary's continuing without recognition from the National University and she had a change of heart about its future. She decided to apply for recognition for St Mary's as a women's college. Sr Benvenuta surmises, 'what finally caused Mother Patrick to send in the application for recognition of St Mary's as a constituent college of the new National University was probably the example of Loreto College, St Stephen's Green and Alexandra.'[64] Alexandra had filed an application to Trinity College for recognition, and intense lobbying followed this decision. A memorial was drawn up by friends of St Mary's for presentation to the governing body of the University College, Dublin; over 3,000 signatures were secured. Archbishop Walsh warned Mother Patrick of the very real possibility of her application's being rejected. The university authorities, he warned, 'have very solid ground to stand upon in opposing the present applications'.[65] If two colleges for women were recognized, that would open the way for others from all over Ireland to look for similar colleges. There is more than a hint of annoyance when Dr Walsh wrote of an awkwardness about two colleges making application. He ended the letter with a further note of warning: 'whoever is responsible for the present deadlock is incurring a very heavy responsibility'.[66] These words may have weighed heavily on Mother Patrick: Sr Cajetan Lyons, who remembered Mother Patrick in her later years, gave as her opinion that Mother Patrick suffered intensely as a result of the whole controversy about women's colleges.

The governing body of the National University was the authority which would give or withhold recognition of any application. Perhaps if the Loreto and Dominican nuns had come to an agreement between themselves to share responsibility for a women's college, they might have been successful. However, lacking cooperation, the cards were stacked against them both. The National University Association of Women Graduates was an influential body which was opposed in principle to all women's colleges. Two of its members, Mary Hayden and Agnes O'Farrelly, were on the governing body of University College, Dublin. At a meeting of the governing body in April 1910, letters protesting against the recognition of all women's colleges were read from the National Association of Women's Graduates and the Teachers Guild of Great Britain and Ireland. A motion was put 'that the College of St Mary's Eccles Street and Loreto, St Stephen's Green, be recognised for women students in Arts'. On a vote, this motion was lost 11/6. A compromise motion was put that 'the governing body consent to the recognition of First University Courses in St Mary's, Eccles Street and Loreto College'. The Governing Body reported to the Senate of the National University of Ireland:

> [h]aving considered the Application for Recognition of St Mary's University College, Eccles Street and Loreto College, St Stephen's Green, the Governing Body of University College, Dublin, does not consent to the recognition of either of these colleges.[67]

There were further attempts by both groups to have a First University Course recognized, but without success. In December 1912 the Senate finally came to a decision which was unfavourable to the nuns. There was a majority opinion both inside and outside the university that there should not be any affiliated colleges recognized either in Dublin or elsewhere. McCartney sums up the situation:

> [t]he case for the recognition of two women's colleges had become difficult to sustain. The two in question [Loreto and Dominican] were strikingly similar: run by orders of nuns, tied to secondary schools, offering the same limited range of courses, with small numbers of students at university level, and dependent largely on part-time academic staff.[68]

Whatever force such arguments possessed, the two orders were undoubtedly acutely disappointed in not having their colleges recognized, though perhaps Mother Patrick felt vindicated. As for relations between the Loreto and Dominican, as Sr Benvenuta comments, 'their dilemma caused no lasting resentment between the two religious orders ... they both set about implementing the alternatives which allowed the setting up of hostels'.[69] At 49 and 77 St Stephen's Green, the Dominican and Loreto nuns respectively set up halls of residence and carried on their ministry in university education in another way. The campaign for university education for women was the main thrust of the Sion Hill and Eccles Street communities in the last fifteen years of the nineteenth and the first decade of the twentieth centuries; professional training for secondary school teachers was yet another educational undertaking involving these two communities. Their response to these needs will be examined in the next section.

ST DOMINIC'S TRAINING COLLEGE, 17 ECCLES STREET

Mother Peter (Mary Jo) McGrath

A further development of the educational work of the Eccles Street Dominicans was the foundation in 1909 of St Dominic's Training College for secondary teachers. This new initiative was begun by Mother Peter McGrath (Mary Jo McGrath), a past pupil of both Dominican College (secondary school) in Eccles Street and of St Mary's University College. During her life-time as a Dominican, Mary Jo taught in Dominican College, and served at least one term of office as prioress of the convent (1909–12). Mary Jo's birth-place was in Tallaght, at the foothills of the Dublin mountains, at that time having a population of 360. The dominant building on the north side of the village was the new Dominican Priory, established in 1856. Tallaght was the centre for studies, or *Studium Generale*, for the young friars preparing for the priesthood. This was the village in which Mary Jo McGrath grew up. We do not know Mary Jo's year of birth, but, calculating from her year of matriculation, it must have been about 1867 or 1868: just twelve years after the coming of the Dominicans to the village. Her family, like those of the other Tallaght people, was greatly influenced by the friars; the Dominican church was the only Catholic church in the area and the McGraths must have attended Mass in the priory. This Dominican influence is evident from the fact that Mary Jo was sent as a boarder to Dominican College, Eccles Street, an influence which was further strengthened for her when she met Mothers Patrick Sheil, Antonina Hanley and other members of the Eccles Street community.

In 1885, Mary Jo was one of the first students to matriculate from Dominican College, Eccles Street. She pursued her studies in St Mary's University and graduated with an arts degree from the Royal University of Ireland. She then entered the Dominican novitiate in Sion Hill and was given Sr Peter as her name in religion which later changed, as was customary at that time, to Mother Peter on her election as sub-prioress and prioress of Eccles Street Convent. Most of her religious life was spent in Eccles Street as teacher and headmistress of Dominican College and as prioress of the convent. At her death in 1917 she left behind the legacy of two institutes of exceptionally high standards – a school run on sound educational principles and a Catholic training college for secondary teachers. A pen picture of her personality was given in *The Lanthorn*; she was, according to the writer,

> an enlightened educator intent on making Dominican College, Eccles Street, even humanly speaking, a success ... [She was] elevated in sentiment, broad of view, constant in policy, unfettered by petty conventions, whole-hearted in every undertaking, in giving, open-handed.[70]

Many of the young graduates, alumnae of St Mary's University College, were employed on the staff of the secondary school in Eccles Street. Both Mother

Peter and Mother Patrick realized that these young graduate-teachers were in need of training in the philosophy, methodology and history of education if they were to be competent teachers in the schools. The 1932 number of *The Lanthorn* gives a synopsis of the history of the training college and Mother Peter's part in its foundation:

> [t]he original idea of opening up a Secondary [Teachers'] Training College in Eccles Street is due to Mother M. Peter McGrath. The initial labours of the enterprise were also hers. When the scheme was fairly afoot, Mother Patrick [Sheil], with her wonted energy, launched into it, and devoted herself to its successful accomplishment.[71]

In the following section of this chapter the state's provision for training colleges for primary teachers is explored, but there was no state provision made for secondary teacher training. Some members of religious orders and secular teachers availed themselves of the training provided by the Cambridge Syndicate and other centres in England. There was at least one graduate of St Mary's University College (her name is not known), who had gone to England early in the 1900s and trained in the Cambridge Syndicate.

In England, for several years prior to 1898, the idea had been canvassed in university circles that teacher training ought to be undertaken by Oxford and Cambridge universities for those planning to teach in secondary schools. For this purpose, a syndicate was formed associated with Clare College and King's College, both in Cambridge.[72] Oscar Browning (1837–1923) was requested to be secretary to the syndicate, which arranged lectures and held examinations and each year awarded certificates on 'the theory, history and practice of education' for those men and women who were planning to teach in higher secondary schools.[73] Browning, a Fellow of King's College for more than thirty years, organized the Cambridge University Day Training College, which became known as The Cambridge Syndicate (1879). Enjoying a high reputation as a pioneer of education, he has been described as:

> one of the generation of teachers who desired many radical reforms, more flexible methods and curricula, less emphasis on rigid time-tables, more importance given to the arts, less time devoted to athletics. In this sphere he was well respected.[74]

Browning was also ahead of his time in his conviction that a student from a working-class background did not necessarily lack potential in academic subjects. Those who studied in the Cambridge Syndicate College were obliged to have read for a degree before attending the one year's course of lectures of the Syndicate. The subjects of these lectures included psychology, the history of education and the theory and practice of education. The students were given practical lessons in classroom management and teaching. Criticism classes were organized in certain approved practicing schools at which students were obliged to conduct classes in the presence of their fellow-students and lecturers and, at the end of each session, have their teaching methods discussed by their peers and supervisors. These sessions were known as 'criticism lessons'.

Several schools in England had connections with the Cambridge Syndicate. Among the approved girls' colleges were Cheltenham Ladies College, the Ursulines School at The Downs, Wimbledon. The examinations of the Cambridge Syndicate were open to non-residents at the university but, before recognizing a training centre for students, inspectors from the Syndicate visited the colleges; their staff members were validated, the courses offered were appraised and, if deemed satisfactory, the college was recognized by the Cambridge Syndicate. In 1898, Sr Bernard Hackett, of the Ursuline Convent in Waterford, applied to Oscar Browning for recognition of their college as a training centre.[75] An inspector, Sir Joshua Fitch, reported favourably on the Ursuline College and recommended that it be given provisional recognition. He was confident that at a later date the students could be presented for the teaching practicals when there would be a 'sufficiency of practicing schools for the syndicate's purposes'.[76] Besides the Ursulines, Loreto College, St Stephen's Green, the Irish Sisters of Charity in King's Inns Street, and Alexandra College in Dublin were also taking advantage of the Cambridge Syndicate's training facilities, mainly as individual institutions. In England, however, there was a reluctance on the part of some of the bishops to have too many Catholic colleges seeking recognition from Cambridge. This is evidenced by a letter dated February 1898 from the inspector J.G. Fitch, to Oscar Browning, in which Fitch referred to an interview he had with Herbert Vaughan (1832–1903), Cardinal Archbishop of Westminster. Fitch reported that,

> Cardinal Vaughan strongly objected to the multiplication in England of Catholic Institutions claiming recognition by the Cambridge Syndicate. Indeed he went so far as to try to exact from me a pledge that you would not for the present at least, sanction any other than the Convent in Cavendish Square.[77]

From the same letter it is clear that there was some difference of opinion between Cardinal Vaughan and the Catholic Archbishop of Liverpool of the day, Dr George Brown. Notre Dame College, Mount Pleasant, in Liverpool, was one such college seeking recognition by Cambridge. Vaughan raised an objection to this, insisting that he wanted, 'one strong, efficient institution for Catholic students in London, with the whole power and influence of the Catholic hierarchy to support it'. Fitch advised 'wary walking' to Oscar Browning, 'seeing that little jealousies and rivalries are not wholly unknown even between Roman Catholic bishops and between the Sisters of different religious orders'.[78] In spite of the opposition of Cardinal Vaughan, the Notre Dame nuns in Mount Pleasant went ahead and their college was recognized by the Cambridge Syndicate.

That incident had a bearing on the Irish scene. When the Dominicans in Eccles Street first applied to Oscar Browning for recognition of their training college, Browning took Fitch's advice and walked warily. He replied to Mother Peter McGrath that he could not give that recognition until the nuns produced a letter from the Archbishop of Dublin stating that they had the archbishop's approval and that the college would be inspected by a person appointed by the Syndicate. Browning's letter was written in September 1904.[79] For some unknown reason, three years elapsed before the matter was taken up again by the Eccles Street nuns. A letter of 25 October 1907 from Mother Peter to Archbishop Walsh of Dublin requested the archbishop's written approval and set out her reasons for their application to the Cambridge Syndicate.[80] A teacher's diploma was necessary for graduates who wished to take up teaching in secondary schools and obtain enhanced salaried positions there. Alexandra College had opened such a training centre and since there was no Catholic college in the capital city, some girls were going for their teacher training to Alexandra College, which advertised its courses widely.[81] Another reason for Mother Peter's request to Archbishop Walsh was that, from time to time, Irish bishops from dioceses outside Dublin had applied to the nuns in Eccles Street for certificated teachers to train nuns of other orders from their dioceses. Mother Peter regretted that they could not supply these teachers. A Catholic college in Dublin, as a centre for teacher training, could be very successful and the superiors in Sion Hill were urging the Eccles Street community to forward the matter.

Archbishop Walsh's reply to Mother Peter, together with the fact that the Alexandra College circulars were not distributed in St Mary's University College, gives us an insight into the clerical mind of the Irish Catholic Church at the turn of the twentieth century. Once more we see the fear of the Catholic clergy and nuns towards Protestants of any persuasion who might adversely influence the faith of young Catholics. Thus the archbishop wrote on 4 November 1907,

> [a]s far as I understand the bearing of your project, it seems to be an admirable one. I assume it does not involve sending the girls to Cambridge. That, I have always understood, has been allowed for *English* Catholics, not for *Irish*. Of course I know that not a few Irish people go there, but it is just like going to Trinity College or the Queen's Colleges. ... If the project does not involve sending the girls to either of the English Universities, I can see no objection to it, and I think it ought to be a great success.[82]

This surely begs the question: if English Catholics could be allowed to attend Cambridge University, why not Irish Catholics?

St Dominic's Training College was the official name given to the new venture. Browning acknowledged the receipt of the archbishop's letter and explained that the Training College would have the formal inspection necessary for affiliation to the Cambridge Syndicate. Since the Dominicans had no suitably qualified mistress of method, Browning suggested that Sr Raphael of the Cavendish Square College, which was under the management of the Congregation of the Holy Child, might recommend a suitable person to Mother Peter. The Cambridge Syndicate nominated a Mr Headen, Senior Inspector of National Schools, to inspect the proposed training college, prior to its recognition.[83] It was more convenient and less expensive for the Cambridge Syndicate to appoint a local person to supervise the approved centres in Ireland. The purpose of the inspection was to ensure that the entrance examination to the new college was up to the standard required by the Syndicate; the practical training as given by the master or mistress of method was adequate; the teaching given in the theory, history and practice of education was sufficient; the practicing school was suitable and run to a proper standard and the training continued for a whole year.[84] Mother Patrick wrote to the archbishop early in December 1907, seeking permission to begin lectures the following autumn since the college must be 'organised and at work' before the inspection could be carried out. The nuns also suggested that, as with other training colleges, a committee of ladies and gentlemen prominent in educational work should be associated with the college. Mother Patrick invited Archbishop Walsh to act as patron or president of the proposed committee, which he declined to do, owing to pressure of work; nor did he sanction the formation of the committee. He had previous experience of one such committee being of no benefit. The archbishop was doubtless referring to the committee of twenty-one men and no women, which had been set up for St Mary's University College, Merrion Square, in 1893.

Mother Patrick wrote to Browning on 24 November 1907, making a plea for recognition even before the inspection was carried out and asking, '[i]n what does the inspection consist?' She argued the case, perhaps a little tetchily, on the grounds that the nuns,

> have now been twenty-five years before the public as a Teaching Institution. We have taken the first place of *all* Women's Colleges in Ireland both as an Intermediate and a University College; our students have carried off the highest prizes that the Royal University of Ireland can offer in Scholarships, Exhibitions, Studentships and Fellowships, and we hoped that such results would dispense us from the Expense of Inspection.[85]

Browning's negative reply to this letter settled the matter; on 3 December 1907 Mother Patrick wrote: '[a]s inspection is a necessary condition for affiliation, we no longer hesitate about it...'.[86] No further plea was made. Unfortunately, after Headen had called at Eccles Street in March 1908, to carry out the inspection and furnish his report, he wrote to Browning that 'the College for which she [Mother Patrick] hopes to gain recognition from the Syndicate does not yet exist'.[87] The Dominicans had purchased a large house, at No. 17 Eccles Street, which they intended furnishing and staffing as a training college and which Mother Peter intended to open in September 1908. Nothing else was in place.

Even so, there must have been dismay in Eccles Street after Headen's visit. Mother Patrick and Mother Peter had set their hearts on opening the college immediately, but not even the reputation of Eccles Street as an educational establishment absolved them from having the college in working order before gaining the Cambridge Syndicate's approval.

In April 1908, the plans for the college were taken a step further; the archbishop had received some papers from the prioress of Eccles Street, Mother Augustine Clinchy, one of which was a draft prospectus for the college. Archbishop Walsh made one general, but telling, comment:

> there is an argumentative tone, running through a good deal of the paper, giving to it somewhat of a combative character. A matter of this kind is often overlooked by the writer of a document, whilst to a reader it may seem particularly prominent. I think the Waterford people would regard a good deal of the paper as an attack on their establishment. This, of course should be avoided.[88]

The 'Waterford people' mentioned must surely refer to the Ursulines, who were already running a training centre for secondary teachers and were affiliated to the Cambridge Syndicate. Unfortunately, there is no extant copy of this 'argumentative' document to which Walsh referred. The archbishop's interest in the project is in keeping with his life-long interest in educational matters. At the end of May he sent further advice about the re-drafted prospectus. The amendments on this occasion were merely of a stylistic nature.

A letter from Browning to Dominican Convent Eccles Street, dated 13 March 1909, gave the long-awaited approval: Browning wrote, '[t]his week it was decided to place the Training Department of the Dominican convent upon the list of Training Colleges recognised by the Syndicate'.[89] The first recorded names of those who qualified in the Cambridge University Syndicate from St Dominic's Training College, Eccles Street, were those of H.K. Hawkins, Nora Meade, M. O'Loughlin, Elizabeth B. Flanagan, Molly Cotter, E.M. Triston, M.T. Triston, R. Dunne and M.M. O'Neill: these ladies were accorded Diplomas in Education in the summer term of 1910. One of the Triston sisters named above became a Dominican, (Sr Clara, of Muckross Park) as also did Elizabeth Flanagan, (An Mháthair Treasa, foundress of Scoil Chaitríona); Molly Cotter was one of the first teachers in Scoil Chaitríona.[90] At a later date, some nuns from other congregations attended the college in order to gain the diploma. Provision of a training facility for these nuns was one of the reasons given some years previously by Mother Peter for the establishment of such a college. Louise Gavan Duffy, one of the graduates who studied for the Diploma in Education in St Dominic's Training College, wrote in 1913:

> [t]he only Catholic women's College in Dublin to offer a course of training to lay secondary teachers and prospective teachers, St Dominic's was

founded five years ago, and, in spite of the want of appreciation and support, which is the common fate of pioneer enterprises, it has done remarkable work already, as well in educating public opinion as in its own immediate sphere.[91]

Not content with the training college which was now established, the nuns in Eccles Street were concerned about two other matters relating to the welfare of their students. The first was the financial drain on their students' pockets, during this year of training when they would not have incomes. A loan fund was opened for those who needed some financial support; small loans were given by the nuns, and the students, having qualified and found employment, repaid the money within a short space of time: an account book is extant with names and amounts borrowed noted.[92] The second matter was the establishment of a Catholic Employment Agency for young, newly qualified teachers who might find it difficult to get employment in Catholic schools through lack of information about job prospects. Again, Mother Patrick Sheil was the prime mover in this. There are copies of nine letters in the Dominican archives which are in reply to a circular which Mother Patrick sent to convents of other orders, not only in Ireland but also in England. In the circular she enquired if the communities were interested in supporting such a venture. Here, once again, one can sense the anxiety to have the students placed in Catholic schools, especially if they went to England. Of the nine replies, seven were positive and one was non-committal, though it wished the venture well, and one expressed some reservations. To date, there is no evidence as to the success or failure of the Catholic Agency, or if indeed it came to fruition even for a short space of time.

When the courses for the Higher Diploma in Education were established in University College Dublin, under the professorship of Dr Timothy Corcoran, SJ, the majority of students in St Dominic's Training College transferred to the new university. The necessity for St Dominic's Training College ceased and University College, Dublin, took over the training of secondary teachers, both men and women. While the Dominicans in Eccles Street were busy with their negotiations for a separate women's university college, their sister Dominicans in Falls Road, Belfast, were requested by the bishop of Down and Connor, Dr Henry Henry, to undertake the management of a women's training college for primary teachers. The story of the establishment of this college forms the final section in this chapter.

PRIMARY TEACHER TRAINING

Campaign for denominational training colleges

For over a period of fifty years from the introduction of the national schools in Ireland (the Stanley System 1831), the training of teachers for the new schools was a cause of contention. The Catholic hierarchy never approved of the Teacher

Training College in Marlborough Street, Dublin, which opened in 1838 for men and 1842 for women, then the only training college in the country. The Catholic bishops' difficulty with the Marlborough Street college was that it was based on the 'united' system, and because it was non-denominational in theory and catered for all Christian denominations, the bishops suspected its credentials. The hierarchy, from the inception of the National Schools, held out against 'mixed' or 'united' schools for the children of their flock, so now also they were determined that the training of Catholic teachers should not be conducted in the same manner. The Model Schools were a training ground for teachers, using a kind of apprenticeship system; they were seen by the bishops as agents of proselytism and as an 'appendage of a general system of training teachers in ordinary national schools'.[93] Thus the bishops forbade the clergy to send young Catholic men and women to the Marlborough Street college and also forbade their appointing teachers who were trained in the college to posts in Catholic schools. The result was that young Catholic men and women could train only through the monitorial system, a course which was lengthy and not of a high standard.

Prior to 1883, two attempts were made to clear these obstacles, and to provide colleges which would be acceptable to Catholics. Lord Carlingford, Chief Secretary, wrote to the National Education Board in 1866 suggesting the establishment of training colleges of a denominational character; in 1883, Earl Spenser, Lord Lieutenant, pointed out to the Board that 66 per cent of employed teachers were untrained. In both cases the advice of these senior figures in the governing of Ireland was ignored. A Royal Commission of Inquiry into Primary Education in Ireland, the Powis Commission, was set up in 1868–70. Its findings regarding training colleges were that the whole system should be placed on a broad base of equality and that training colleges under voluntary or religious bodies should be established.[94] Cardinal Cullen and Powis were of one mind on having denominational colleges on equal status with the Marlborough Street College, but both Cullen's and Powis's recommendations also went unheeded. The question of training colleges acceptable to Catholics was treated as a matter of urgency only in the 1880s, under Gladstone's government. Cardinal McCabe, Cullen's successor as Archbishop of Dublin, initiated the foundation in Dublin of two training colleges for Catholic teachers: St Patrick's, Drumcondra, in 1875, under the Vincentian Fathers; and a college under the Sisters of Mercy in Baggot Street in 1877. Until 1883 both of these colleges were financed solely by the Catholic Church. In later years, Archbishop Walsh in his book, *Chief Grievances,* was to emphasize the fact that the Sisters of Mercy took up the task of teacher training 'purely as a work of benevolence, and altogether out of their own private and personal resources'.[95] Walsh argued further that the Model Schools' claim to excellence, and the lack of grants to other schools, gave the Model Schools an advantage in the perception of parents, which induced them to send their children to those schools in preference to others less well endowed. It could be argued that, while the monitorial system was in operation, a training system of limited value was supplying the needs of the Catholic schools. Where there were schools providing a monitorial system, the government did not feel the urgency of financing state-endowed training colleges for Catholics; this monitorial system was operating in many girls' convent schools and boys' monastery schools which were managed by the religious brotherhoods.[96]

The Powis Report admitted that the percentage of Catholic teachers who went for training was not large. Bishop Dorrian of Down and Connor diocese, in his evidence to the Royal Commission, gave his opinion that, 'one system of training cannot turn out teachers qualified to enter any school, indiscriminately, the tone of the school, the style of literature and religious training must be left in the hands of the clergy.'[97] Dorrian went further and admitted to the Commission that the bishops would be glad to receive any reasonable assistance if a system of separate training schools were established. He was aware that in England grants were given to training colleges of all denominations: '[w]hat is done for England, should in justice be done for Ireland', he commented. The Treasury estimates for 1882–3 provided £110,500 to support forty-two training colleges in England and Wales, while Ireland received £7,755 from the Treasury for the Marlborough Street institution only.

In 1883, in response to the Catholic bishops' campaign for denominational training colleges, Lord Lieutenant Earl Spencer requested the Irish Chief Secretary, George Trevelyan, to address the matter of teacher training in Ireland. Trevelyan announced that the government was prepared 'to encourage and facilitate the establishment in Ireland of Training Colleges under local management, by authorising the National Education Board to make grants towards their maintenance'.[98] In fact, the denominational colleges, when they first got government recognition, were not given equal financial treatment with the Marlborough Street college; students in the government college were given their training free of charge, while the newer denominational colleges were obliged to charge £16 per annum for the one-year course and £20 per annum for the two-year course, which were at the time substantial fees.

It must be remembered that from the introduction of the Stanley Education system in 1831, the Catholic hierarchy was continuously working to gain control over the schools in the dioceses. The bishops' efforts were successful: in their opinion a major factor in the promotion of the Catholic ethos in national schools was the training of teachers in Catholic colleges also under their authority. Colleges totally controlled by the Commissioners of Education did not satisfy the bishops.[99] St Patrick's College for men, Drumcondra, Dublin,was established in 1883. Our Lady of Mercy College in Baggot Street was also recognized for grant aid by the National Education Board in 1883. The Church of Ireland College, situated in Kildare Place, which was co-educational, 'went into connection' with the commissioners in 1884; that is, the college was recognized as state-aided and its students' qualifications were accepted by the Board of Education. In the same year, another college for men was established in Waterford under the management of the De la Salle Brothers. It had taken the government forty-three years to acknowledge and recognize training colleges which were acceptable to the Catholic bishops. By 1896 the need for women's training colleges had become an urgent necessity. It was this urgency which made the bishop of Limerick, Dr Edward O'Dwyer, and Dr Henry Henry, successor to Dr Dorrian, in Down and Connor, request the Commissioners' permission to establish women's colleges in their respective dioceses.

ST MARY'S TRAINING COLLEGE, BELFAST 1900

The recognition of Our Lady of Mercy Training College in Baggot Street and of St Patrick's College in Drumcondra paved the way for Dr O'Dwyer and Dr Henry to apply for a training college in each of their dioceses in 1896. Conditions in both the north and south of the country demanded that training colleges for women should be a priority with the government. It was against the background of an expanding Catholic Belfast that the Dominican nuns had first come to Falls Road in 1870 and, when permission for a women's training college was granted to Dr Henry, the Dominicans were approached by the bishop to undertake the administration and staffing of the college. According to the Belfast newspaper the *Irish News*, the nuns had gained 'a splendid record as educationalists'.[100] O'Dwyer of Limerick, in his letter to the Commissioners of National Education, gave his reasons for siting a college in his diocese: the Catholic women's college in Dublin (the Sisters of Mercy College in Baggot Street) could not cater for the needs of the whole country; Limerick city 'is the centre of railway lines running into the counties of Clare, Tipperary, Kerry, Cork and Waterford' and was therefore 'well situated for the purpose'.[101]

If Bishop O'Dwyer was pressing the need for a women's training college in Limerick on the grounds that it would serve the needs of the surrounding counties in the south-west of Ireland, Bishop Henry of Down and Connor diocese might have emphasized that the Catholic population of Belfast was increasing. In the first decades of the nineteenth century the population of the province of Ulster was predominantly rural, but owing to the success of the Irish linen trade abroad, there was a decline in the small home-based woollen and linen industries, which gave way to factory-based methods of the production of textiles. Increasing numbers were drawn to centres in Belfast where factory and mill work, especially for women, was available. Marianne Elliott estimates that between 1839 and 1917, there was a ten-fold increase in the numbers employed in the textile mills in Belfast:

> [a]s early as the 1830s Belfast had ten steam-powered spinning mills, four of them in the already recognisable Catholic Falls Road. By 1861 there were thirty-two mills and the port had begun its legendary expansion to accommodate the textile trade. ... Belfast's sectarian geography was already defined by these mills.[102]

Some of the mills were located at the top of Springfield Road, and at Broadway, in the general area of Falls Road. Elliott also claims that there was a change in organized Catholicism in Belfast as a response to the growth in the Catholic population. The building of chapels, convents and other social institutions, she writes, 'further defined the Catholic areas and increasingly provided a social outlet for the often dreary lives of the Victorian working class'.[103]

Thus the time had come for new national schools for Catholics and for a Catholic teacher-training college in Belfast. The Catholic bishops realized that for the success of their campaign, the Catholics of Ireland should be made aware of the disparity between the generous financing of the English training colleges and the reluctance of the government to accept the need for equal grants for Catholic training colleges in Ireland. The Commissioners, for their part, accepted the fact that the 'great majority of the teachers employed in the national schools are still untrained', and in May 1897 Sir Daniel Harrel, of the Chief Secretary's Office, reported:

> [the] Commissioners of National Education have, in connection with the establishment of training colleges in Belfast and Limerick, officially represented that the annual supply of trained candidates for teacher-ships is about half the number requisite to fill vacancies.[104]

As a result of these negotiations, both the colleges in Limerick and in Belfast were sanctioned simultaneously and two new Catholic training colleges were added to the existing three: Mary Immaculate College in Limerick under the direction of the Sisters of Mercy and St Mary's College, Belfast, under the Dominican Sisters in Falls Road. The sanction for the licences is dated 10 May 1897.[105] The foundation stone of Mary Immaculate College, Limerick, was laid on 8 September 1899, that of St Mary's College, Falls Road, Belfast, on 27 October 1899. It could almost be said that these two colleges were 'twin foundations'. There seems to be no doubt that the bishops of Limerick and of Down and Connor had acted together in sending their applications for financing their colleges to the Board of Education in Dublin and the Treasury in Whitehall.

A letter dated 29 September 1900 from A. Hamilton, Secretary in the Office of National Education, Dublin, to Bishop Henry, informed him that the Commissioners of National Education had 'ordered that Saint Mary's Training College, Belfast, be recognised'.[106] No documents are available to certify the legal agreement reached between the nuns in Dominican Convent, Falls Road, and the diocese of Down and Connor about the obligations of each party with regard to the site for the building and the structure itself. Years later, in 1934, Plunkett Dillon, a member of a Dublin firm of solicitors, John L. Scallon & Co., wrote to the then Dominican prioress general, Mother Colmcille Flynn, clarifying to some degree the legal situation regarding the land used for the building of St Mary's in Falls Road, Belfast. In the course of the letter Dillon wrote:

I find that between August and December 1897, the late Mr Terence O'Reilly was in very close personal correspondence with Mother Ignatius [the then prioress of Falls Road convent] and that he was in Belfast for an interview with her and I believe, with the Bishop, the late Dr Henry, on the 30 December 1897. It is unfortunate that the correspondence was of a private and purely personal nature and consequently no records were kept, for reasons which you can understand. ... I can state what Mr O'Reilly was advising Mother Ignatius in August 1897, with regard to the agreement between the convent and the Bishop.[107]

Plunkett Dillon stated that land was bought by the convent, part of which was leased to the bishop some time in 1889 or early 1890. Certain very specific conditions were laid down which included such matters as the agreement for the management of the college, which should be endorsed by the diocese on behalf of the bishop's successors. Further, the erection of the college was the bishop's responsibility together with its cost; the community of Dominicans in Falls Road had the right to approve of the plans and were entitled to have included in them such conveniences and accommodation as they might consider necessary. If for any reason the community ceased to manage the college, the bishop or diocese should compensate the community for loss arising from discontinuance. In the event that the Training College and land attached should be offered for sale at any time, first option to purchase should be given to the convent. Finally, the bishop should provide all necessary furniture, educational and other appliances, instruments and books, as required by the community, and would undertake to continue to supply the same as and when required thereafter. In her centenary book on Mary Immaculate College, Limerick, *Passing on the Torch*, Sr Loreto O'Connor gives the details of the foundation of the Limerick college: the land for that college was jointly purchased by the bishop of Limerick and the Sisters of Mercy, the college building itself being modelled on Notre Dame College in Mount Pleasant, Liverpool.

EQUALITY OF FINANCIAL GRANTS TO THE TRAINING COLLEGE

There remained a curious anomaly in the provision of state grants to the training colleges in Ireland.[108] Three of the Catholic bishops campaigned for equality of treatment for their Catholic colleges: Archbishop Walsh of Dublin, Bishop O'Dwyer of Limerick and Bishop Foley of Kildare and Leighlin, the last named being also the Catholic bishops' representative on the Board of Education. The inequality arose in the funding for the building, furnishing, repairs upkeep of the buildings and for the maintenance of the students in training. The Marlborough Street College was built and equipped by the government, and the administrators were free to use the college income for educational purposes. One example of the disparity in financial aid to the colleges was that the Catholic colleges were granted only three-quarters of their annual expenditure, not the full 100 per cent which Marlborough Street was given. Government stipulations were:

> the grants per student would only be forthcoming on the certain conditions, one of which was that subsequent to the student's successfully qualifying as a national teacher, he or she was engaged for two years in a recognised school and was favourably reported on by the inspector.[109]

The import of that clause was that the later training colleges did not get their grants for any particular group of students until two years had passed from their qualification, at which point their financial obligation to the state as trained teachers had been fulfilled. Archbishop Walsh had campaigned for 'justice and equality, not one iota less' for St Patrick's and Baggot Street colleges in 1890, when Chief Secretary Arthur Balfour ordained that, 'all training colleges in Ireland, Catholic and Protestant denominational and undenominational [are] to be placed on a footing of absolute equality as regards the financial assistance afforded by the State'.

When the time came for establishing the Limerick and Belfast colleges, the Board of Education made a new agreement about financial aid to Mary Immaculate College, Limerick, and to St Mary's College. Both Bishops O'Dwyer and Henry accepted this new agreement at the time and did not insist on having the more financially favourable conditions of the 1890 Dublin agreement applied to their new colleges, and both were to regret their acceptance. Morrissey in his biography, *Bishop Edmund Thomas O'Dwyer*, contends that it was Bishop Henry who suggested they should fight 'for the privileges the Dublin Colleges enjoy' but neither bishop chose to admit that he had agreed to the 'precise financial conditions laid down by the Commissioners before their training colleges were sanctioned'.[110] That did not prevent O'Dwyer from complaining publicly about the perceived injustice; on the occasion of the laying of the foundation stone of Mary Immaculate College he drew attention to the different approach of the state to financing the Limerick, Waterford and Belfast colleges. O'Dwyer pointed out to the gathering that these three colleges were excluded from the benefits given to the Dublin Catholic colleges, though they were under the same Board of Education, and were establishing colleges which would deliver the same training programme to the students. 'What once was granted' he argued, 'can be granted again'. Bishops Henry and O'Dwyer, along with Sheehan of Waterford, persisted in their efforts. O'Dwyer wrote to the Commissioners, 'surely you will put us in the provinces on the same footing financially with the colleges in Dublin'.[111] Henry confided to O'Dwyer that because St Mary's College was 'built very cheaply', he was fearful that the Belfast case for further financial help from the Commissioners would be weakened.[112] It was not until 1911 that the three colleges, Limerick, Waterford (De La Salle Brothers' college) and Belfast attained financial parity with the other colleges, denominational and non-denominational.

Bishop Henry blessed and officially opened St Mary's College on 23 September 1900. The building was described at length in the report in the Belfast *Irish News* on the following day. It was three storeys high, with a double flight of granite steps leading to the main door and entrance hall, which was tiled with tessellated work. An exhibition hall was to the left of the main door. The floors were of polished oak block and, with admirable common sense on the part of the planners, a hydraulic lift to the upper floors and a fire-proofed staircase were installed. Another feature of this 1900 ultra-modern building was the grand staircase in Portland stone, lighted with coloured and painted lights with emblematic figures representing grammar and knowledge. The study hall was graced with an arcade of oriel windows and there were also four well-furnished, spacious classrooms, a laboratory, a gymnasium and a library. An infirmary and convalescent rooms were isolated from the college proper, while a separate wing with its own entrance was provided for the nuns who were members of the resident staff.[113] Both Mary Immaculate College and St Mary's buildings were impressive and both still serve the educational needs of young men and women entering the teaching profession; nineteenth-century architects and the bishops believed in good structures and these have stood the test of time.

COLLEGE ORGANIZATION AND CURRICULUM

There is a striking similarity surrounding the initial stages of the foundation of the Limerick and Belfast women's training colleges. It would be of great interest to compare the educational approach of the two religious orders to the work of teacher-training in their respective colleges; unfortunately, the archives of Mary Immaculate College in Limerick are not available for research purposes at present and, in the case of St Mary's Training College, Belfast, there is a lack of contemporaneous documents or correspondence which might give more detailed information. We do know that the Sisters of Mercy and the Dominicans were intent on seeking advice about their new undertakings. O'Connor wrote of a visit made by Sr Angela Burke, superior of the Sisters of Mercy, to teacher-training colleges in England in order to gather 'information about the various aspects involved in running a training college'. One of the Limerick nuns, Sr Paul Quinlan, spent a year at Mount Pleasant Teacher Training College in Liverpool in preparation for her new work as principal of Mary Immaculate Training College, Limerick.[114] The Dominican convent archives in Falls Road, Belfast, 1896 record:

> [a] Training College for Teachers being in contemplation, it was considered advisable that two of the community should visit some educational establishment for the purpose of acquiring information on the most modern plans for buildings made for training colleges.[115]

12. Students of St Mary's College, Belfast, 1900

In 1896, the prioress and sub-prioress of Dominican Convent visited colleges in Belfast and Dublin, Mount Pleasant in Liverpool, Downhill, Glasgow, Wandsworth in south-west London, and Cambridge. The Dominicans certainly made an extensive tour of colleges, but there is no record of their having sent a nun specifically to train at that time in preparation for the task ahead, as did the Sisters of Mercy. There is no record of anyone either going abroad, or visiting the Sisters of Mercy college in Baggot Street, for this sole purpose. This seems strange, especially since Mother Francis Kennedy, the first principal of the college, was one of the two visiting England and Scotland.

Mother Francis Kennedy was the pupil who, in 1870, transferred from the Cabra boarding school to be the first boarder in the newly founded Falls Road boarding school. At the end of her secondary schooling, she entered as a postulant in the Dominican community in Falls Road. As the first principal of St Mary's Training College she was also professor of languages: the title 'professor' seems to have been automatically given to all who taught in the college. Members of the first staff were: Sr de Ricci McLornan, vice-principal and named professor of writing, spelling and punctuation; and Sr de Paul Bean, who acted as bursar. Three other nuns, Srs Martha Mallon, Benedict Coyle and Bernard McGettigan, were assigned from the Falls Road community to manage the household affairs of the college. Laywomen were designated as professors of arithmetic and book-keeping, methodology, that is, the practice of teaching and English composition, English literature, grammar, geography, reading and history, kindergarten teaching, drawing, needlework and cutting out of fabric to patterns, music, and cookery and laundry work. Two laymen graced the staff, Sergeant Croft, the drill instructor, and H. Lappin Esq., professor of elementary science.[116]

Mary Immaculate College in Limerick followed the general format of teaching as experienced by the Sisters of Mercy on their visit to the Notre Dame College in Liverpool. Great stress was indeed placed on the practice of teaching. For example, every two weeks each member of staff prepared ten students for teaching practice.[117] Since all the colleges were financed by the Treasury in London and were subject to the regulations of the Board of Education for curricular studies and examinations, all of them were pursuing the same curriculum. It is not possible to draw many comparisons between Mary Immaculate College in Limerick and St Mary's College, Belfast. The basic subjects were taught in both colleges. However, St Mary's College register had columns marked out for 'special subjects': French, Irish, Latin, Instrumental Music and Practical Cookery, and the number of students who opted for each of these subjects was noted. No one in fact studied French, Latin or Practical Cookery. On the other hand, piano and harmonium were very popular, and Irish gained in popularity as the years passed. Under the influence of the Gaelic League, the Commissioners of National Education in Ireland consented to place the Irish language on an equal footing in the schools with the teaching of Latin, Greek and French, and this at least in part, probably accounted for the number of students in St Mary's who chose to study Irish as an optional subject. 'Kindergarten' as a 'subject' was introduced in St Mary's in 1911; experimental physics was taught in Mary Immaculate. In both colleges nuns and lay people shared the teaching.

Prior to the establishment of teacher-training colleges, the monitorial system was used to introduce potential candidates to the work of teaching in national schools. Monitors were graded as junior or senior; at the age of eleven years, boys and girls were selected, usually by local school inspectors and teachers, each to serve three years training. They taught, under supervision, the lower classes for three hours each day while joining in lessons for the remainder of the day and they also received one hour's instruction from the principal teacher after school hours. Senior monitors were appointed at the age of fourteen years and served for four years. Pupil-teachers were appointed from the ranks of senior monitors. The highest grade of subordinate teacher was the assistant, who was usually a senior monitor who had completed his or her four year training course.

On the evening of 16 September 1900, the first students to arrive and be registered in St Mary's came from Castlerea, Co. Roscommon. They were Annie Dillon, Mary Bleakley and Mary Keagan, and were followed on the following morning by Rose Anne McCurry from Cushendall, Co. Antrim. The initial

13. Mother Francis Kennedy, 1858–1933, St Mary's Training College, Belfast

enrolment of 100 women students came from twenty dioceses in Ireland. Of the total number, eighteen students belonged to that class of certified teachers referred to above who entered for a one-year course, while eighty-two entered for the two-year course. In the first decades of the century, the students were either monitors who had passed the Queen's (later King's) scholars' examination or were certified teachers, and so took the full two-year course. This system of admission continued until the 1930s, when students were accepted from the new high or 'secondary' schools if their senior school examination certificate results were satisfactory.

Mother Francis Kennedy was principal of St Mary's continuously from 1900–18, and again from 1924–26 and from 1929–32. She died in April 1933. An appreciation of her work was written at the time of her golden jubilee of profession in 1925; it recalled that she had 'a keen business capacity ... [and] her achievements on behalf of education, particularly in its higher spheres, were long recognised by all sections of the community'.[118] Many of her former students attended her funeral to honour one who 'had shed lustre on their profession'. The College continued to train women candidates during the years of the First World War. With the partition of Ireland in 1921, St Mary's was the only teacher training college in Northern Ireland, and came under the control of the Northern Ireland Ministry of Education in 1923 when the new Unionist-dominated government ceased to recognize the qualifications of teachers trained in any of the colleges in the Irish Free State. The Dominicans remained on the teaching staff until the late 1990s: almost 100 years of service had been given to the education of teachers in Belfast.

CONCLUSION

Three educational establishments involving the Dominican nuns in Ireland have been examined in this chapter: St Mary's University College, Dublin; St Dominic's Training College for secondary school teachers in 17 Eccles Street, Dublin; and St Mary's Training College for national school teachers in Belfast. All three enterprises sought to further the higher education of women in the late nineteenth and early twentieth centuries. The foundation of St Mary's Training College in Belfast was undertaken in collaboration with, and at the invitation of, the bishop of the diocese of Down and Connor, Dr Henry. The initiative for the two Dublin colleges, while taken with the permission and encouragement of the Archbishop of Dublin, came from the nuns' own anxiety to cater for education of women at university and post-graduate level. How well did these ventures into third level education fulfil the aspirations of those who began them and of those who participated in them?

In St Mary's College, Belfast, the Dominicans undertook to manage and staff a college for the training of primary school teachers. The nuns had no previous experience of such a college and so it was for them a pioneering project. As an educational work, the college was under government control: financing, staffing and curriculum of the college were all dictated by the Board of Education in Dublin. The nuns were there at the request of the diocese and while they had responsibility for the day-to-day running, ultimately they answered to two outside agencies, the bishop of the diocese and the Board of Education. In the early days of state-controlled training colleges, there was not any great difference between one training college and another. We saw how even in the establishment of St Mary's, its sister college in Limerick was licensed in an identical letter sent to both bishops on the same day. Bureaucracy dictated both to the Sisters of Mercy and the Dominicans how the colleges would be organized, the time given to the subjects on the curriculum, the fees paid by the students, the holidays allowed and the salaries of the staff. In so far as the Dominicans were concerned, they set up the college as an environment for young women who had chosen primary teaching as their vocation. As a Catholic college, the atmosphere was rooted in the practices of the faith; religious emblems and statues were common in the corridors and lecture rooms. Not only the nuns, but the bishop expected the students to be practising Catholics and as such, they would have had a very thorough training in the doctrines of the church and in catechetics.

The Dominican role in the college was to be present as teachers and lecturers, guide the students in their studies, and afford them pastoral care when required. The Dominican presence was perhaps the only distinguishing mark; the ethos of the school or college is an elusive element. It can be experienced by those who are part of the college, either as staff or students but is very difficult to define.

St Mary's University College was set up in Eccles Street in 1884, later transferred to Merrion Square and Muckross Park, but finally returned to Eccles Street in 1903. St Mary's had the distinction of being the first Catholic women's university college in Ireland.[119] While Mother Patrick Sheil was the inspirational figure behind the idea of providing a centre for Catholic women to pursue university courses, Mother Clare Elliott and the community in Sion Hill had the courage to allow the community in Eccles Street to set up the college. As a centre, it had its trials and upheavals; it was difficult to finance such a college, especially as some of the students who were educated there were not able to pay high fees. The nuns were fortunate in having members of their own community who were capable of teaching courses at university level, especially Latin and modern languages, but they had distinguished outside lecturers on their staff also, Dr William Delany SJ and Eamonn de Valera among them. Mother Patrick Sheil and her colleagues in the community supported the thrust of the arguments for women's higher education and were prepared to work and finance it. Mother Patrick had a change of mind about women's colleges when it became apparent that Loreto College St Stephen's Green were applying for recognition as a women's college, when University College, Dublin had been validated as a constituent college of the National University of Ireland. Patrick Sheil applied also for recognition; in the event, neither college succeeded.

St Dominic's Training College, Eccles Street, was set up in conjunction with the Cambridge Syndicate – another Dominican initiative to provide an educational service for women. The college closed when the Higher Diploma in Education was begun in University College, Dublin. If one were a Dominican nun living in the second decade of the twentieth century, one might have taken a pessimistic view. St Mary's University College and St Dominic's Training College were no longer functioning, and to those who were participants it might have seemed that the nuns had failed to sustain what they had begun. To those who are looking back on the story, a very different landscape emerges. The Dominicans were very active agents in changing the prospects of women who sought higher education but had no hope of attaining it. Were St Mary's University College not there in the 1890s, many women would have had no chance of gaining university degrees. St Mary's University College filled that vacuum, and the possibility of having professional training for secondary teaching was the logical step forward that St Dominic's Training College provided.

NOTES

1. D. McCartney, *UCD, A National Idea. The History of University College Dublin* (Dublin: Gill & MacMillan, 1999), p.1. Cited henceforth as McCartney, *UCD*.
2. Ian Ker, *John Henry Newman, A Biography* (Oxford: Oxford University Press, Oxford Lives Series, 1988), pp.376–7.

3. J.H. Newman, *The Idea of a University* (New York: Doubleday, Image Books edition, 1959).
4. Ibid., pp.61–2.
5. D. Gwynn, *A Hundred Years of Catholic Emancipation (1829–1929)* (London: Longmans, Green & Co., 1929), p.165.
6. McCartney, *UCD*, p.8.
7. Gwynn, *A Hundred Years of Catholic Emancipation*, p.165.
8. McCartney, *UCD*, p.4.
9. McCartney, *UCD*, p.8.
10. A.C.F. Beales, 'John Henry Newman', in A.V. Judges (ed.), *Pioneers of English Education* (London: Faber and Faber, 1952), p.140.
11. McCartney, *UCD*, p.17.
12. T.J. Morrissey, *Towards a National University, William Delany SJ (1835–1924)* (Dublin: Wolfhound Press, 1983), p.35.
13. McCartney, *UCD*, p.24.
14. See T.J. Morrissey, *William J. Walsh, Archbishop of Dublin, 1841–1921* (Dublin: Four Courts Press, 2000), pp.210–31 for a comprehensive account of the events leading to the establishment of the National University of Ireland 1909.
15. Morrissey, *William Walsh, Archbishop of Dublin*, pp.210–31.
16. J. Logan, 'Governesses, Tutors and Parents: Domestic Education in Ireland, 1700–1888', *Irish Educational Studies*, Vol. 7, No. 2, (1988), p.5.
17. M. Byers, 'The Higher Education of Women', *The Englishwoman's Review of Social and Industrial Questions*, Vol. 12 (1881), pp.413–33.
18. M. Byers, 'Higher Education of Women', *Transactions of the National Association for Promotion of Social Science*, 1881, pp.413–33 (p.426).
19. A. Oldham, 'Women and the Irish University Question', *New Ireland Review* (January 1897), pp.257–63 (pp.257–9).
20. L. Daly, 'Women and the University Question', *New Ireland Review*, Vol. 17 (March–August 1902), pp.74–80.
21. N. Meade, 'Women in Universities', *Irish Educational Review*, Vol. 1, No. 4 (1908), pp.236–43; N. Meade, 'Women in Universities, A Rejoinder', in *New Ireland Review*, Vol. 1, No. 6 (1908), pp.355–61.
22. AUCD, National Association of Women Graduates, Minutes of Meeting, March 1902, Dublin.
23. Ibid.
24. M. Hayden and H. Sheehy Skeffington, 'Women in University – A Reply', *The Irish Educational Review*, Vol.1, No. 5 (1908), pp.242–83 (p.283).
25. M. Hayden and H. Sheehy Skeffington, 'Women in University – A Further Reply', *Irish Educational Review*, Vol.1, No. 7 (1908), pp.410–18.
26. OPSH, *Sion Hill Annals*, p.150.
27. OPC, *Cabra Annals*, p.147.
28. McCartney, *UCD*, p.72.
29. Akenson, D.H., *The Irish Education Experiment; the National System of Education in the Nineteenth Century*, eds T.W. Moody, J.C. Beckett, Studies in Irish History series, Vol. VII (London: Routledge and Kegan Paul, 1970), p.177.
30. NLI., *The Dublin Almanack*, 1843, List of Barristers.
31. NLI., *Thom's Directory*, 1841 (Dublin: Pettigrew & Oulton), List of Barristers.
32. Sr Benvenuta MacCurtain, 'St Mary's University College', *University Review*, Vol. 3, No. 4 (Dublin: Newman House, 1964), pp.33–47 (p.35).
33. OPE, Anon., 'St Mary's University College', *The Lanthorn*, Year-Book of Dominican College, Eccles Street, Vol. 7 No. 2 (Dublin: published privately, 1932), p.183. Articles written by members of the community were not usually attributed to named individuals.

34. The elected office-holders in Dominican convents in the nineteenth century were: a prioress, a sub-prioress, and three other members of the community known as 'discreets', or, in modern terms, 'councillors'. The group had responsibility for implementing the important business of the house.

35. Morrissey, *William J. Walsh, Archbishop of Dublin,* p.350.

36. Ibid. p.351.

37. OPG, E7/22. Unsigned copy of an undated letter.

38. OPG, E7/1: Walsh to Clare Elliott, 5 August 1893.

39. DDA, Folder 356/7, Walsh Correspondence; letter from Mother Michael Corcoran to Archbishop Walsh, 17 July 1893.

40. OPE, Undated and untitled newspaper cutting among the Eccles Street papers.

41. OPSH, *Sion Hill Annals,* pp.193–8. OPE, Eccles Street Papers: List of nominees to College Council. Nine members of the council were members of the Senate of RUI, two were Commissioners of Education, and ten were heads of colleges and schools.

42. OPSH, *Sion Hill Annals,* p.283.

43. McCartney, *UCD,* p.22.

44. DDA., Walsh Papers 1894, Box 356/8; folder 363/2. Letter from Mother Imelda, prioress of Dominican Convent, Eccles Street, to Archbishop Walsh. Emphasis in the original.

45. OPG, *The Lanthorn,* Vol. 7 No. 2, p.184.

46. Sr Benvenuta, 'St Mary's University College', p.40. See Appendix 6, Prospectus, St Mary's University College.

47. DDA, Walsh Papers, Augustine Clinchy to Walsh, Box 364 /2.

48. OPSH, *Sion Hill Annals,* p.291.

49. OPM, Letter from Eleanor Butler to the prioress dated 3 December 1925.

50. BPP, *Report of Royal Commission on University Education in Ireland* (Robertson Commission), H.C. 1902, xxxi.

51. McCartney, *UCD,* p.74.

52. BPP, *'Robertson Commission', Report,* H.C. 1903, xxxi, xxxii. See also tabulated synopsis earlier in this chapter, p.126.

53. BPP, *'Robertson Commission', Report,* H.C. 1902, xxxi, pp.317–18.

54. Hayden and Sheehy Skeffington, 'Women in University – A Reply', p.277.

55. NLI, Mss. Room, Ms. PO3, 9145, M. Hayden, *Diary,* Feb. 1896.

56. OPG, Copy of Memorial to Right Hon. G. Balfour, MP, Chief Secretary to Lord Lieutenant for Ireland. Undated.

57. BPP, *'Robertson Commission' Report,* Evidence of Mary Hayden on behalf of the Dominicans in St Mary's University College, pp.357–9. My emphasis.

58. Ibid., p.358. Emphasis in original.

59. Ibid., documents submitted to the Commission, p.365.

60. Ibid., Report, Evidence of Mary Hayden on behalf of St Mary's College, p.358.

61. See Figure 3, University Structures, p.126.

62. A. Birrell, *Things Past Redress* (London: Faber and Faber, n.d.), p.194.

63. Sr Benvenuta, 'St Mary's University College', p.44.

64. Ibid.

65. OPG, Letter of Archbishop Walsh to Mother Patrick, 4 July 1910.

66. Ibid.

67. AUCD, Minute Book of Governing Body, University College, Dublin, 19 April 1910.

68. McCartney, *UCD,* p.81.

69. Sr Benvenuta, 'St Mary's University College', p.45.

70. OPE, 'In Memory of Mother Peter, O.S.D.', *The Lanthorn,* 7, Vol. 2, No.2 (1917), p.220.

71. OPE, 'St Mary's University College', *The Lanthorn,* Golden Jubilee Number, 1932. p.195. The sentence in the quotation referring to Mother Patrick explains why the letters relating to the college were written sometimes by M. Peter McGrath and sometimes by

M. Patrick Sheil. Mother Peter McGrath's health was not robust and, though a younger woman, she predeceased Mother Patrick by nine years.

72. Ian Anstruther, *Oscar Browning* (London: John Murray, 1983). A full account of the Cambridge Syndicate and Oscar Browning's involvement in it is given by Anstruther.
73. Ibid., p.151.
74. CUL, Educ 3/2–22, Box 1.
75. CUL, Educ. 3/14–3/22, Sr Bernard Hackett to Oscar Browning, 21 February 1898.
76. CUL, Educ. 3/19–3/22, Fitch to Oscar Browning, 17 Feb. 1898.
77. Ibid., February 1898.
78. Ibid.
79. OPG, D1/1, Browning to Mother Peter McGrath, September 1904.
80. DDA, Box 381/2–8 Folder 381/6, Mother Peter to Archbishop Walsh, 25 October 1907.
81. Alexandra College sent out circulars to the students in St Mary's University College. Mother Peter did not distribute the circulars 'lest anyone might be tempted to avail themselves of the opportunity offered.'
82. OPG, File D1/1, Archbishop Walsh to Mother Peter McGrath. (Emphasis in the original.)
83. OPG, File D1/1, Oscar Browning to Mother Peter, 24 November 1907.
84. OPG, File D1/1, Mother Augustine Clinchy, prioress of Eccles Street Convent, to Archbishop Walsh, 15 November 1907.
85. KCC, OB 14–18, Mother Patrick to Oscar Browning, 10 March 1908. (Emphasis in the original.)
86. KCC, OB 14–18, Mother Patrick to Oscar Browning, 3 December 1908.
87. KCC, OB 14–18, Headen to Browning, 21 March 1908.
88. OPG, E/7 Archbishop Walsh to Augustine Clinchy, prioress of Eccles Street, 31 May 1908.
89. OPG, Browning to Dominican Convent, Eccles Street. 13 March 1909
90. OPE, Result sheet of Teachers' Training Syndicate, Cambridge, June 1910.
91. OPE, L. Gavan Duffy, 'A Year in St Dominic's', *The Lanthorn,* Vol. 1 No. 1, 1913.
92. OPE, Copy book containing the students' accounts.
93. W. Walsh, *Statement of Chief Grievances of Irish Catholics in the Matter of Education* (Dublin: Browne and Nolan, 1890), p.64.
94. P.J. Dowling, *History of Irish Education* (Cork: Mercier Press, 1971), p.124.
95. Walsh, *Chief Grievances,* p.127. A comprehensive account of the history of teacher training and the Catholic bishops' misgivings about it, is given by Walsh, pp.97–206.
96. The term 'convent and monastery schools' was used by the Commissioners of Education as a descriptive phrase for schools run by women religious and religious brotherhoods, respectively.
97. BPP, 1870 xxviii, *Report of Royal Commission of Inquiry into Primary Education* (Powis Report), Evidence of Bishop Dorrian. Par. 8741, Index to minutes.
98. Trevelyan's letter quoted in Walsh's *Chief Grievances,* p.119.
99. See note 97 above re Bishop Dorrian's evidence to the Powis Commission.
100. Naf, *The Irish News* (Belfast), 24 September 1900. Report of the opening of St Mary's Training College, Falls Road, Belfast.
101. NAI, Chief Secretary's Office, Registered Papers (CSORP). Letter of Bishop Edward O'Dwyer to Commissioners of Education, October 1896. Cited in Loreto O'Connor, *Passing on the Torch,* p.5.
102. M. Elliott, *The Catholics of Ulster. A History* (London: Penguin Press, 2000), p.322.
103. Ibid.
104. NAI, Letter from Sir Daniel Harrel, Chief Secretary's Office Registered Papers (CSORP), Dublin, to the Treasury in Whitehall, London, no. 7222; cited in O'Connor, *Passing on the Torch,* p.6.
105. NAI, CSORP. Note: There are four documents relevant to the two colleges in Limerick and Belfast listed in the index of registered papers, but access to the papers is not possible as they are currently noted in the National Archives of Ireland as 'not found'.

106. OPFR, Letter of A. Hamilton, Office of National Education to Dr Henry, Bishop of Down and Connor.

107. OPFR: J. Plunkett Dillon to Mother Prioress General, Dominican Convent, Cabra, Dublin., 1 September 1934.

108. J. Rushe, 'Bishop O'Dwyer of Limerick 1886–1917 and the Educational Issues of His Time' (unpublished Master's Thesis, University College, Galway, 1980), section 6.5. Dates of connection of the Training Colleges in Ireland with Board of Education.

1838	Marlborough Street, Dublin, male and female (m/f)	Nondenominational.
1889	St Patrick's, Drumcondra, Dublin (m)	Catholic.
1883	Srs Of Mercy, Baggot, Street, Dublin (f)	
	Transferred to Carysfort 1903	Catholic.
1884	Kildare Place Dublin (m/f)	Church of Ireland.
1891	De La Salle Waterford (m)	Catholic.
1900	St Mary's, Belfast (f)	Catholic.
1901	Mary Immaculate, Limerick (f)	Catholic.

109. P.J. Walsh, *William J. Walsh, Archbishop of Dublin* (Dublin: Talbot Press, 1928), p.466.

110. T.J. Morrissey, *Bishop Edward Thomas O'Dwyer 1842–1917* (Dublin: Four Courts Press, 2003), p.250.

111. Walsh, *William J. Walsh, Archbishop of Dublin* cited in Rushe, 'Bishop O'Dwyer of Limerick 1886–1917 and the Educational Issues of his Time', section 6.34.

112. Ibid., section 6.43.

113. NAF. Address of Bishop Henry, *The Irish News,* 24 September 1900.

114. O'Connor, *Passing on the Torch,* p.9.

115. OPFR, Convent Annals, Red covered copybook, 1896, p.85.

116. OPFR, Annals of Dominican Convent Falls Road, September 1900.

117. MIUC, J. Rushe, 'Bishop O'Dwyer of Limerick 1886–1917 and the Educational Issues of his Time', (unpublished master's thesis, University College, Galway, 1990) section 6.41.

118. OPR, Ms. St Mary's Training College collection, 'Golden Jubilee Gathering'.

119. Akenson, *Irish Education,* p.177.

4

Widening Horizons

QUIS DOCUIT IPSAS MAGISTRAS?

The above adaptation of the old Latin tag, *Quis custodiet ipsos Custodes*,[1] introducing this final chapter, sums up queries one might have about the preparation and training of Dominican nuns themselves for the variety of educational work which they undertook between 1820 and 1930. Who taught the teachers, especially in the first three-quarters of the nineteenth century? In the early nineteenth century Irish Catholic schools were conducted by people, whether lay or religious, who had little if any formal training as teachers. As noted in Chapter 3, it was not until the 1880s that training colleges for Catholic primary teachers were established in Ireland, and university education was opened to women in Ireland only in 1879.

The postulants (candidates) who had a desire to teach and who applied for admission to the Dominican Order from 1820–1930 could be divided approximately into three groups: those who came to the convents before the era of Teacher Training Colleges or the possibility of university education for women; those who came from the era of the Intermediate Education [Ireland] Act 1878 up to and including the First World War, some of whom benefited from the early days of university education and lastly, those who came post-First World War, when the educational opportunities for women were more assured. For this last group, assuming their finances allowed, it was no longer unusual to have had an academic education with either a university degree or a teacher's primary training certificate and diploma before committing themselves to religious life.

DOMINICAN TEACHING NUNS 1820–78

The three divisions of time given above are not definitive; they are chosen as a convenient way of dividing the groups of nuns according to their likely patterns of education. Anne Columba Maher, her niece, Catherine de Ricci Maher, and grand-niece, Bertrand Maher, came from a 'strong farmer' family in Co. Carlow. The period 1814–20 was the beginning of the era of the Mahers, when Columba had her first term of office as the young prioress who moved the ailing and depleted community from Clontarf to Cabra, and thus gave the Dominican women in Dublin a new lease of life. A member of the Maher family was in a position of influence in the Cabra convent continuously from 1814 until the death of Mother Bertrand Maher in 1929. Other members of that extended family were in positions of authority in Cabra's daughter-houses, Kingstown and Belfast. The Maher family was related also to Paul, Cardinal Cullen, and to Patrick, Cardinal Moran, of Sydney, Australia. Other members entered Dominican convents in Ireland during the nineteenth and twentieth centuries. The family influence was felt not only in Dominican convents but also among the secular clergy and in a variety of religious houses, male and female, both in Ireland and abroad. Maher/Cullen was a kind of ecclesiastical dynasty.

By 1820 the old eighteenth-century Anglo-Irish connection in the Dominican convents in Dublin had weakened to be replaced by women, many of whom came from farming, professional and business families. The era of the landed gentry was thus replaced by communities whose members came from well-to-do families who could afford the dowries expected of them when daughters entered convents. Most of those who entered were past-pupils of the schools; some had no training for teaching before entering, others spent time in a 'finishing school on the Continent'. At the end of century the prospectus for Cabra Convent noted:

> [t]o secure the ablest teachers, and the most approved methods, some members of the Community took out their diplomas for teaching, both in theory and practice, in the Cambridge University, and went through a complete course of training in Bedford College, London, while others fitted themselves for their work by a prolonged residence on the Continent.[2]

The point is made that the nun-teachers in the school were trained for their work. Within the novitiate and in their early years of teaching, the young nuns were given instruction by experienced teachers in the community, a kind of in-house training supplemented by teaching from professionals who were invited to give lectures and courses. There are not many written records of these courses, but oral tradition has it that priority was given to philosophy and Catholic doctrine, to ensure the carrying out of the Dominican ministry of preaching the Gospel through their work in the classroom. The prioresses and their councils were careful to give the 'apprentice' teachers a broad education in music, art and literature. This was true of all the Dominican convents of the period.

CULTURAL INFLUENCES

The Cabra and Sion Hill annals record examples of the conscious and positive effort of the communities to create an atmosphere of appreciation of art and music within the convents; convents founded later in the century carried on that tradition. Taylor's Hill and Cabra convents both have collections of copies of works of art in paintings and prints; their collections of church vestments and

14. Sr Concepta Lynch, 1874–1939

silver-ware date back to the seventeenth and eighteenth centuries. Community members who were talented in art and music were encouraged to develop their gifts. Examples are Sr Margaret Joyce of Taylor's Hill, who has left an embroidered altar-frontal of great beauty dating from 1726; Sr Vincent Hogan, a member of the Cabra community 1887–1908, who produced beautifully illuminated books which are preserved in the archives; and the work of Sr Concepta Lynch (1874–1939) of the Kingstown (Dún Laoghaire) community whose work lives on in the Celtic Oratory, which is preserved and is now included in the town's shopping centre. In recent years Dún Laoghaire-Rathdown County Council has given financial help and encouragement for the restoration and security of the oratory, which the civic authorities rightly consider a national treasure of Celtic art. Etienne Rynne, a noted archaeologist, writing about Sr Concepta's work says,

> there is nothing cold or functional about Sr Concepta's art as used so magnificently in the Oratory of the Sacred Heart. ... Sr Concepta had apparently an unerring eye for good taste in the exploitation of strong colours. ... Without fail she has successfully managed to counter-balance the power of her oranges, greens, whites and reds with more muted browns, purples, blues and blacks. One is comfortably absorbed into the decorated Oratory, rather than overwhelmed by it.[3]

Sr Stanislaus McCarthy (1850–97) of Sion Hill had a gift for poetry; inherited from her father, Denis Florence McCarthy, also a poet, who wrote for Thomas Davis's newspaper, *The Nation*. Sr Stanislaus' collected poems, published after her death as *Songs of Sion*, are mostly of a religious character.[4] Over the years there were also excellent musicians among the teaching staffs in the convents. Mother Clement Burke (1879–1944), of Eccles Street, was renowned as a singing teacher; she had trained in Germany before entering in Sion Hill in 1900. She it was who gave encouragement and tuition to the internationally acclaimed La Scala opera singer Margaret Burke Sheridan, and other noted Irish singers. Reference has been made to the original work of Sister Hyacinth McAuliffe in Taylor's Hill who, in her teaching in the boarding school in the 1860s, used her own original note-books for teaching history and arithmetic. Both nuns and pupils attended occasional lectures; part of the summer holidays was given up to courses. Some examples of musical recitals and lectures in 1913 are: Verdi's Requiem; Newman's Dream of Gerontius; Joan of Arc by Madame Guérin, Officier de l'Instruction Publique; Masterpieces in Art by Rev. Dr Beecher; Athens by Dr D'Alton, Maynooth College; Irish Music by Arthur Darley; Einstein's Theory of Relativity by Dr Pádraig de Brún.[5]

For enclosed Dominican nuns, one of the beneficial results of the admission of women to university education was that some of their graduate-past pupils entered in the convents where they had been at school. A document of 1922 formulated what had been the unwritten policy of the Dominican convents after the admission of women to university. 'The Training of Sisters as Teachers' stated, '[we] have as a general rule, required that Postulants for our Order should have obtained their B.A. Degree or its equivalent before entrance. We intend in the majority of cases to maintain this standard.'[6]

Between 1889 and 1940, a period of fifty-one years, at least forty-one postulants who were graduates entered the novitiates in Cabra, Sion Hill and Wicklow.[7] This does not include those who joined the order in the Galway, Belfast and Kingstown (Dún Laoghaire) houses. The educational contribution of some of the early graduates – Mothers Peter McGrath, Gonzales Stone, Peter Flynn and An Mháthair Treasa Ní Fhlanagáin – is well known within the Dominican Congregation, and reference has been made to them in preceding chapters. In their own life-times they were acclaimed as having furthered the cause of Irish women's education in various ways. When these young graduates entered the Dominican convents, each house was still an autonomous unit, with its own internal government of prioress and council, under the local bishops. New thinking filtered through to the communities, both through the mediation of outside forces and from within the convents themselves. Had the time come for new structures which would allow for more cooperation, even amalgamation, between the Dominican convents in Ireland?

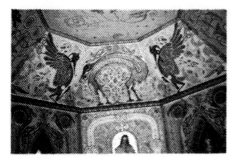

1. Triptych on frieze above the altar.

2. Strutting bird – detail of triptych above the altar.

3. Corner of the Oratory showing the floor, the design of which is based on the back panel of the Shrine of St Patrick's Bell.

4. Bird-headed quadruped – central detail of triptych above the altar.

15. Detail of triptych in Celtic Oratory, Dún Laoghaire

AMALGAMATION OF DOMINICAN CONVENTS 1928

The question of amalgamation was raised from about 1907 onwards. Two Irish Dominican priests, Frs Louis Nolan and Finbar Ryan, were working separately and together for the amalgamation of the Dominican convents within Ireland. Fr Nolan, who lived in Rome, was appointed a Consultor to the Congregation for Religious; in that capacity he was in a position to help with the negotiations, both within the Dominican Order and with the Vatican, if the nuns were willing to amalgamate. Fr Ryan lived in Dublin and was convinced that amalgamation would further the sphere of influence of the Dominican nuns in Ireland. There is strength in unity. The idea of an amalgamation of the convents of Dominican women was spoken about freely within the communities, but it would mean a very big upheaval in the lives of the nuns, an upheaval which some of the members thought could not be justified. A celebration of two events in Dominican Convent Cabra brought the idea closer to realization: 1917 was the bicentenary of the foundation, from Galway, of the original Dublin convent in Channel Row, and 1919 was the centenary of the foundation of Cabra from the convent in Clontarf. Both anniversaries were celebrated together in 1919 because the aftermath of the Easter Rising prevented an earlier celebration.

Another and perhaps more compelling consideration was argued in favour of closer cooperation and unity: the new Code of Canon Law was promulgated in 1918. An anonymous writer in *Weavings* cites Louis Nolan:

> [w]ould not the materialisation of this idea [amalgamation] be a grand and worthy outcome of your centenary celebration? It would certainly be in accordance with the spirit of the Church and the spirit of the Order ... and now seems the opportune moment, not only because of your centenary celebrations, but also, since the Constitutions of the different religious bodies are to undergo examination with a view to bringing them into harmony with the new Code of Canon Law.[8]

Finbar Ryan's role was played out in Ireland where he was well acquainted with the personalities of the women involved and the histories of the convents. This was a radical change for all concerned and Ryan 'would advise, cajole, entreat, but never command'.[9] The decision was for the nuns themselves to take: every Sister in each convent voted in the autumn of 1927. When the Archbishop of Dublin, Dr Edward Byrne, came to preside at this voting in Eccles Street, Mother Patrick Sheil, the person responsible for St Mary's University College, was in frail health in the infirmary. The archbishop went there and received her vote; it was the last great act of faith which Mother Patrick made in her lifetime of dedication to the cause of the Dominican ministry in education. On 14 February 1928, the Decree of the Sacred Congregation of Religious formally recognized the Congregation of the Irish Dominican Sisters. A general chapter (an assembly) of delegates from the Cabra, Sion Hill, Belfast, Wicklow and Dún

Laoghaire convents and their respective daughter-houses, Sutton, Eccles Street, Muckross Park and Portstewart, was held in April 1928. Mother Colmcille Flynn was elected to the office of first Prioress General, and Dominican Convent Cabra was nominated as the mother-house. Amalgamation was not total: both Taylor's Hill in Galway and Siena Convent, Drogheda, remained autonomous. At the time, the Siena Convent community was considering closing the school and reverting to a purely contemplative form of Dominican life, which they did in 1930. The Taylor's Hill community's dilemma was their canonical position as a part of the Order under the jurisdiction of the Master-General and his vicar in Ireland. O'Neill writes: '[t]hey were confronted with the question of renouncing their actual membership of the Order in favour of affiliated membership of a Congregation'.[10] The decision in 1928 was to remain autonomous under the jurisdiction of the Master General of the Order. The Taylor's Hill community joined the Congregation in 1970.

The overriding consideration for amalgamation of the convents was primarily to keep in tune with the Church's thinking on religious life at that time; but inevitably there were other effects, foreseen and unforeseen. In particular, each convent lost its autonomy and power to make decisions on major issues. Novices were received into a central novitiate in Cabra and after profession were assigned to convent communities by the Prioress General and her council. Financial matters were subject to scrutiny by the general council of the Congregation. Raising of loans for building purposes, allocation of personnel, transfer of personnel, decisions about the number of nuns required to staff schools, extension of school buildings; these matters were all now subject to the decision taken at general council level. The big difference in the life of individual nuns was that a member of the Congregation could be transferred from one convent to another, a challenge some found difficult to accept. Those who entered the Congregation after 1928 knew in advance that these new regulations were in place and accepted them as part of their vocational choice and commitment. On the positive side, change can be enriching. There was more social interaction between members of the new congregation and the schools had certainty about future personnel; new members brought new ideas and suggestions for improving the systems already in place, while discussion among a wider pool of people resulted in more diverse approaches to problem-solving. Personnel could be moved from one place to another according to the needs of the schools. The recruitment to the Congregation increased and the deployment of teaching sisters helped to improve standards, especially when opportunities for specialized training were availed of.

In January 1929 a meeting was held with thirteen head-mistresses of the schools and the new general council of the Congregation. The main purpose of the meeting was to set out some guide-lines for a common educational policy. The guide-lines were to be arrived at by the 'interchange of ideas and ... [in order] to select the most perfect manner and methods of imparting to [those] who go out from our schools, the same principles by which we ourselves are animated.'[11] This meeting of headmistresses became an annual event in the life of the Congregation and was a forum for exchange of ideas and discussion of matters relating to the work in the schools. It was one of positive results of amalgamation which helped to form a bond between the Sisters in the various houses of the Congregation and helped to create a unity in their approach to educational matters, though it was always stressed that the aim was never uniformity.

RELATIONS WITH THE DEPARTMENT OF EDUCATION

The relationship which developed between the Eccles Street community and the educational authorities after the 1878 Intermediate Education [Ireland] Act grew from the school's reputation, the opening of St Mary's University College and the educational opportunities it afforded for university education for women. As already mentioned, the Ursuline, Loreto and Dominican Orders were seen as pioneers in this work in the last decades of the nineteenth century. The in-house training within the Dominican convents developed and expanded in a more formalized way, which in turn led to the Commissioners of Education inviting the nuns in Eccles Street to set up summer courses in 1909, primarily for the continuing education of nuns throughout the country and not exclusively for Dominicans. Apart from other considerations, Eccles Street as a base for conferences was ideally situated, near the centre of the city, with good public transport close by. 'Summer Schools for Nuns' was the title given to the courses, which were of three weeks duration in July each year. There was ample accommodation for visiting nuns to stay as the boarders' bedrooms were vacant in the summer-time. The 1925 syllabus stated:

> [t]he Dominican College Summer School course of Lectures was inaugurated in July 1909, with the approbation of His Grace the Archbishop of Dublin. The object of the School is to provide opportunity for Nuns, engaged in Secondary teaching throughout the country, of studying up-to-date methods of education in important subjects of the School programme. Particular attention is given to the teaching of religion, the lectures having special reference to the Bishops' Syllabus of Religious Instruction for Secondary Schools; conferences on matters of general educational interest for Catholic teachers are arranged as time and other circumstances allow.[12]

These courses continued well into the 1930s and were given by university professors and lecturers and well-known clergymen. Catholic faith, which included scripture, apologetics and sacred liturgy was given priority; Gregorian music was also taught. The secular syllabus catered for courses in Irish, mathematics, geography, history (Irish and European), English literature and domestic economy. Besides these subjects, social science and music – including pianoforte playing – were also catered for. The courses were approved by the education authority, and after the Government of Ireland Act by both the Northern Ireland ministry of education and by the Irish Free State Ministry of Education and Department of Agriculture and Technical Instruction.[13] In conjunction with the nuns' summer school, an 'Irish Holiday School for Children' was set up in 1929. Nuns attending the summer school had an opportunity of seeing the practice of teaching by modern methods, carried out through the medium of Irish, in religion classes, singing, dramatic art, local history and geography, cookery and housewifery, drill, dancing and games.

Mother Reginald Lyons, prioress of Eccles Street and, after 1928, a member of the general council of the Congregation, was personally well-known to the officials of the Department of Education. Many of the higher civil servants had served under the British administration and were aware of the successful summer courses for nuns, which Mother Reginald had initiated. As a result of these courses, the nuns in Eccles Street had contacts with convents of all Orders throughout the country. In the early spring of 1929, Dr Butler, Assistant Commissioner representing the minister for education, called to visit Mother Reginald and requested that she

> confer with the Heads of a few of the more important convent schools, mentioning the Ursulines, St Louis, and Loreto, as to the possibility of the Nuns sending representatives to the Meetings in Hume Street, referred to in the enclosed circular.[14]

The circular referred to requested assistance in framing programmes and examination papers and in fixing the standard of marking. The prioress-general in Cabra consulted with the Archbishop of Dublin, Dr Edward Byrne (1921–40), who 'thought it important that the opportunity for the Nuns' participation in the framing of Educational Schemes should be fully availed of'.[15] The archbishop also favoured the formation without delay of a Nuns' Association of Headmistresses. This was to be an association similar to the Catholic Headmasters' Association (CHA).[16]

Clearly, the time had come by May 1929 for the nuns to take responsibility for their own affairs, and to organize themselves into a cohesive body which would have authority to represent all the convent secondary schools in any discussions or representations made to the bishops, the Department of Education, the teachers, unions or other revelant bodies. From the limited documentation in the archives, one cannot establish whether it was the archbishop or Mother Reginald who suggested the Nuns' Association of Headmistresses, but the internal evidence suggests that Mother Reginald seized the opportunity to go ahead with plans to set up such an organization. In May 1929 she sent her own separate circular to all the houses of the Cabra Dominican Congregation, informing the convents of Dr Butler's proposal and the archbishop's permission to proceed; at the same time she reported on the preliminary meeting held in April 1929.[17]

Mother Reginald's memorandum recorded that sixteen nuns from eight convents attended the meeting, which was held in Dominican Convent, Eccles Street. One sister from each of the Saint Louis, Sisters of Mercy, Ursuline, Society of the Sacred Heart and Dominican congregations was selected as representatives to attend the Department of Education's meeting in Hume Street, in the offices of the secondary branch of the Department. Each delegate was to lead the discussion for one of the subjects: Irish, mathematics, history, English and geography. Though the primary object of the meeting in Eccles Street was the selection of representatives, from the point of view of later events, item 3 on the agenda – '[t]o take steps towards the formation of an Association of Heads of Convent Schools' – was to have lasting effects for the teaching Orders in Ireland.[18] This was the seed which blossomed into the Conference of Convent Secondary Schools (henceforth referred to as CCSS), an organization which was to serve the Catholic convent schools of Ireland until almost the end of the twentieth century.

CONFERENCE OF CONVENT SECONDARY SCHOOLS

The first meeting of the CCSS was held in Eccles Street on 17 May 1929. From the beginning, the archbishop gave every support and encouragement to the newly formed conference. At the time Dr Byrne, who was in failing health, was unable to preside in person over the meetings and he appointed a Vincentian priest (Congregation of the Mission), Dr Cullen, president of St Patrick's Training College, Drumcondra, to represent him. It was typical of the period: the patriarchal attitude of the Church authorities; the readiness of the nuns to comply with the wishes of the archbishop; and the automatic assumption that it was appropriate or even necessary to have a cleric as chairperson at a meeting of a body of nuns who were making decisions about the administration of their own schools. In fact, the custom of having a representative of the Archbishop of Dublin chairing the annual general meeting of the CCSS continued for decades. The scope of the conference was set out in a letter to all the convents in Ireland which had secondary schools. The purpose of the conference was:

> to facilitate the interchange of ideas and information on all school matters; e.g. Teaching, Examinations, Internal Management and Organisation generally;
>
> to watch over Catholic interests in all matters concerning our schools, and to take such steps as may be considered advisable to procure the due considerations of such interests.[19]

As might be expected, the formation of the Conference of Convent Secondary Schools was considered necessary to direct policy in Irish Catholic convent secondary schools, but there were other objectives set out, including that of

16. First meeting of Conference of Convent Secondary Schools 1929 (CCSS)

balancing 'lay organisations and [resisting] the tendency to State and lay interference and aggression' in the education of Catholic girls.[20] Here again we can detect the continued fear of the religious losing control of the schools to either state or other outside bodies. That fear was further reflected in the convents' reaction to the Vocational Education Act of 1930. The Act provided for a state-funded technical education of boys and girls who did not wish to have an academic secondary education or who could not afford to attend fee-paying secondary schools. The business transacted at this first inaugural meeting of the CCSS in May 1929, however, centered on the practicalities of organizing the new association. Membership, the formulation of rules, the election of officers, formation of a standing committee and membership fees were matters for discussion and decision.[21]

Sixty-five convents were represented at the first AGM of the Conference in 1929. The nuns came from all over the Twenty-Six Counties. Over 119 filled the hall in Eccles Street, while 'letters of sympathy with the movement and of regret for inability to attend' were received from seventeen convents.[22] Dr Cullen, CM, chairing the meeting, reminded the nuns during the proceedings that the CCSS would give them the opportunity for the discussion of all matters in connection with education, would clarify and strengthen the Catholic view-point, and be a power for good throughout the country. He further pointed out the necessity of being alive to the trends of modern thought and ideas. Among the many speakers from the floor in the afternoon session was Mother Gonzales Stone of Muckross Park, one of the early graduates of St Mary's University College, Eccles Street. Though there is no record of Mother Gonzales' thoughts at this inaugural meeting. One might assume that she was proud to be associated with the new movement, remembering her days in St Mary's University College; the struggle then was for the right of women to attend university. The work of Mothers Patrick Sheil, Peter McGrath and the others who had spent themselves in keeping the fire of women's educational rights alight had borne fruit in this new manifestation of women religious, claiming to have their views on education formally recognised by both Church and state.

Voting for the officers of the CCSS was not for individual nuns but for congregations; voting was on a *pro rata* basis, according to the number of votes cast for each congregation. The congregations thus elected nominated their own representatives and these took their places on the standing committee. Before declaring the results of the voting, Dr Cullen, as chairman, proposed that a congregation receiving forty to fifty votes should have one representative on the standing committee; one getting double that number, eighty to ninety, two representatives, and for treble the number of votes, three representatives should be allowed. The proposal was carried unanimously. Voting for the offices of president, secretary and treasurer was separate from that of the standing committee. The result of the voting is set out below:

Table 5 Results of Voting at CCSS 1929

Congregation	Votes	Members on Standing Committee
Dominicans	127	3
St Louis	95	2
Ursuline	80	2
Sacred Heart	76	1
Srs of Mercy	57	1
Brigidine	44	1[23]

In the first year, Dominicans were elected to the three offices. Mother Reginald Lyons OP was elected president and continued to hold the presidency until 1942, when she had taken up office as prioress-general of the Cabra Dominican Congregation. Mother Reginald addressed a letter, dated 17 June 1930, to the convents in Northern Ireland who administered secondary schools. She reported on a standing committee meeting where 'it was unanimously agreed that all the convent secondary schools in Northern Ireland should be invited to join the Conference'.[24] The offer was not taken up and there is no documentary evidence to explain why the invitation was not accepted at that time. It may have been that the convents in Northern Ireland were in the early stages of adjusting to the new political situation after partition and the changes in their educational system which followed. The earlier connection with the Catholic Headmasters' Association (CHA) was retained; the nuns adopted a modified version of the rules of the men's association as their own. In fact, though, given that the nuns now had their own organization to debate and put

17. Mother Reginald Lyons, 1878–1962, first president of CCSS

forward ideas relating to their work in the schools, they still continued to relay their suggestions and decisions to the Department of Education and the Teaching Bodies through the CHA. Doyle concludes, 'until the early 1960s the CHA unofficially accepted responsibility for negotiating on behalf of the nuns'.[25]

Throughout the decades the CCSS as an organization continued as a forum for the convent secondary schools. Each year the annual general meeting was held over a period of two days in June or July. In the 1930s and 1940s the venue was either Dominican College, Eccles Street or Sacred Heart Convent, Mount Anville, Dundrum, Dublin. A set pattern developed over the years: the day began with a High Mass in the convent chapel, followed by a general meeting at which the reports from the standing committee and treasurer were read. An address was given by the chairman, who was always a nominee of the Archbishop of Dublin, usually a high ranking diocesan cleric or one involved in education. The subject of the chairman's address was generally of a religious educational nature. Examples over a number of years are: Catholic Traditions in Education; The Role of Women in Society and Formation of Character. Doyle summarizes the nuns' concerns in the first decade of the CCSS's existence:

through the 1930s their attention was devoted to the importance of music, art, physical education and sports and all cultural activities including radio, cinema and drama, on teaching methods and 'how to improve learning'.[26]

Mother Reginald Lyons' presidential addresses were on matters arising from the agenda of the standing committee meetings held during the previous twelve months. The subjects ranged from programmes for subjects on the curriculum, teaching through the medium of Irish, the debate about the script used in written Irish (Roman or Gaelic), teachers' salaries, government grants, insurance matters, and negotiations in train with the Department of Education. Doyle writes that in the 1930s and 1940s the CCSS showed 'a marked independence of the Department of Education', by refusing to agree to a standardized entrance examination to secondary schools; the nuns claimed that this would be an undue interference in their schools.[27] Through the formal addresses and the discussions from the floor, the members of the CCSS were given a broad perspective on the educational concerns of the day; topics of philosophical, curricular and administrative interest were chosen both for presentation and discussion. In this way, the whole body of nuns who were involved in secondary education kept themselves abreast of educational matters, while at the same time they were building up, through the CCSS, an association which would be capable of negotiating with the Department of Education and others; not from the stand-point of any one religious order or congregation, but as a united body which had an informed collective opinion and was, as far as possible, of one mind about educational matters.

OLD AMBITIONS REAWAKENED

One of the subjects addressed by the CCSS in the early 1930s was the training of nuns as primary, secondary and domestic economy teachers. In fact, a ghost from the past reappeared in 1931 – the proposition of having a separate constituent college of the National University of Ireland, for nuns only, where the women religious upon graduation could take a course leading to a Higher Diploma in Education. The item appeared on the agenda of the CCSS at its annual general meetings in 1932 and 1933. The matter thus became not only part of the history of the Dominicans but also an issue for the CCSS. In those same years, the suggestion was also made that a new training college be opened in Galway, to train nuns as primary teachers. Again the Dominicans were approached, this time by the bishop of Galway, Dr O'Doherty. O'Neill cites the record of the – as yet inconclusive – opening moves:

[t]he bishop of Galway, Dr O'Doherty who is a friend of Mother Colmcille's, the Prioress General, was invited by her to visit Cabra when the question of the Training College, and his application to have the Dominican Congregation in charge, was discussed. No definite answer was given then.[28]

Taylor's Hill Convent had not at the time joined the new Cabra Congregation. When the officials in the Department of Education in Dublin realized this, they withdrew the invitation to the Dominicans to open the new college. No explanation was given for this withdrawal but it is likely that it came about because the Sisters of Mercy in Carysfort College, Dublin extended their accommodation for student-nuns and were then able to increase the number trained each year from twenty to fifty. In relation to the training of nuns as domestic economy teachers, in 1933, it was agreed between the Department of Education and the Dominicans that St Catherine's Domestic Science College, Sion Hill would enrol a class of student-nuns every three years. This minuted agreement was thus: '[a] group of twelve nuns may be taken every third year who must complete their three years course before another group is taken'.[29]

For years, the recurring debate about a separate university college for nuns as a constituent college of the National University of Ireland (NUI) under the management of the Dominicans in Eccles Street continued. The nuns had indeed never abandoned the idea and their hopes were that they would be able once more to take up university education, even if it were confined to a college for nuns. A typescript document in the CCSS archives, dated 11 October 1921, records the Dominicans' response to a bishops' circular on the training of sisters as teachers:

> [w]e propose that the professional training ... be obtained by attendance at St Dominic's Training College, Eccles Street which was established in 1907 with fullest sanction of Archbishop Walsh and [was given] recognition by Cambridge University Training Syndicate in 1909. ... Our Order is enclosed; the sisters are debarred from attendance at University College Dublin, and from the Higher Diploma in Education. We now propose to seek from NUI recognition of St Dominic's as a Recognised College with examinations the same as those of University College Dublin.[30]

The nuns promised in the same reply to run courses for religious instruction on lines laid down by the Institut des Hautes Etudes, Fribourg, Ecole de Formation Religieuse. Music, art and domestic science would be included in the curriculum. The Dominicans were willing to finance the college entirely from their own congregational resources and from the students' fees. Their document stated that all the bishops' questions 'which concern our work as a teaching order' were answered.

Another reference to a separate university college for nuns occurred in October 1928, when Mother Reginald Lyons in a letter to an unnamed bishop – probably Archbishop Byrne of Dublin – made the observation that the difficulty as set out was in finance, 'and for this the Dominican Congregation are prepared to be responsible'. The last mention of a separate university college was at the general chapter of the Congregation in 1934; the Dominicans were still seeking to have their own training college for nuns, stating the 'urgent and growing necessity of securing qualifications for our young sisters'. The reason given was that only fourteen postulants with university degrees out of a total of sixty-seven choir nuns had entered within the period 1929–34. Unlike the pre-amalgamation period, where each convent had to staff only its own schools, the new congregation now had an obligation to provide teachers for all the Dominican schools under its jurisdiction. Obviously, those without qualifications would require training. Mother Reginald reported that within those years (1929–34), 'unceasing efforts' had been made to obtain a recognized constituent university college or the recognition of a first year course done 'in our own house of studies'.[31]

The renewed request for a constituent college was not successful. In 1933 Mother Reginald had an interview with Professor Corcoran, SJ, of University College Dublin in which Corcoran pointed out that, following proposed future legislation in Dáil Eireann, University College, Dublin might lose a certain amount of autonomy. The university authorities were at that time 'unable to deal with other matters less pressing or momentous'.[32] This interview between Professor Corcoran and Mother Reginald Lyons is the last recorded reference to the Dominicans' seeking to set up a separate constituent college of the university for women including nuns. This constant return to 'lobbying' for a constituent college of the university shows the determination of the new general council of the congregation to keep control not only of their own schools, but also, if possible, of the third-level education of their young nuns. In this instance, though they had the backing of the CCSS in later years, they failed. In the 1940s, the rule of enclosure was modified to allow young Dominican nuns to live in Dominican Hall, St Stephen's Green, and attend University College, Dublin in order to study for degrees and the Higher Diploma in Education.

It is difficult to separate the interests of the Dominican Congregation, especially in the matter of teacher training at the time, from the interests of the whole body of nuns in Ireland. The Dominicans, recently amalgamated into a congregation, intent on observing the Dominican rule of enclosure to the full, pressed long and hard to have their own university college and campus. Their young nuns could then attend this college and not go outside the enclosure of the convent grounds. The CCSS continued to work for the good of all the teaching congregations and nothing that touched on the ministry of teaching was omitted from its deliberations. Meetings with the nuns' lay colleagues, through the Association of Secondary Teachers of Ireland (ASTI), became more frequent. Practical matters of common interest such as conditions of employment, draft form of contract and tenure of office of lay teachers were generally the subject of negotiation. Discussions between the ASTI and members of the CCSS touching on the profession of teaching were a common occurrence: a proposed council of education and changes in the secondary school programme are examples of some of the items which appeared on the agendas of the CCSS annual general meetings.

A later by-product of the CCSS was the formation of the Catholic Women's Federation (CWF), an association of the past-pupils' unions of the convent secondary schools of Ireland, whose object was developed from the early-twentieth-century concept of Catholic Action. The aim of the CWF was to involve the younger past pupils in voluntary social work for the poor, and the broader ideal of promoting,

> [t]he social and educational interests of women and [establishing] friendly relations with groups of women of other religious denominations. The Federation is affiliated to the National Women's Council of Ireland and the World Union of Catholic Women's Organisations.[33]

There is within that statement more than a hint of an ecumenical dimension to the work of the Catholic Women's Federation.

The formation of the CWF was a direct response to Pope Pius XI's call to Catholic Action in his encyclical letter *Non Abbiamo Bisogno*, or in its English language version, *Concerning Catholic Action*, which was published in 1931.[34] In an address given at the 1931 AGM of the Conference of Convent Secondary Schools, Canon MacMahon of Clonliffe College defined Catholic Action as

> the organised co-operation of priests and laity in the apostolate of the Church in the defence of religious and moral principles; the development of a sound social action under the guidance of the hierarchy and above all political parties so the Catholic life may be restored to individuals, to families and to society.[35]

From its beginning, the CCSS had as its aims the exchange of ideas and information on all matters relating to schools, in teaching, examinations, management and general organisation, and the provision of a forum where these ideas might be expressed. The natural development was interaction with others in the educational field, Church authorities, the Department of Education and teachers' unions. These objectives were achieved over the years. The path was not always smooth nor the encounters with their partners in education always amicable, but much was achieved by the Conference of Convent Secondary Schools until it and other similar organizations merged in the 1980s. The Dominican nuns are proud of the part they played in its beginnings and for many years afterwards, and of the influence they had through the Conference in furthering the course of Catholic education in Ireland. Eileen Doyle, in *Leading the Way*, has this to say:

> [t]he contribution of the Irish Dominican nuns to the education of girls and to the history of the CCSS was considerable. St Dominic's Training College was opened in the convent in Eccles Street in Dublin in 1909 and within twenty years more than 100 nuns from several congregations had been prepared for their teaching diplomas. Thus the Dominicans were highly regarded among the female teaching orders as leaders in education,

and when a managerial body for the voluntary secondary schools run by nuns was to be established, they were to the fore.[36]

After the formation of the Cabra Congregation of Dominican Sisters, a more unified approach was made to educational policy within the congregation itself. Annual meetings of the headmistresses of schools were held, but a marker was laid down in the first of these in January 1929. In the second session under the heading 'Educational Policy', the object was clearly stated:

> [t]o collect the accumulated experiences of all our schools and teachers, and from this common stock to select the most perfect manner and methods of imparting to the large body of people who go out from our schools the same principles by which we ourselves are animated.[37]

A warning was given against sudden or ill-considered changes including transplanting the customs of one house or school to another; unintelligent imitation of others in their ideas and methods, which could degenerate into mere competition with other schools, even their own. These warnings are fully in line with the Dominican ethos of respecting the individuality of people, having an independent approach to solving problems, and of being united in ideals, without imposing uniformity on the schools. Freedom was given to each school to continue its own approach, while keeping within the general policy of the congregation. This policy was stated as that of giving the pupils a broad all-round education; the subjects taught should be chosen for their formative and cultural value rather than for mere examination purposes. However, and in keeping with the climate of the times, what today would be considered a very unecumenical rule was laid down: 'the children attending our schools shall not be prepared for entrance to Protestant or non-Catholic Colleges, e.g. Trinity College'.[38]

In 1930 it was decided to set up a house of studies for the young nuns who had entered the congregation without any teaching qualifications. The object of the house of studies located in the convent in Sion Hill was to prepare the Sisters for entrance to either university or teacher training college. The necessity for such a house was of short duration and the courses there ended in 1934.[39] Here again, the motive for setting up a house of studies in Sion Hill at that time could be interpreted as the Dominicans once more hoping that such a house could later, perhaps, be recognized as a constituent college of the National University of Ireland. A further step in forwarding the educational thrust of the new congregation was the appointment of a directress general of studies. The directress of studies paid an annual visit to each school and, as a means of assessing standards, a single congregational examination was set, from 1935 for the congregation's private junior schools and from 1936 for first and second year pupils in the secondary schools. The policy of a congregational internal school examination did not last long; the Dominican tradition of each school's autonomy won out over the attempt at uniformity. Summer courses in Irish and science were organized for 'our young nuns', and it became common practice to allow the sisters to go to educational conferences and to take advantage of courses in further education both at home and abroad.

ALUMNAE OF DOMINICAN SCHOOLS AND COLLEGES

As with most educational institutions, Dominicans can claim to have educated many students with varied personalities, intellectual abilities, talents and gifts. Understandably many of the students who are best remembered are those whose talent and ability were outstanding, who became well-known in academic, literary or social circles and of whom some written records exist. One might make a judgement on the Dominican system of education using these as exemplars, but it must not be forgotten that many girls passed through who later lost touch with their friends and their old schools, but nevertheless personally lived very happy, quiet and contented lives. Some there are, undoubtedly, who may have seemed failures to many. It is to be hoped that these latter, whatever their difficulties, were helped along the road of life by their years in the Dominican schools. In the following paragraphs, some attempt is made to evaluate the schools as seen through the eyes of past-pupils or other commentators. Mary Macken in 'Women in the University and College' wrote,

> [i]n a fine pioneering spirit and at much sacrifice, the Dominican St Mary's College, accommodated since 1886 in the Eccles Street Schools, was transferred, under the famous Mother Patrick, to Merrion Square. ... The new college in Merrion Square soon made academic history, for, in ... one bare year after Junior Fellowships were first opened to competition, Mary T. Hayden won the Fellowship in English and History, and Katherine Murphy that in Modern Languages. Both gave St Mary's as their 'College', Mary, however, bracketing St Mary's and Private Study with Alexandra.[40]

Linking Alexandra with St Mary's University College in this way was a generous gesture by Mary Hayden and points to the reality of life for those who pursued the cause of university education for women. Protestant or Catholic, the women were at one in their desire to establish their right to equal status with the men students. While there was rivalry between the various women's colleges, there is evidence that Mother Patrick Sheil and Miss White, Lady Principal of Alexandra College, communicated amicably with each other on educational matters. The barriers between the Protestant schools and the nuns were slowly coming down, surely a good result of all the work which went into the cause of the higher education of women in Ireland.

Mary Hayden, Hanna Sheehy Skeffington, Norah Meade, Mary Jo McGrath, Annie Stone, Nora Monaghan, Louise Gavan Duffy, these are just seven names taken from the long list of young women who were past-pupils of St Mary's

University College. These particular ladies achieved much in the course of their lives; Mary Jo McGrath and Annie Stone as Dominican nuns, working in Eccles Street and Muckross Park respectively, Nora Monaghan as a Sister of Mercy, first Principal of the prestigious Preparatory College in Tourmakeady, Co. Mayo. Hanna Sheehy Skeffington was internationally famous for her championing of the right of women to vote, and suffered a gaol sentence in 1912 in Mountjoy for her activities in the Irish Women's Franchise League. Hanna's life was dedicated to questioning issues relating to 'socialism, nationalism and feminism in the first half of the [twentieth] century'.[41] Mary Hayden, also a campaigner for women's rights, co-founded the Irish Association of Women Graduates and later was a Senator of the National University of Ireland and Professor of History in University College, Dublin. Louise Gavan Duffy, an early convert to the ideals of the Gaelic League and those of Pádraig Pearse, founded Scoil Bhríde in St Stephen's Green in 1917, the first girls' Irish medium primary school in Dublin. Louise sat on the Gaelic League's executive council. Her part in the Easter Rising was, appropriately for a woman at that time, making tea upstairs in the GPO for the men, while Pearse and the Volunteers made war on the British army in O'Connell Street.

Nora Meade clashed with both Mary Hayden and Hanna Sheehy Skeffington on the question of separate colleges for women under-graduates. This controversy has been recorded in the previous chapter. Nora later became the first woman journalist on the staff of the *New York World*. Other past students took different paths in life: Mary Boardman ran a high school in Madras and became an inspector for the education authorities there. May Davoran, a non-graduate past-pupil, became a Trade Union official and activist. Margaret Burke Sheridan's career as an opera singer was launched from Eccles Street under the tuition of Mother Clement Burke, who herself had studied voice production in Germany. These women were outstanding as leaders and activists in many causes at a time when an independent Ireland was evolving.

There was a natural pull among these graduates towards the academic life, but how does one account for their involvement in the various campaigns for women's higher education, the vote, in trade unionism and other controversial movements? Perhaps the answer lies in a quotation from Eleanor Butler, a past pupil of Muckross Park:

> [t]he spirit of earnestness, calm and deep, of courage and generosity in the cause of better education of Catholic womanhood had been, and is, the moving spirit of Sion Hill. It had called Sion Hill into being, had drawn to its community a band of gifted and splendid women whose enthusiasm burned at white heat.[42]

Hanna Sheehy Skeffington recalled that her education in Eccles Street had given her 'great independence of thought and action'; Patricia Herbert, already quoted, spoke of the broad cultural education she received in Scoil Chaitríona, in which

18. Sr Stanislaus McCarthy, 1849–97

European languages and culture were included in the curriculum. Words such as 'energy, capability, spirit, sympathy' are used to define the human qualities of the nuns which made the schools places where the young women were encouraged to use their talents and gifts to the full. Mother Patrick Sheil, in St Mary's, is recognized as the moving spirit, the giant labourer who could find ways and means to carry every project into execution.

The Dominican spirit in the schools of the order is not easy to define. Sr Bede Kearns in an article in *The Lanthorn*, 'The Spirit of Eccles Street' wrote, 'it is easier to talk about the spirit of [a school], exemplifying it by memories and anecdotes, than to write an article in which it is defined and committed to cold print'.[43] Bede recorded the views of past pupils on their recollections of their school days: phrases and words serve better to give some sense of what being a Dominican pupil meant. 'A spirit of trust; magnanimity; practised rather than preached, manifested in a breadth of vision which looked beyond the here and now'; 'a great feeling of unity and encouragement from the older girls and especially from the community and teaching-staff'; 'enlightenment and kindness'; 'knowledge was made interesting and exciting and over-competitiveness was frowned upon'; 'a feeling that each one of us was an individual and treated as such'.

19. Sr Gonzales Stone 1867–1944

20. Unnamed graduate students, Muckross Park 1901–02

Sion Hill, Eccles Street, and particularly St Mary's University College have been singled out in this book, but the same could be said of the other Dominican schools. These three schools had the good fortune to have sufficient documented evidence to prove their case. In recent times, Mary McAleese, the present President of Ireland, and past pupil of St Dominic's, Falls Road, Belfast summed up her perception of Dominican education as she experienced it:

I owe an extraordinary debt of gratitude to those women; I acquired a lot of things at St Dominic's that have lasted with me. The world I grew up in was that women were circumscribed in terms of roles that they were permitted to play. But in this school [St Dominic's] things were different. We had very strong women, women who gave us a role model that in many ways contradicted the opportunities and systems we had come from. In their own quiet way, without ever preaching, they articulated a view of strong women ... women who were professional, women who were administrators, ... women who were opinionated. They were respected and one was aware of the respect, the awe in fact, by which they were held by so many civil servants and policy makers. These were women who contributed to the whole debate on education. ... We were ... among the first generation of young women [in Northern Ireland], who could legitimately hope to go out into the professions in large numbers. ... It was the nuns who encouraged us to have that vocation.[44]

President McAleese's words testify that the spirit which animated Mother Patrick Sheil and her contemporary Dominicans is evidently alive and alert in our day. The question could be posed: what if Mother Patrick and her colleagues had not provided the opportunity for higher education for the women of the 1880s in Dublin? The Loreto nuns in St Stephen's Green were there, ready, capable and willing to provide that service and the women would not have been denied access to further education. The fact is that both the Dominicans and the Loreto nuns were in Dublin and the Ursulines in Cork at a time when Catholic women were ready to take advantage of the colleges opened for them, and Ireland is the richer for having these Orders working, if not always together, then at least on parallel lines.

NOTES

1. Juvenal, *Satires 6,* 'Who will guard the Guardians?'
2. OPC, *Cabra Annals,* p.148.
3. OPGA, Etienne Rynne, *A Shrine of Celtic Art* (Dublin: private publication, n.d.), p.8.
4. OPGA, Illustration 12, S. McCarthy, *Songs of Sion,* (Dublin: Browne & Nolan, 1898).
5. OPE, *The Lanthorn,* Year Book of Dominican College, Eccles Street, Vol. 1, 1913 and following numbers.
6. OPG, 'The Training of sisters as Teachers'. Typescript of a paper drawn up in 1922.
7. A count was made of those who entered these three novitiates and whose names were recorded in *The Lanthorn,* the Year Book of Dominican College, Eccles Street, 1913–40, inclusive.
8. Anonymous, 'The Propitious Moment – Amalgamation', in *Weavings: Celebrating Dominican Women* (Dublin: Dominican Sisters, 1988), p.19.
9. L. Corr, *Dr. Finbar Ryan OP* in *Weavings,* p.23.
10. R. O'Neill, *A Rich Inheritance* (Galway: Dominican Sisters, 1994), p.191. On pp.176–97 Rose O'Neill gives a full account of the Taylor's Hill community's dilemma about the amalgamation of the Dominican convents in Ireland in 1928 and their decision to join the Congregation of Irish Dominican Sisters in 1970.

11. OPS, Minutes of Meeting of Dominican Headmistresses, Dominican College, Eccles Street, January 1929, p.3.
12. OPE, Syllabus, 'Dominican College, Eccles Street, Dublin, Summer Courses, July 1925'.
13. OPE, Syllabus, 'Summer Courses, July 1922'.
14. OPS, Letter of Mother Reginald to the prioresses of the Dominican convents, 1 May 1929.
15. Ibid.
16. CHA was founded in 1878 to be a voice for Catholic boys' schools and colleges. Eileen Doyle, *Leading the Way* (Dublin: Secretariat of Secondary Schools, 2000), pp.82 and following.
17. OPS, Mother Reginald, letter to Dominican convents, 1 May 1929.
18. Ibid.
19. SCSS, CCSS; 1929/30 file, Minutes of Meeting 17 May 1929.
20. SCSS, CCSS; 1929/30 file, Suggested General Agenda for the Meeting of Heads of Schools. Secondary Schools, 17 May 1929.
21. Ibid.
22. OPS, Minutes of meeting of CCSS, 1929.
23. SCSS, CCSS; 1929/30 file: Typescript notes of inaugural meeting 17 May 1929.
24. SCSS, CCSS; 1929/30 file: Copy of Mother Reginald's letter to convents in Northern Ireland.
25. Doyle, *Leading the Way,* p.90.
26. Ibid.
27. Ibid.
28. O'Neill, *A Rich Inheritance,* p.148.
29. T.A. Flynn, 'The Involvement of the Dominican Sisters of Sion Hill Convent in Third Level Education, with special reference to St Catherine's College of Domestic Science, 1929–1962' (unpublished Master's dissertation, University of Dublin, Trinity College, 1996), p.17.
30. SCSS, Typescript in the CCSS archives, in file dated 1929/30.
31. OPG, Acts of Second General Chapter 1934, sub-sections 17, 21, and 21(a)
32. SCSS, CCSS; 1933 Report of Annual General Meeting, 1933.
33. Dublin Diocesan Guidebook 2002 (Bray: Brendan Byrne and Associates, 2002). Note on the Catholic Women's Federation, p.221.
34. OPC, Pope Pius XI, Encyclical Letter, *Non Abbiamo Bisogno* (London: Catholic Truth Society, pamphlet H 207, 1931).
35. SCSS, CCSS; 1931 Report of Annual General Meeting; address of Canon MacMahon.
36. Doyle, *Leading the Way,* p.94.
37. OPS, Document, 'Minutes of Meeting of Dominican Headmistresses Held at Dominican College, Eccles Street, 13–14 January 1929', p.3.
38. OPG, Acts of the First General Chapter, 1928, sub-section 15 (b), (g).
39. OPSH, Document S.H.6/1–2b.
40. Mary M. Macken, 'Women in the University and College', in M. Tierney (ed.) *Struggle with Fortune* (Dublin: Browne & Nolan, 1954), pp.142–65, p.149.
41. M. Luddy, *Hanna Sheehy Skeffington,* (Dundalk: Dún Dealgan Press, Historical Association of Ireland *Life and Times Series* No. 5, 1995), p.53.
42. Transcript of Eleanor Butler's speech given at Past Pupils Reunion Day in Muckross Park, 16 February 1918.
43. Bede Kearns, OP, 'The Spirit of Eccles Street', *The Lanthorn,* Centenary Year, 1982, pp.29–33, pp.29, 31.
44. M. McAleese, 'President McAleese visits Villa Rosa', *Far and Near* (Dublin: Bulletin of Irish Dominican Province, June 1999), p.3.

5

Conclusion

We should have shrivelled up and died,
As wintered berries past their prime.[1]

The present group of women known familiarly as the 'Cabra Dominicans' could cite this couplet and apply it to themselves were their story but a recital of an institution's history. It is more than that: it is the story of the survival of an institution in which successive generations of women dedicated their lives to follow the call of the Gospel, 'come follow me' and, in that following, engage in the ministry of teaching.[2] There was ample cause for our forebears to shrivel up and die: their early seventeenth and eighteenth-century history was a succession of alternate times of despair and hope, as religious persecution in the era of the Penal Laws swung intermittently between relentless priest-hunting and periods of dubious toleration. Later generations of Dominican women in the late eighteenth and early nineteenth centuries could also have shrivelled up as 'wintered berries past their prime', this time through poverty, harsh application of the law, old age, and a serious fall in the number of new members joining the order.

The year 1820 was chosen as a key moment for a starting point because the move from Clontarf to St Mary's Dominican Convent, Cabra, Dublin in December 1819, was a new beginning. The nuns who arrived in Cabra from Clontarf had personally survived the hardships and poverty of their time both in Clontarf and, before that, in Channel Row. The story is confined to the Dominicans' educational work in Ireland and its object is to discover what, if any, contribution the Dominicans made to education, particularly to the education of girls in the country from 1820–1930. All sectors of educational work were explored and it was not always an easy path to follow.

It must be kept in mind that Columba Maher, the prioress, had in December 1819 only four companions, one a novice, when they arrived from Clontarf to their new convent in Cabra. The nuns had few resources; their house had been bought by the sale of debentures, which left the nuns with very little money either in the form of investment income or earned income. This was the financial situation of the five nuns when they began their ministry to the poor children of the area; their first school a poor school. This was new and unexplored educational territory for women of an Anglo-Irish background but who were now poor themselves, few in number, ageing, and with an uncertain future before them. It soon became clear to Columba Maher that the community's presence in Cabra was of very little significance to the authorities in the archdiocese of Dublin. This led to the momentous decision to apply for their transfer from the jurisdiction of the Master General of the Dominican Order to that of the Archbishop of Dublin, Daniel Murray; a decision interpreted by some as a betrayal of the Dominican way of life. Whatever criticism the nuns received for their action, it is clear that the archbishop's support helped to stabilize the community. In 1841 their school was connected with the Stanley system of national schools, the numbers in the community increased and the nuns opened a boarding school which in time became one of the leading schools of its kind in the country. Archbishop Murray was very much involved with the Stanley system of national school education, and it must surely have been at his suggestion that the nuns applied to have their poor school connected to the scheme.

As the century moved on, in 1847 in the later stage of the Great Famine, Mother Columba Maher also committed her community to the education of deaf girls. St Mary's School for the Deaf, Cabra was in time internationally acclaimed as having special expertise in this branch of education. Cabra's success as educators and their particular way of religious life drew a further increase in postulants. The increased numbers in the community allowed the nuns to make foundations, not only in Mount Street, Kingstown and Belfast, but also in South Africa, Australia and New Orleans. These foundations were always at the invitation of the local bishop or of someone acting in his name. The invitations were a sign that the nuns' work as educators was well regarded and their way of life had the approval of the hierarchy.

In the primary sector, six national schools were under Dominican management: this number is small, considering that there were, in all, thirteen Dominican communities running schools during all or part of this period. In the mid-nineteenth century three schools closed: Siena Convent, Drogheda; Taylor's Hill, Galway; and St Mary's Convent, Cabra, Dublin. All three were in difficulties with the Board of Education. Was this a failure on the part of the nuns who were responsible for the schools' management? The research evidence shows that in two cases out of three, the inspectors reported that the standard of teaching was low, there was poor attendance, and in one case even the standard of hygiene was bad. A mitigating factor for the nuns in Siena Convent was that the poor attendance of pupils was due to the poverty of the families and the lack of clothing for the children. In Taylor's Hill, Galway, the nuns themselves were in poor health and few in number. Cabra's closure was on a point of principle: the manager, Mother Catherine (de Ricci) Maher, refused to interpret in a strict manner the law relating to prayer during the period of secular teaching. Cabra's closure lasted for twenty-five years, but the school was re-admitted to the national school system with what amounted to a retreat by Mother Catherine Maher. She not only verbally promised to obey the rules in future, but was obliged to put her promise in writing.

While accepting that these were reasonable explanations of the closure of the schools, we also became aware that the nuns in Taylor's Hill opened a private fee-paying junior school about this time. It seems strange that the nuns, while pleading lack of personnel to teach in the national school, were able to staff the private fee-paying junior school. The real reason may have been that the income from the fee-paying school might have been greater than that from the national school and the nuns had no other means of livelihood. On the whole, looking at the question of Dominican national schools over the span of 100 years, it seems that the Dominicans' preference was for private fee-paying junior schools, as being more in their tradition. There were exceptions for families in straightened financial circumstances who attended these junior schools, but the schools were certainly perceived to be for families who were relatively well-off.

Another area in which the Dominicans had difficulties was with their industrial classes in national schools. Industrial classes were for children who did not have the opportunity of secondary education and were taught a trade, mainly needlework and the use of sewing machines. In the case of Dominican schools the industrial classes were attached to the national school and did not have a boarding section. Kingstown school was the most successful; its industrial class survived for many years. The experiment in Sion Hill in the 1860s is both surprising and puzzling. Here, there seems to have been a conflict about the preferred type of school with which the community felt comfortable and, again, the fee-paying junior day school won the day.

The support for this theory depends on an interpretation of the *Sion Hill Annals*. It has to be admitted that the nuns attempted to provide for the poorer section of the population, and while the good-will of some of the community was there, good-will alone is not sufficient to make a successful, viable school. There was need for a cooperative effort from the whole community and on the evidence, this would not have been forthcoming. Another factor which may have influenced the Sion Hill nuns at this time was the presence of a community of Sisters of Mercy in the parish of Booterstown, who were running a very good national school close by. While researching this episode of the poor school with an industrial bias, it was surprising to find that many of the Sisters now living had never heard of this attempt to open a poor school. Is this a sign of inherited collective amnesia?

St Mary's School for Deaf Girls was unique in that it was a pioneering work for the Dominicans who, since 1847, continue to educate girls with hearing impairment. From the beginning the nuns insisted on having the requisite training, and made a determined effort to acquire the specialist skills which were necessary for success. Going abroad to France at a time of hardship and famine in Ireland meant that Sisters Magdalen and Vincent, the two pioneers in the work, had to rely on the money collected by Fr McNamara to finance their journey. St Mary's School for Deaf Girls was one centre where the industrial training was very successful. The vocational department, as it was called, opened in 1863 when lace-making, dress-making, tailoring and embroidery were introduced.

A more contentious decision was that taken about oralism. A congress for teachers of the deaf in Milan in 1880 called on all schools for the deaf to introduce oralism, that is, the teaching of lip-reading and speech for those children who could benefit from new methods. No one from Cabra attended that congress but there must have been some discussion about its findings, because it was decided that St Mary's School for the Deaf should follow a strictly manual approach to language development. Why were there no representatives from Cabra attending the Milan conference? There is no reference to it in the Cabra annals and history does not record the reason for this decision by the Dominicans. The challenge came years later, in the 1950s, when parents demanded that the method of teaching the children to communicate using only sign-language was no longer adequate for their deaf children's future. In 1930, the closing date of this study, manual communication was the only method in use in St Mary's School; the older girls' opportunity for future employment was in the trades areas of dress-making, embroidery and machine sewing or in domestic service.

The struggle with lack of money and personnel which had dogged the nuns' early years in the 1820s and 1830s gave way to change, a change marked by a blossoming out from the Cabra, Sion Hill and Kingstown communities, those new foundations already mentioned. In these new convents in Ireland, the nuns carried on the teaching tradition of the Galway and Siena convents, Channel Row and Cabra. In the mid-nineteenth century the emphasis was on the education of the young lady, already treated of at length. The Dominican boarding schools of the era were no different from any others in their curricular choices. The advertisements placed in the *Catholic Directories* of the mid-nineteenth century prove this. Dominicans like to think that any differences there may have been lay in the spirit of the Dominican schools.

The big challenge came with the introduction of the Intermediate Education (Ireland) Act of 1878. To enter students for the examinations, or not, was the big question which many found difficult to answer. The weight of public opinion was not in favour of the new system and some bishops added their voices against the examination system for girls. Here again, we see the Sion Hill nuns making another effort to break through the prejudices of the day, this time successfully. The Sion Hill community was the first Dominican community to accept that the time for change had come. Not only did they welcome the examination system, they also launched a new foundation in Eccles Street, originally thought to be for orphaned girls whose parents had lost the means of providing for their future. Very quickly Mother Patrick Sheil accepted the idea of public examinations and successfully set about creating a school where girls would, with deliberate intent, be prepared for the Intermediate examinations of the Board of Education. Mother Patrick had exceptional qualities which fitted her for this new approach to education and she led the Dominicans along the way. In Chapter 2 it was shown how the community in Sion Hill was enthusiastic about the new programmes and examinations begun by the Board of Education, but were not immediately encouraged by the Archbishop of Dublin to pursue the matter.

The parents of the majority of pupils in Sion Hill were in agreement with the archbishop and did not wish to have their daughters enter for the examinations. When the opportunity arose to open a house in Eccles Street, did Mothers Antonina and Patrick set their hearts on proving that this new foundation would benefit the pupils best, if they were given the chance to study for the Intermediate examinations? The nuns were aware of the climate of opinion which looked to the day when young women could attend university and educate themselves for the professions. Though not taking any active part in the public debate about higher education for women, they surely had a very deep interest in the outcome. This new school would give the nuns the opportunity to break down the prejudices which were behind the parents' thinking. Dominican College Eccles Street with its success in the examinations and its university classes in Eccles Street, was the first Catholic girls' school to provide suitable university courses. The girls entered for the examinations of the Royal University with acclaimed success. This was undoubtedly a great break-through for the education of Catholic girls in Ireland because the Eccles Street pupils came not only from the city of Dublin, but there were boarders in the school from all parts of the country.

Mother Patrick and her companions failed in their attempt in 1909 to have St Mary's University recognized as a constituent college of the new National University of Ireland, but it is doubtful if in their hearts the Dominicans were convinced that women's colleges were the best solution for the university education of their students. The evidence given on the Dominicans' behalf to the Robertson Commission by Mary Hayden makes that clear. Why then, did the nuns try so hard to gain recognition for their own college? If the Loreto Sisters were to gain this recognition and not the Dominicans, Mother Patrick and her community would have been aggrieved. The question of cooperation between the two orders seems not to have been given serious consideration, or if it had been given, I have found no evidence to prove it. The oral testimony of Sr Cajetan tells us that Mother Patrick 'suffered greatly in her old age about the university question'. What a pity that she who had done so much for women's education should have had this gnawing grief.

Two teacher training colleges were added to the Dominican group of schools and colleges in the period 1900–09: St Mary's Training College for national school teachers in Falls Road, Belfast and St Dominic's Training College for secondary teachers in Eccles Street, Dublin. St Mary's was part of the national government scheme to supply trained teachers who were in short supply in primary schools throughout the country. For Mother Francis Kennedy and her staff in Belfast this too was unknown ground but they accepted the challenge and carried through a very successful college. St Dominic's Training College for graduates who wished to become teachers in secondary schools was launched by Mother Peter McGrath in cooperation with Mother Patrick in 1909. This college was a logical outcome to the university classes; most of the students graduated with a BA degree and for women in the late nineteenth and early twentieth centuries, teaching was one of the few options open to them. Success in teaching meant having a post-graduate course in the theory and practice of education. St Dominic's College was housed in Eccles Street and added to the long line of buildings in Dominican ownership which formed the streetscape until the late 1980s. These two colleges were very much a part of the Dominican nuns' efforts to cover all the sectors in the education of young women, from primary schools to third level. It showed the commitment which the nuns brought to their ministry in education. While the group of schools and colleges in Eccles Street gained a nationwide reputation for outstanding work in the field of women's education, the other Dominican schools accepted the Intermediate examinations in time and all offered the advantages of recognized national certification for their pupils.

The unforeseen result of the Dominicans' work in education in the early years of the twentieth century was the formation of summer-schools for nuns begun by Mother Reginald Lyons. The summer-school obviously was the seed of the future Conference of Convent Secondary Schools. The work of the Conference was of immediate benefit to all the convent schools in Ireland, which chose to become members. From that Conference sprang the power to negotiate with the other bodies involved in education and to bring the influence of the vast body of women religious who taught in secondary schools to bear on all aspects of education. The Conference of Convent Secondary Schools was recognized and respected by the hierarchy, the Department of Education and the professional associations of lay teachers. Other orders and congregations shared in the policy-making and administration of the Conference and from its annual general meetings, a bond was thus formed between congregations, which helped to give the group a unity and strength which individual convents could never have achieved.

To conclude this chapter, one can only take an overall view of these 'medieval nuns' who had come to Cabra in 1819, few in number, short in resources, uncertain of their future. From the group of five led by Columba Maher in 1819 to a thriving congregation of Dominicans with twelve convents and schools attached in 1930, was a mighty leap. No one in Mother Columba's group could have imagined such a transformation. In the intervening years the Dominican nuns had their failures, their aborted attempts to help the less fortunate in society, but they also had their glory days, when they succeeded and were proud to be one of the agencies which brought the education of women from the gentility of the drawing-room to the classrooms and academic lecture-halls of schools and colleges. They pioneered Catholic education for deaf girls, supported the thrust towards the revival of the national language in Scoil Chaitríona, and initiated in 1930 in north Belfast a school with a commercial and academic programme to suit the needs of the time. St Dominic has as one of his titles *Lucerna Christi*, the lantern or lanthorn of Christ. The Cabra Dominican nuns and their descendants battled through poverty, uncertainty and closure of schools, to emerge once again and be a lanthorn through which the Christian message of the truth of the Gospel would shine in all their schools throughout the country. To take up the theme of survival from Nancy Williams,

> We overflow with secret sap,
> We are the bearers of the seed.
> We endure by our consent,
> We mid-wife to each other's dawns and dusks.[3]

This is of course the *raison d'être* of Dominican ministry.

NOTES

1. Williams, N. and Roach, J., 'Survival', *Whooping Crones, God Songs for Women* (Springfield, Oregon: Catherine Joseph Publications, 1996), p.27.
2. *New Testament,* Matthew 4:19.
3. Williams, 'Survival', (adapted), p.27.

Appendix 1

Dates and locations
Dominican convents in Ireland
(See also Maps 1 and 2 pp. ii and 39)

Date	Location	Comments
1644	Galway	1717 A group moved to Dublin
1717–1808	Channel Row, Dublin	Moved to Clontarf in 1808
1722	Siena Convent, Drogheda (School 1722–1930)	In 1930, Siena Dominican nuns became a contemplative community and closed the school
1808–1819/20	Clontarf, Dublin	Moved to Cabra in December 1819
1819/20	Cabra, Dublin	
1836–1840	39, Lr Mount Street, Dublin	Moved to Sion Hill in 1840
1840	Sion Hill, Blackrock, Co. Dublin	
1842–67	Usher's Quay, Dublin	Convent closed in 1867. School given over to and amalgamated with Kingstown
1847	Kingstown/Dún Laoghaire	
1870	Falls Road, West Belfast	
1870	Wicklow	
1882–1984	Eccles Street, Dublin. 1. Dominican College 1882–1984 2. Scoil Chaitríona 1928–72 3. Commercial College 1930–78	St Mary's University College moved to 28 Merrion Square 1893. 1. Convent and Dominican College moved, 1984 to 204 Griffith Ave. 2. Moved, 1972 to Mobhi Road. 3. Closed in 1978
1893–1900	St Mary's University College and High School, 28, Merrion Square, Dublin	Convent closed 1900. University classes moved to Muckross Park
1900	Muckross Park, Donnybrook, Dublin	St Mary's University College 1900 and returned to Eccles Street 1903
1912–2005	Sutton, Co. Dublin	Convent closed 2005. School still in operation
1917–1999	Portstewart, Co. Derry	Convent closed in 1999. School still in operation
1930	Fortwilliam Park, North Belfast	

Appendix 2

Notice of foundation of institute for education of orphan girls in Eccles Street, Dublin

INSTITUTION

FOR

𝔉ree 𝕮atholic 𝕰ducation

FOR THE ORPHAN GIRLS OF

𝕿he 𝖀pper and 𝕸iddle 𝕮lasses

(THE FIRST ESTABLISHED IN DUBLIN)

𝖀nder the 𝕻atronage of

HIS EMINENCE THE CARDINAL ARCHBISHOP OF DUBLIN
THE MARCHIONESS OF LONDONDERRY
THE COUNTESS OF GRANARD
THE LADY O'HAGAN
THE LADY FRENCH
THE LADY NUGENT, Ballinlough Castle
THE LADY DE VERE
THE LADY NETTERVILLE
THE LADY O'DONNELL
THE HON. MRS O'HAGAN.

In our dear Catholic Ireland, here especially in this City of Dublin, the just rights of the poor have ever been fully recognised.

Open any Directory, and glance at the long lists of Catholic Charitable Institutions, see the numerous Orphanages – the Asylums for Deaf Mutes – the Blind, etc. all amply sufficient to prove how well our fellow citizens have entitled themselves to a share in that benediction promised to those who "understand concerning the needy and the poor".

But there is another class for whom as yet no special provision has been made in this City – the poor, not by birth, but by misfortune – the Orphan Children of respectable parents. In the upper and middle classes, amongst our friends and intimates, which of us has not known cases where a Father and Mother dying, and leaving their little ones unprovided for, had to look forward to the time when those children, so tenderly and carefully nurtured, would have to depend on the charity of strangers and perhaps be placed in Orphanages destined only for the lower classes, and thus lose that position in society to which birth entitled them.

What a blessing for such parents in their last moments, could they hope that friends were at hand to act as parents to those children, to educate them in a manner suitable to their birth, while at the same time enabling them to support themselves hereafter in a respectable manner.

Some such considerations as the above have led to a general desire for the establishment of a Catholic Institution for the Free Education of the Orphan Girls of respectable parents. No such Institution exists in Ireland.

The Christian Brothers, and the O'Brien Foundation, have done much to supply this want as regards Boys; it is needless to refer to the numerous advantages which the Protestant minority enjoys in this respect, for Catholic Orphan Girls of the class above named nothing has as yet been done.

These words are printed in the hope that they may meet the eyes of some generous and wealthy person able and willing to assume the honourable post of Founder. Once established, there are very many who will be delighted to aid and further this most deserving charity. The project has been laid before the Cardinal Archbishop, who has given it his blessing and warm approval, declaring it much needed, especially as a counterpoise to the numerous Free Protestant Institutions now existing.

Intending benefactors are invited to lay their views before His Eminence the Cardinal Archbishop of Dublin, or the Very Rev. Canon Farrell, P.P. Booterstown, who will receive and attend to such communications.

A leading Educational Establishment in the Dublin diocese, long convinced of the urgent necessity existing for a Foundation similar to that herein projected, is willing to assume its organisation and direction, when set on foot.

Appendix 3

Dominican Orphanage

OF

OUR LADY OF SION,
18 & 19 ECCLES STREET,
DUBLIN.

The premises Nos. 18 and 19 Eccles Street were purchased in December, 1882, by one of the most charitable of our citizens, for the purpose of establishing an Orphanage for the maintenance, education, and advancement in life of the orphan daughters of parents of the mercantile, professional, or private gentlemen class, who have seen better days, and were, by reverse of fortune, left without the means of maintaining themselves or providing for their children.

The main object of the Orphanage is to impart to the girls received into it an education similar to that of the higher class educational establishments, and to give a thorough and special training for the important duties of governesses. Such of the girls received into it as show no aptitude for teaching, are trained for the industrial and civil posts open to females.

The Orphanage is under the management of the Nuns of the Dominican Order, who reside in the Orphanage, superintend and manage it gratuitously. The Orphanage has no fund for its maintenance, and depends altogether for its support on the contributions of the charitable. The only means which the Nuns have of supplementing the contributions of the charitable are the emoluments arising from a Day School conducted by them.

Children suitable for admission to the Orphanage are selected by the Nuns, a preference being given to the most deserving objects, and those recommended by persons giving an annual donation of not less than £20 towards the support and maintenance of the Orphanage.

The Orphanage is under the patronage of:

His Eminence the Cardinal Archbishop of Dublin.

The Holy Sacrifice of the Mass will be offered on the first Friday of every month and daily prayers by the Community and Orphans for our Benefactors, living and dead.

Appendix 4

Copy of Letter from Archdeacon MacMahon, Vicar General
Archdiocese of Dublin
to
Mother Antonina Hanley
Prioress, Dominican Convent Eccles Street
26 April 1883.

St. Michan's
April 26th/83

Dear Sr. M. Antonina,

I got your kind note on Monday morning and would have acknowledged it at once only as usual one thing or another continually interfered.

I am sure you did not intend to add to my burdens and even tho' you did I would willingly bear them if I thought they were expedient, but that is the point we differ on.

I told you as well as I could my reasons for not wishing to mix myself up with your projects. It is not any dislike to yourselves or to your Institution.

I am sure you never intended nor would wish to Interfere with any other Community or Institution. But indirectly I fear you will – a great number of the class you contemplate are the very class which make up St. Joseph's – and if you take them for what that Institution asks and strives to get tho' alas it is too often disappointed, don't you think that the friends of the applicant would naturally think to get them into what they consider the more respectable school? And thus St. Joseph's would be deprived of that support which would help and enable them to admit others, 'tho deserving who could pay nothing. If you had part of Miss O'Brien's Bequest – a funded sum at your back – then indeed you might and should undertake, tho' very prudently, such an undertaking.

But the moment you come into the Parish to set out with an appeal – I don't think it wise as I said. I fear it would injure your day school. Why, if it goes abroad that yours is only a higher class of orphanage, I don't know would the people be so ready to send their children or go to other places.

There are so many orphanages already in the Parish that I really tremble at the idea of another. It may be all very good at the start, but believe me, costs very much as it goes along. Be wise, be prudent, let your day school take root.

You will meet no doubt, as you go along, with children of that class you are intended for. You will do the best you can for them but don't implicate yourselves.

You remember I said this from the very beginning of this work. I spoke it and wrote it to Mother Clare and to every Sister I spoke to on the subject. So you must see I am not inconsistent or variable in my opinion.

I _wish_ you _well_. I will and must _pray_ for you as portion of my flock – you know I blessed your house – even in a deluge – I hope the dews of heaven will descend on it and that it will be for years to come a holy Sion in the Parish of Saint Michan and St. Joseph.

With kindest regards to the Sisters
Believe me,
Yours sincerely in J.C.
J. McMahon P.P.
Archdeacon.

Appendix 5

St Mary's University College Prospectus

St Mary's University College

AND
High School
28, MERRION SQUARE, NORTH,

Conducted by the Dominican Sisters.

FOUNDED 1893 FOR THE HIGHER EDUCATION OF LADIES,

UNDER THE PATRONAGE OF
HIS GRACE THE MOST REV. DR WALSH, Archbishop of Dublin.
COLLEGE COUNCIL;

President – His Grace the Most Rev. Dr Walsh, *Archbishop of Dublin.*

Members of the Senate of the Royal University of Ireland

The Most Rev. J Healy, D.D. LL.D., *Coadjutor Bishop of Clonfert*

The Right Hon. Christopher Palles, LL.D., *Lord Chief Baron of the Exchequer of Ireland, Commissioner of Intermediate Education in Ireland.*

The Right Hon. The O'Conor Don, LL.D., *Commissioner of Intermediate Education in Ireland*

The Right Hon. Christopher T. Redington, M.A. D.L., *Vice-Chancellor Royal University of Ireland.*

The Right Rev. Mgr. Molloy, D.D. D.Sc., *Rector of the Catholic University of Ireland*
The Rev. William Delany, SJ, LL.D.

Francis R. Cruise, Esq., M.D.

Sir Christopher J. Nixon, M.D. LL.D.

Edmund Dease, Esq., M.A., D.L.

Commissioners of Education in Ireland.

The Most Rev. R. Browne, D.D., *Bishop of Cloyne*

Richard Paul Carton Esq., Q.C.

Heads, &c., of Colleges and Schools.

The Most Rev. N. Donnelly, D.D., *Bishop of Canca, Vice-President, Royal Irish Academy of Music, Dublin.*

The Very Rev. Robert Carbery, SJ., *President, University College, St. Stephen's Green, Dublin.*

The Very Rev. J. Botrel, C.S.Sp., *President, University College, Blackrock, Dublin.*

The Very Rev. Peter Byrne, C.M., *President, St. Patrick's College, Drumcondra, Dublin.*

The Very Rev. Thomas Hardy, C.M., *President, St. Vincent's College, Castleknock, Dublin.*

The Very Rev. J.A. Moran, S.M., *President, Catholic University School, Leeson Street, Dublin.*

The Rev. T. Finlay, SJ M.A., F.R.U.I., *University College, St. Stephen's Green, Dublin.*

The Rev. Richard Bodkin, C.M., *St. Vincent's College, Castleknock, Dublin.*

The Rev. H. O'Toole, C.S.Sp., *Dean of Studies, University College, Blackrock, Dublin.*

The Rev. L. Healy, C.S.Sp., *Dean of Studies, Blackrock College, Dublin.*

Prospectus

ST MARY'S UNIVERSITY COLLEGE AND HIGH SCHOOL has been founded for the purpose of affording Catholic Ladies complete facilities for Higher Education in all its branches. In the College, Students will be prepared in all the subjects included in the Intermediate and University Programmes. No public examinations, however, will be compulsory. Students can make their own choice among the various subjects included in the College Course and there will be provided a well-organised system of College Examinations, by which their success in study can be efficiently tested.

The College Curriculum will include the ordinary subjects of the Intermediate and University Courses; and, in addition, Music – Instrumental and Vocal and the other subjects indicated in detail further on. Students who have made a Two Years' Course at the College, and have satisfied the examiners as to their proficiency, will be awarded a College Certificate.

The teaching Staff will consist of distinguished Graduates of the Royal University, and of eminent Professors; also of members of the Dominican Community, whose success as teachers has been so amply demonstrated by the results of the Intermediate and Royal University Examinations for the last eight years. The Assistant Staff will include a number of former Students of the College who have distinguished themselves most highly during their College Course, and have been especially successful at the Intermediate and University Examinations.

The general course of studies in the College will be directed by the College Council, composed of University Graduates, and gentlemen of distinguished position in the educational world, under the presidency of his Grace the Archbishop of Dublin.

There will be a Tutorial Committee consisting of the principal members of the Teaching Staff, who will form a deliberative Council to advise regarding all details of the teaching work of the College. For Catholic Students an advanced course of Religious Instruction will form a very important part of the programme.

SUBJECTS OF COLLEGE LECTURES

Religious Knowledge
Arithmetic and Book-keeping
Celtic Language, Literature and History
Chemistry
Dancing and Calesthenics
Drawing – Freehand and Model
  in Light and Shade, from Casts
  and Models
Education, Theory and Practice of
Elocution
English Language and Literature
French Language and Literature
German Language and Literature
Geography, Physical, Political,
  Historical
Greek Language and Literature
History, Ancient and Modern
Hygiene

Italian Language and Literature
Languages (Comparative Study of)
Latin Language and Literature
Logic
Mathematics –
  Algebra, Trigonometry, Geometry
Music, Instrumental and Vocal
Natural Science, Botany, Geology,
  Zoology
Painting in Oils and Watercolour
Perspective
Philosophy, Mental and Moral
Physiology
Physics, Mathematical and
  Experimental
Political Economy
Shorthand and Type-writing
Spanish Language and Literature

PROFESSORS AND LECTURERS

Rev. E. Delany SJ, LL.D.
C. Doyle Esq. M.A., F.R.U.I.
P. Gavin, Esq. M.A., R.U.I.
V. Steinberger, Esq. M.A., F.R.U.I.
A. W. Cerf, Esq., M.A., T.C.D.
J. Gibney, Esq. M.A. (University
  Student-Gold Medallist) R.U.I.
P.A.E. Dowling, Esq. B.A., R.U.I.
W. Magennis Esq. M.A.
  (University Student) F.R.U.I.
Robert Donovan, Esq. B.A., R.U.I.
W.P. Coyne, Esq. M.A., R.U.I.
Hugh O'Donohoe B.A., R.U.I.
J.W. Bacon, Esq., B.A. R.U.I.
M.J. Conran
J. Smeeth, Esq.

Monsieur Loup
Signor Esposito
Signor Papini
Brendan Rogers, Esq. Organist,
  Pro-Cathedral, Marlborough Street.
Jos. Robinson, Esq. R.I.A.M.
Miss O'Hea
Mlle. Decoudin
Miss Mary O'Hea.
Miss Hayden, M.A., R.U.I.
Miss Murphy M.A. (Student), R.U.I.
Mme Leggett-Byrne
Mr Clarke (Drill Sergeant)
The Members of the Community of
  St Mary's University College

Bibliography

PRIMARY SOURCES

Manuscripts and archival material

National Library of Ireland (NLI)
Kildare Street, Dublin 2

Larcom Papers: Ms. 7649, 7650, 7651,
Collection of newspaper clippings on Irish affairs, nineteenth century.
Sheehy-Skeffington Papers:
Ms 24164, Transcript of Radio Interview, 1940s. No date given: Hannah Sheehy Skeffington with Dr Dixon.
Ms. 33,603 (4), Correspondence: Hannah Sheehy Skeffington and Mother Patrick Sheil Dominican Convent Eccles Street, 1904.
Ms. PO3, 9145, M. Hayden, *Diary*, Feb. 1896.

National Archives of Ireland, Bishop Street, Dublin 8 (NAI)

Files relating to National Schools.
ED1/28, Dominican Convent, Cabra Convent School.
ED1/29, Dominican Convent, Cabra Female School.
ED1/30, Dominican Convent, Cabra School.
ED1/32, Dominican Convent School, Cabra.
ED1/34, No. 87, Dominican Convent School, Taylor's Hill, Galway.
ED1/58 No. 103, Dominican Convent School, Siena, Drogheda., Co. Louth.
ED1/97 No. 33, Dominican Convent School, Wicklow.
ED2/15 Folio 145, Dominican Convent School, Cabra.
ED2/121 Folio 93, Dominican Convent School, Cabra.
ED2/104 Folio 92, Dominican Convent School, Siena, Drogheda.
ED2/136, Folio 84, Dominican Convent School, Taylor's Hill, Galway.
ED9 File 5235, Dominican Convent School, Kingstown (Dún Laoghaire).
ED9 File 15029, Dominican Convent School, Kingstown.
ED9 Folio 92, Dominican Siena Convent, Drogheda.
Chief Secretary's Office, Registered Papers (CSORP), Dublin, Letter from Sir Daniel Harrel to Treasury, Whitehall.
Chief Secretary's Office Registered Papers (CSORP), Letter of Bishop O'Dwyer to Commissioners of Education, October 1896.

Dublin Diocesan Archives (DAA)
Archbishop's House, Drumcondra, Dublin 9

Archbishop Daniel Murray Papers 1823–52.
Archbishop Paul Cullen Papers 1852–78.
Archbishop Edward McCabe Papers 1878–85.
Archbishop William Walsh Papers: 1885–1921.
Archbishop Edward Byrne Papers. 1921–40.

Archives, University College Dublin
Belfield, Dublin 4 (AUCD)

GV 2/1 Minute Book of Governing Body, University College, Dublin, 1910/11.
NUWAG 1/1 Newspaper cuttings – death of Hanna Sheehy Skeffington.
NUWAG 1/3 National Association of Women Graduates and Candidate Graduates,
    Minute Book, January 1902.
NUWAG 2/1 Minute Book, National Association of Women Graduates 1912.

Archives, Mary Immaculate College, Limerick (MIUC)

Mary Immaculate Training College, Limerick, College Annual 1927 and
    following years.
Report of Commissioners of National Education, No. 69, 1902 (Dublin: HMO,
    1903).

Dominican Archives

NOTE: Except in the case of the Dominican Generalate and the Dominican Irish
Region House, which are placed first and second in the following list of Archives,
all other Dominican Convent archives and collections are in alphabetical order of
postal areas.

1847–1960s of the Kingstown (Dún Laoghaire) convent. The Portstewart
convent is now closed. All available archival material from the foundation of the
school in 1917 to the closure of the convent in the 1990s is also held in the Irish
Region archives. More recent school archives are held in Dominican College,
Portstewart, Co. Derry. Due to change of location, none of these archives have
to date been classified.

Irish Dominican General Archives (OPG)
Contact address: General Archivist, Dominican Sisters, 5 Westfield Rd., Dublin
    6W, Ireland.

Constitutions of the Congregation of Dominican Sisters, Cabra, Dublin (Private
    publication 1947).
Register of St Mary's University College and High School 1893–1912.
P. Flynn, *Dominican Ideals in Education*, (pamphlet, private publication, no date).

OPG
Box D1/1
Letters: Oscar Browning to M. Peter McGrath Eccles Street, September 1904 and 1907.

Letter: Archbishop Walsh to M. Peter McGrath, n.d.

Letter: M. Augustine Clinchy, to Archbishop Walsh 15 November 1907.

Box E/7
Letter: Mary Hayden to Mother Gonzales Stone, Dominican Convent, Eccles Street, 28 May 1911.

Documents: Formal applications to University College Dublin for recognition of St Mary's University College as a constituent college for women.

Letter: Archbishop Walsh to M. Augustine Clinchy, Sion Hill Convent, 31 May 1908.

Letter: Oscar Browning to prioress of Dominican Convent, Eccles Street, 13 March 1909.

Box E7/1:
Letters: Archbishop Walsh to various Dominican prioresses and others, relating to educational matters 1893–94.

Box E7/2:
Minutes of meeting of college council of St Mary's University College, December 1894.

Box E7/21–36:
Letter of Archbishop Walsh to Mother Patrick, 4 July 1910.

Letters: Archbishop Walsh and Mother de Ricci Harkin, 19 October 1911.

Undated letter: Mother de Ricci Harkin to prioress of Sion Hill Convent.

Box E7/22:
Undated, unsigned, copy of circular letter to benefactors of St Mary's University College.

Originals of correspondence received by the Dominican nuns from clergy and laity whose support was solicited for the recognition of St Mary's University College, 1909.

Anonymous typescript paper, 'The Training of Sisters as Teachers', 1922.

Constitutions of Irish Dominacan Sisters, Cabra, (Private publication, 1947).

Boxes dated 1927–28:
Acts of the First General Chapter of the Congregation of Dominican Sisters Cabra, 1928.

Acts of Second General Chapter of the Congregation of Dominican Sisters Cabra 1934.

Copy of memorial to Right Hon. G. Balfour, MP, Chief Secretary to Lord Lieutenant for Ireland. Undated.

Dominican Irish Region Archives (OPR)
Contact address: Region Archivist, 10 Ashington Grove, Navan Road, Dublin 7. Due to change of location this archive holds the following five unclassified collections:

(a) Kingstown (Dún Laoghaire) Convent dating 1847–1960s.
    Letters: 1869–70, Monsignor McCabe to Fr O'Doherty.
    Fr O'Doherty to Fr O'Rourke.
    'School Rules' (ms. notebook).
    Account Book from Usher's Quay school 1845–52.
(b) St Mary's Training College, Falls Road, Belfast, Co. Antrim.
    Report: St Mary's Training College, Belfast, Session 1900–01.
    Ms. St Mary's Training College, Belfast, 'Golden Jubilee Gathering'.
    Other materials from St Mary's Training College Falls Road, Belfast are held
    in the present library of St Mary's University College, Falls Road, Belfast.
(c) Dominican Convent, Portstewart is now closed. All the available archival
    material from the foundation of the school in 1917 to the closure of the
    convent in the 1990s is held in the Dominican Irish Region archives. More
    recent school archives since closure of convent are held in Dominican
    College, Portstewart, Co. Derry.
(d) Dominican Convent, Santa Sabina, Sutton, Dublin 13.
    Book of Annals of Santa Sabina.
    Minutes of Meetings of Dominican Headmistresses, Dublin, January 1929.
    Letter: Mother Reginald Lyons to prioresses of Dominican convents, 1 May
    1929.
(e) Dominican Convent, Portstewart, Co. Derry, Collection
    Advertisement for the convent school 1917.
    Document: Scheme for Management, Control, and Regulation of Dominican
    Convent Portstewart, Co. Londonderry.
    Newspaper (unidentified) cutting, relating to the school, June 1935
    School Prospectus 1920s.

Dominican Convent, St Mary's, Cabra, Dublin 7 (OPC)

*Annals of the Dominican Convent, Cabra with some Account of its Origins,
    1647–1912.* Compiled by Mother Imelda Kavanagh (Dublin: published
    privately 1912)
Account Book, Boarding School 1872–1940.
Catholic Registry – 1837–1930s.
Record of Prizes, 1909–10.
National School Roll Books, 1870s, 1880s.

Dominican Convent, Falls Road Convent, Belfast, BT12 6AE (OPFR)

Annals of Dominican Convent, Falls Road, Belfast (edited version) from 1870.
Conventual council Minutes 15 November 1916.
Letter: Dr MacRory to M. Paul Bean, 30 January 1917.
Letter: J. Plunkett Dillon to Prioress General, Dominican Convent, Cabra,
    1 September 1934.
Letter: M. Reginald Lyons to Prioress of Falls Road convent, 5 September 1950.

Letter of A. Hamilton, Office of National Education, to Dr Henry, Bishop of Down and Connor.

Dominican Convent, Iona House, 28 Fortwilliam Park, Belfast, BT15 4AP (OPFW)

The Irish News, 15 September 1930; proof copy of advertisement for school.
The Irish Weekly and Ulster Examiner, 15 September 1930.
Times Educational Supplement, 29 September 1930. These two latter papers carried reports of the opening of the new school in Fortwilliam Park.
Dominican Convent Annals, Fortwilliam Park.
Minute Book, Governing Body, Dominican College, Fortwilliam Park, 1942.

Dominican Convent, 204 Griffith Avenue, Dublin 9 (OPE).
(This convent's archive is held in the Eccles Street collection).

Book of Annals, Sion Hill.
Ms. Annals, Dominican Convent, Eccles Street, September 1928.
Circulars: *Dominican Orphanage of Our Lady of Sion, 18 & 19 Eccles Street.*
The Lanthorn, Year Book of Dominican College, Eccles Street, published annually, 1913–1972 with special numbers for convent's golden jubilee 1932 and centenary 1982.
Anon. 'In Memory of Mother Peter, OSD', *The Lanthorn*, Vol. II No. 2 1917
Anon, 'St Mary's University College', *The Lanthorn*, Golden Jubilee Number, 1932.
Copy book containing details of St Dominic's Training College students' Loan Scheme accounts.
Gavan Duffy, L., 'A Year in St. Dominic's, *The Lanthorn*, Vol.I No.1, 1913.
Kearns, B., *The Lanthorn, Centenary Year* 1982.
Kearns, B. *Dominican Approach to Education* (Unpublished pamphlet, n.d.).
List of nominees to St Mary's University College Council, 1893.
Letters: Monsignor MacMahon to M. Antonina Hanley, 1883.
Obituary notice of M. Clare Elliott, undated and untitled newspaper cutting [1904].
Raffle ticket – original.
Results of Public Examinations, Dominican Convent of Our Lady of Sion, Eccles Street, published annually 1884–c.1913.
Result sheet of Teacher Training Syndicate, Cambridge, June 1910.
Syllabi of Summer Courses for Teaching nuns held in Eccles Street, 1909–30s.
Partial set of syllabi in archives.
Prospectus: 'Institution for Free Catholic Education for the Orphan Girls of the Upper and Middle Classes' (Eccles Street).

Dominican Sisters, Dún Mhuire, 461 Griffith Avenue, Dublin 9 (OPGA)

Sr. S. MacCarthy, *Songs of Sion* (Dublin: Browne & Nolan, 1898).
Scoil Chaitríona File: Contains various press cutttings and articles relating to Scoil Chaitríona.
E. Rynne, *A Shrine of Celtic Art*, The Oratory of the Sacred Heart, Dún Laoghaire.

Dominican Convent, Muckross Park, Donnybrook, Dublin 4 (OPM)

Annals of Muckross Park.
Letter: Eleanor Butler to prioress of the convent, 3 December 1925.

Dominican Monastery, Siena Convent, The Twenties, Drogheda, Co. Louth (OPD)

Account Book 1840.
Ms. Annals, 1847, 1851.
Ms. Annals of the Convent of St Catherine of Siena, Drogheda, Co. Louth 1853.
Ms. Synoptic edition of Annals.
Council Book 1860.

Dominican College, Newbridge, Co. Kildare (OPN)

Newbridge College Quaterly (Newbridge College, Co. Kildare, 1947).
Newbridge College Annual (Newbridge College, Co. Kildare, 2002).
Newbridge College Magazine, (Newbridge College Co. Kildare, Summer 1900).

Dominican Convent, Sion Hill Blackrock, Co. Dublin (OPSH)

Keogh, *Irish Catholic Directory*, 1873.
St Catherine's College, Sion Hill, Prospectus – 1910.
Document 6/1–2b, Document – House of Studies for Young Dominican Nuns.
Book of Annals, Sion Hill Convent, Blackrock (Dublin: Browne & Nolan, 1904).

Dominican Convent, Taylor's Hill, Galway (OPT)

School Annals, 1859.
B4/2 Visitation Report of Provincial, Fr B.T. Russell, 1859.
Ms notebooks of Sr Hyacinth McAuliffe, History and Mathematics.

Dominican Convent, Wicklow (OPW)

Photocopy – Resolution of Town Commissioners, Wicklow, 1869.
M. Clarke, *Wicklow Parish.* (1944).
Souvenir Programme Dominican Bazaar Wicklow, 1910.
Sr T. Dwyer, *Dominican Convent Wicklow, Centenary 1870–1970.*
Ms. Annals Dominican Convent, Wicklow, 1870.
School Report Books, 1907–23.
Anon. *Guide to Wicklow*, 1914 (no publisher named).
School Roll Books 1880s.

Archives of other Religious Orders and Congregations

Institute of the Blessed Virgin Mary, Loreto Archives, (LSG)
55 St Stephen's Green, Dublin 2

Anon. Résumé of Mother Michael Corcoran's Life, 1888–1918.

Society of Sacred Heart, Mount Anville, Dublin 14 (SSHA)

Pamphlet 496, *Life at the Sacred Heart.*
Pamphlet 497, *Children of the Sacred Heart.*
Disciplines et usages du Pensionnat, (Customs and Code of Discipline of the Boarding School).
Règlements Des Pensionnats (*Rules of the Boarding Schools*).
(Orleans: Alex Jacob, 1852).

St Louis Archives and Heritage Centre, Monaghan (SLA)

Unattributed cutting, 1872 'Children's Hospital, Temple Street, Dublin.
Réalt na Mara, School Year Book, 1918/1919.
Reflections, School Magazine, Clochar Louis, Muineachán (Dublin: Folens, n.d).

Vincentian Fathers, Sybil Hill, Raheny, Dublin 5 (VFR)

T. McNamara, Ms (pages unnumbered), 'Memoirs of Congregation of the Mission in Ireland, England, and Scotland 1867'

Cambridge University Library Archives (CUL)

Collections relating to Cambridge Teacher Training Syndicate.
EDUC 3/2–22 Box 1 Oscar Browning and Cambridge Syndicate 1878.
EDUC. 3/14–3/22 Correspondence: Sr Bernard Hackett and Browning 1898.
EDUC. 3/19–3/22 Correspondence: Fitch to Browning 1898.

King's College, Cambridge Archives (KCC)

Oscar Browning Papers:
OB 14–18: 1907–08 Browning's correspondence with:
    Sandymount Academical Institute, Dublin;
    St Angela's Ursuline Convent, Cork;
    Mother Patrick, Dominican College, Eccles Street;
    Mr Headen, Inspector of Schools.
OB2/134: 1908–13 Browning: miscellaneous correspondence.
OB 2/109: 1909 Browning and Ursulines, Waterford.

Secretariat of Catholic Secondary Schools, (SCSS) Emmet House, Milltown, Dublin 14

Archives of the Conference of Convent Secondary Schools:
File 1929/30: Suggested agenda for Meeting 17 May 1929.
Minutes of Meeting 17 May 1929.
Typescript notes of inaugural meeting 17 May 1929.
Copy of Mother Reginald Lyons' letter to convents in Northern Ireland.
Dominican nuns' reply to the bishops' circular re: the training of nuns as teachers.

Report of Annual General Meeting, 1931. (Canon MacMahon's address).

Report of Annual General Meeting, 1933.

File 1942, Mother Bertrand Byrne, prioress Dominican Convent, Falls Road, Belfast, accepting the affiliation of Dominican schools in Northern Ireland to the CCSS.

Official Publications

Public Records Office, Northern Ireland, Balmoral Avenue, Belfast (PRONI)

Collection relating to St Catherine's Primary School, Falls Road, Belfast.

1831, T. 1068–17, Letter from Lord Anglesey to Lord Stanley, 2 Nov. (copy).

1875–78, *National School Register*, Dominican Convent, Falls Road, Belfast.

195/5/1, Observations and Suggestions of District Inspector, St Catherine's Primary School, Falls Road, Belfast, 1876.

195/5/3, *Roll Books and Inspectors' Report Books*, various years between 1901–50, St Catherine's Primary School, Falls Road, Belfast.

British Parliamentary Papers: (BPP)

Irish Statutes and Bills

(i) Pre-Act of Union, 1801:

1710, 8 Anne, c.3: *An Act to prevent the further growth of popery.*

1746, 19 George II, c.7: *An Act for licensing hawkers and pedlars and for the encouragement of English Protestant Schools* [Charter Schools].

1782, 7 George III, c.4: *Catholic Relief Act, Ireland.*

(ii) Post Act of Union:

1831, (286) I, A bill for the establishment and maintenance of parochial schools and the advancement of the education of the people in Ireland.

1878, 41 and 42 Vic. C.66, *Intermediate Education (Ireland) Act.*

1898, First Report, Intermediate Education (Ireland), Act

Government Reports and Letters

1812–13, (21), vi, Fourteenth report from commissioners of the board of education in Ireland in view of the chief foundations, with some general remarks, and result of deliberation.

1813–14, v, 34, Letter of John Leslie Foster to Board of Education, Ireland.

1825, (433), xii, First Report of Commissioners of Education Inquiry, (Ireland).

1826–27, xiii, Letters of John Leslie Foster to Board of Education, Ireland.

1826, Report of Commissioners of Education (Ireland).

1828, (341), iv, Report from select committee to whom reports on the subject of education in Ireland were referred.

1834, (70), xl, First Report of commissioners appointed by the Lord Lieutenant to administer funds voted by parliament for the education of the poor of Ireland.

1837–8, (701), vii, Report of select commission on condition of foundation schools and education in Ireland.

1857–8, (22), Part 1, Report of Her Majesty's Commissioners appointed to inquire into the endowments, funds, and actual condition, of all schools endowed for the purpose of education in Ireland.

1858, (25), Part 2, Report of Commissioners of National Education.

1864, Vol. IV, Report of Commissioners of National Education; Accounts and Papers, Convent Schools.

1870, (28), Part 1, Report from Commissioners of Education, (Ireland), [Powis Report].

1878, (275) iii, 41 and 42 Vict. c.66, Intermediate Education (Ireland) Act.

1898, First Report, Intermediate Education (Ireland), Commission, (Palles Report).

1902, Royal Commission on University Education (Robertson Commission) H.C. 1902, xxxi.

1905, Report, on Intermediate Education in Ireland, (28) (F.H. Dale and T.A. Stephens).

Government Reports, Republic of Ireland

1960 Council of Education Report (Government Publications, Dublin).

Newspaper Features and Articles (NFA)

Christian Examiner and Church of Ireland Magazine, 2nd. series, iv, No. XXVI, October 1835 and 3rd series, ii, November 1837.

Freeman's Journal, 5 December 1888.

Irish Catholic, 5 July 1890.

Irish Times, 24 September 1890.

Irish Catholic, 29 October 1892.

Freeman's Journal, 24 October 1894.

Freeman's Journal, 21 October 1898.

Irish News (Belfast), 24 September 1900.

Freeman's Journal, 1 September 1901.

Irish Weekly and Ulster Examiner, 15 September 1930.

Times Educational Supplement, 29 September 1930.

Irish Times, 24 September 1990.

Nineteenth-century printed reference sources

Almanacks and Directories

Battersby's Catholic Directory (Dublin: Battersby, 1852).

Catholic Directory and Almanack (Dublin: O'Sullivan, 1840).

Complete Catholic Registry, Directory and Almanac 1836 to 1900 (Dublin: Mullany).

Complete Catholic Registry, Directory and Almanack (Dublin: W.J.B., 1862).

Dublin Almanack, 1843.
Dublin Directory 1837 (Dublin: Pettigrew and Oulton, 1837).
Dublin Diocesan Guide Book (Bray: Byrne and Associates, 2002).
Dublin Post Office Calendar (Dublin: G.P.O., 1834).
Gentleman's and Citizen's Almanack (Dublin: Watson, 1799).
Irish Catholic Directory, Almanack and Registry. (Dublin: Keogh, 1869, 1871, 1873).
Thom's Official Directory of the U.K. and Ireland.
    Index of Citizens of Dublin and Street Directory, published annually, from the nineteenth century to the present time.
Watson's Almanack (Dublin: Hope, 1844).
Wilson's Dublin Directory (Dublin: various years).

Papal Encyclicals

Pope Pius X, *Acerbo Nimis*, Encyclical Letter on Teaching of Christian Doctrine 1905 (CCD English edition 1946).
Pope Pius XI, *Non Abbiamo Bisogno (Concerning Catholic Action)*, (London: C.T.S. pamphlett No. H 207, 1931).
Pope Pius XI, *Divini Redemptoris (Atheistic Communism)*.
    Encyclical letter (Oxford: Catholic Truth Society, 1937).
Pope Pius XI, *Divini Illius Magistri (Christian Education of Youth)*, Encyclical Letter (Oxford: Catholic Truth Society, 1937).

PRIMARY SOURCES, PRINTED BOOKS

Annals of the Dominican Convent of St. Mary's Cabra, 1647–1912 (Dublin: Published privately, 1912).
Annals, Sion Hill Convent (Dublin: Browne and Nolan, 1904).
Aquinas, Thomas, *Quaestiones Disputatae de Veritate, Truth*, Translated by J.V. McGlynn, in three volumes, Vol.II (Chicago: Henry Regnery company, 1952).
Aquinas, Thomas, *Summa Theologica*, II-II. Translated by the Dominican Fathers of the English Province (London: Burns Oates and Washbourne, 1920).
de Burgo, T., *Hibernia Dominicana, sive Historia Provinciae Hiberniae Ordinis Praedicatorum* (Cologne: Metternich Press, 1762. Reprinted Farnborough, 1970).
Humbert of Romans, *Legenda S. Dominici*, Walz (ed.), MOPH, XVI (Rome: Monumenta Ordinis Praedicatorum Historica, 1935).
Newman, J.H., *The Idea of a University* (New York: Doubleday, Image Books edition, 1959).
O'Heyne, J., *Epilogus Chronologicus* (Louvain: 1706).
    English Translation, Ambrose Coleman, *Irish Dominicans of the Seventeenth Century* (Dundalk: Wm. Tempest, 1902).
The Catechism of the Catholic Church (London: Geoffrey Chapman, 1944).
The Code of Canon Law, in English translation (London: Collins, 1983).

SECONDARY SOURCES

(a) Books

Akenson, D.H., *The Irish Education Experiment, The National System of Education in the Nineteenth Century*, in series *Studies in Irish Education*, T.W. Moody, ed. by J.C. Beckett, T.D. Williams, Volume VII (London: Routledge and Kegan Paul, 1970).

Anon, *Celebration of Dominican Education* (Dublin: Dominican Education Office, 2000).

Anstruther, Ian, *Oscar Browning* (London: John Murray, 1983).

Armour, N., 'Isabella Tod and Liberal Unionism in Ulster, 1886–96', in A. Hayes and D. Urquhart (eds), *Irish Women's History* (Dublin: Irish Academic Press, 2004).

Ball, F.E., *History of the County of Dublin*, in six volumes (Dublin: Greene, 1905, HSP Library series, first impression 1902).

Beales, A.C.F., 'John Henry Newman', in A.V. Judge (ed.), *Pioneers of English Education* (London: Faber and Faber, 1952).

Beckett, J.C. and R.E. Glasscock, *Belfast, Origin and Growth of an Industrial City* (London: British Broadcasting Corporation, 1967).

Birch, P., *St. Kieran's College, Kilkenny* (Dublin: Gill and Son, 1951).

Birrell, A., *Things Past Redress* (London: Faber and Faber, n.d.).

Black, W., 'Industrial Change in the Twentieth Century', in J.C. Beckett and R.E. Glasscock (eds), *Belfast, Origin and Growth of an Industrial City* (Belfast: British Broadcasting Corporation, 1967).

Blacker, B.H., *Brief Sketches of the Parishes of Booterstown and Donnybrook* (Dublin: Herbert, 1960).

Boase, F. (ed.), *Modern English Biography*, Vol.II (Truro, 1897).

Bourke, U.J., *Life of Archbishop McHale* (New York: Kennedy, 1902).

Boyle, K., interview in *Convent Girls,* J. Bennet and R. Forgan (eds), (London: Virago Press, 2003).

Branca, P., *Women in Europe Since 1750* (London: Croom Helm, 1978).

Breathnach, D. and M. Ní Mhurchú, *Beathaisnéis a hAon* [Biography One] (Baile Atha Cliath: An Clóchomhar, 1986).

Broderick, T. and R. Duggan, *St. Mary's School for Deaf Girls, 1846–1986* (Dublin: St Mary's School for Deaf, 1996).

Burke Savage, R., *A Valiant Dublin Woman* (Dublin: Gill & Son, 1940).

Burstyn, J., *Victorian Education and the Ideal of Womanhood* (New Jersey: Rutgers University Press, 1984).

Catholic Encyclopedia for School and Home (New York and London: McGraw-Hill, 1965).

Catholic Encyclopaedia [*New*], Vols. I, XI (New York: McGraw-Hill, 1966).

Clarke, M., *Wicklow Parish* (Wexford: English and Co. 1944).

Clear, Caitríona, *Nuns in Nineteenth Century Ireland* (Dublin: Gill and Macmillan Dublin, 1987).

Clear, Caitríona, *Women of the House* (Dublin: Irish Academic Press, 2000).

Colum, Mary, *Life and the Dream* (Dublin: Dolmen Press, 1966).

Connolly, Seán, *Religion and Society in Nineteenth-Century Ireland* (Dundalk: Dún Dealgan Press, 1985).

Coolahan, John, *Irish Education, History and Structure* (Dublin: Institute of Public Administration, 1981).

Coolahan, John, *The ASTI and Post-Primary Education in Ireland, 1909–1984* (Dublin: Cumann na Meanmhúinteoiri, Eire, 1984).

Costello, N., *John McHale, Archbishop of Tuam* (Dublin: Talbot Press,1939).

Crean, E., *Breaking the Silence, Education of the Deaf in Ireland 1818–1996* (Dublin: Irish Deaf Society, 1997).

Cullen, Mary (ed.), *Girls Don't Do Honours, Irish Women in Education in the 19th and 20th centuries* (Dublin: WEB, Dublin 1987).

Cullen, M. and M. Luddy, (eds), *Female Activists, Irish Women and Change 1900–1960* (Dublin: Woodfield Press, 2001).

Cullen, M. and M. Luddy, *Women, Power and Consciousness in Nineteenth-Century Ireland* (Dublin: Attic Press, 1995).

Daly, Mary E., *Dublin, Deposed Capital: A Social and Economic History, 1860–1914* (Cork: Cork University Press, 1985).

Dominican Sisters (eds.), *Dominican Sisters Cabra, 1819–1994; Celebrating 175 Years* (Dublin: Private Publication, 1994).

Doolan, A., *The Revival of Thomism* (Dublin: Clonmore and Reynolds, 1951).

Dowling, P.J., *A History of Irish Education; A Study in Conflicting Loyalties* (Cork: Mercier Press, paperback edition, 1971).

Doyle, E., *Leading the Way* (Dublin: Secretariat of Secondary Schools, 2000).

du Bard, N.E. and M.K. Martin, *Teaching Language-Deficient Children* (Cambridge, MA: Educators' Publishing Service, 1997).

Durcan, T.J., *History of Irish Education from 1800* (Bala Merioneth: Dragon Books, 1972).

Elliott, M., *The Catholics of Ulster. A History* (London: Penguin Press, 2000).

Enright, S., 'Women and Catholic Life in Dublin, 1766–1852', in J. Kelly and D. Keogh (eds), *History of the Catholic Diocese of Dublin* (Dublin: Four Courts Press, 2000).

Fenning, H., *The Irish Dominican Province*, 1698–1797 (Dublin: Dominican Publications, 1990).

Ferriter, D., *The Transformation of Ireland 1900–2000* (London: Profile Books, 2004).

Forristal, D., *The Siena Story 1722–1997* (Drogheda: Siena Convent, 1999).

Foster, R.F., *Modern Ireland 1600–1972* (London: Penguin Books, 1989).

Gilbert, J.T., 'Hugh Boulter (1672–1743)', *The Dictionary of National Biography* Vol. II (Oxford: University Press, 1921–22).

Gillespie, R., *The Sacred in the Secular; Religious Change in Catholic Ireland* (Colchester, Vt: St Michael's College, 1993).

Gillespie, R., *Devoted People: Belief and Religion in Early Modern Ireland* (Manchester: Manchester University Press, 1997).

Greene, David, 'The Founding of the Gaelic League', in Seán O Tuama (ed.), *The Gaelic League Idea*, Thomas Davis Lectures series (Cork: Mercier Press, 1969).

Griffey, N., *From Silence to Speech* (Dublin: Dominican Publications, 1994).

Gwynn, D., *A Hundred Years of Catholic Emancipation (1829–1929)* (London: Longmans Green & Co. 1929).

Hayes, A. and D. Urquhart (eds), *The Irish Women's History Reader* (London: Routledge, 2001).

Hickey, D.J. and J.E. Doherty, *A New Dictionary of Irish History from 1800* (Dublin, Gill & Macmillan, paperback edition, 2005).

Hicks-Beach, Victoria, *Life of Sir Michael Hicks-Beach*, Vol. 1 (London: Macmillan & Co., 1952).

Holy Bible, Revised Standard Version (London: Nelson, 1966).

Holy Bible, Good News edition (Swindon: Bible Society, 1976).

Hope, C. *The Treble Almanack* (Dublin: Hope, 1835).

Hoppen, K.T., *Ireland since 1800: Conflict and Conformity* (London: Longman, 1989).

Howley, E., *The Universities and Secondary Schools of Ireland with Proposals for their Improvement* (Dublin: Evening Post, 1871).

Hoy, Suellen and Margaret MacCurtain, *From Dublin to New Orleans: The Journey of Nora and Alice* (Dublin: Attic Press, 1994).

Hufton, O., *The Prospect Before Her* (London: Harper Collins, 1995).

Hutchinson, J.H., *The Dynamics of Cultural Nationalism. The Gaelic Revival and the Creation of the Irish Nation State* (London: Allen & Unwin, 1987).

Jones, M.G., *The Charity School Movement* (Cambridge: Cambridge University Press, 1938).

Jordan, Alison, *Margaret Byers, Pioneer of Women's Education* (Belfast: Institute of Irish Studies, The Queen's University, n.d.).

Joyce, W.S., *The Neighbourhood of Dublin* (Dublin: Skellig Press, 1988, new edn).

Judges, A.V., *Pioneers of English Education* (London: Faber and Faber, 1952).

Kelly, D.P., *The Sligo Ursulines, The First Fifty Years*, 1826–1876 (Sligo: Ursuline Sisters, n.d.).

Kelly, James and Daire Keogh (eds), *History of the Catholic Diocese of Dublin* (Dublin: Four Courts Press, 2000).

Keogh, D., *Edmund Rice, 1762–1844* (Dublin: Four Courts Press, 1999).

Ker I., *John Henry Newman, A Biography* (Oxford: Oxford University Press, [Oxford Lives Series,] 1988).

Kerr, D., 'Dublin's Forgotten Archbishop: Daniel Murray, 1786–1852', in J. Kelly and D. Keogh (eds), *History of the Catholic Diocese of Dublin* (Dublin: Four Courts Press, 2000).

Kennelly, B. (ed.), *The Penguin Book of Irish Verse* (Harmondsworth: Penguin Books, 1970).

Kingsmill Moore, H., *An Unwritten Chapter in the History of Education* (London: Macmillan & Co., 1904).

Komonchak, J., M. Collins and D.A. Lane (eds), *The New Dictionary of Theology* (Dublin: Gill and Macmillan, 1987).

Larkin, Emmet, *The Roman Catholic Church and the Creation of the Modern Irish State, 1878–1886* (Philadelphia PA: The American Philosophical Society, 1975).

Larkin, Emmet, *The Roman Catholic Church in Ireland and the Fall of Parnell 1888–1891* (Raleigh, NC: University of North Carolina Press, 1979).

Lee, J.J., *Ireland 1912–1985, Politics and Society* (Cambridge: Cambridge University Press, 1989).

Lewis, Samuel, *History and Topography of Dublin City and County* (Dublin and Cork: Mercier Press, 1980).

Loreto Sister, *Joyful Mother of Children; Mother Francis Mary Teresa Ball* (Dublin: Gill & Son, 1961).

Lucey, M.F. (Roynane), 'School Days in Cabra Recalled, 1936–1940', *Dominican Sisters, Cabra, 1819–1994, Celebrating 175 Years* (Cabra: Dominican Convent, published privately, 1994).

Luddy, M., *Hanna Sheehy Skeffington* (Historical Association of Ireland, *Life and Times Series*, No. 5, Dundalk: Dún Dealgan Press, 1995).

Luddy, M., *Women and Philanthrophy in Nineteenth-Century Ireland* (Cambridge: Cambridge University Press, 1995).

Luddy, M. and C. Murphy (eds), *Women Surviving: Studies in Irish Women's History in the Nineteenth and Twentieth Centuries* (Dublin: Poolbeg, 1990).

MacAfee, D.C.I., *Concise Ulster Dictionary* (Oxford: Oxford University Press, 1996).

MacSuibhne, P., *Paul Cullen and His Contemporaries* (Naas: Leinster Leader, 1972), Vol. V.

McCartney, Donal, *U.C.D., A National Idea. The History of University College Dublin* (Dublin: Gill & Macmillan, 1999).

McElligott, T.J., *Secondary Education in Ireland, 1870–1921* (Dublin: Irish Academic Press, 1981).

McGarry, P.S., 'Penal Laws', *Catholic Encyclopaedia* Vol. III (New York: McGraw-Hill, 1966).

McGrath, M., *The Catholic Church and Catholic Schools in Northern Ireland* (Dublin: Irish Academic Press, 2000).

Mandonnet, P., *St. Dominic and His Work*, translated by M.B. Larkin (St Louis, MO and London: Herder Book Co., 1945).

Marland, Michael, (ed.), *Sex Differentiation and Schooling* (London: Heinemann Educational Books, 1983).

Martin, R., *The Historical Development of Dominican Spirituality*, translated by A.M. Townsend (Milwaukee WI: Bruce Publishing, 1934).

Moody, T.W. and J.C. Beckett, *Queen's, Belfast 1845–1949, the History of a University* (London: Faber & Faber, 1959), Vol. I.

Moore, H. Kingsmill, *An Unwritten Chapter in the History of Education, being the History of the Society for the Education of the Poor in Ireland,*

Generally Known as the Kildare Place Society, 1811–1831 (London: Macmillan & Co., 1904).

Morrissey, Thomas J., *Towards a National University, William Delany SJ (1835–1924)* (Dublin: Wolfhound Press, 1983).

Morrissey, Thomas J., *William J. Walsh, Archbishop of Dublin, 1841–1921: No Uncertain Voice* (Dublin: Four Courts Press, 2000).

Morrissey, Thomas J., *Bishop Edward Thomas O'Dwyer 1842–1917* (Dublin: Four Courts Press, 2003).

Nichols, Aidan, *Dominican Gallery, Portrait of a Culture* (Leominster, Herefordshire: Gracewing, 1997).

Nowlan, Kevin B., 'The Gaelic League and other National Movements', in Seán O Tuama (ed.), *The Gaelic League Idea, Thomas Davis Lectures series* (Cork: Mercier Press, 1969).

O'Brien, G. (ed.), *The Collected Essays of Maureen Wall* (Dublin: Geography Publications, Templeogue, 1989).

O'Brien, M. Cruise, *The Same Age as the State* (Dublin: O'Brien Press, 2003).

Ó Buachalla, Séamus, *Education Policy in Twentieth Century Ireland* (Dublin: Wolfhound Press, 1988).

Ó Céirín, K. and C., *Women of Ireland, A Biographic Dictionary* (Kinvara, Galway: Tír Eolas, 1996).

O'Connor, Anne V. and Susan M. Parkes, *Gladly Learn and Gladly Teach. A History of Alexandra College and School, Dublin 1866–1966* (Dublin: Blackwater Press, n.d.).

Ó Cuiv, Brian (ed.) *A View of the Irish Language* (Dublin: Stationery Office, 1969).

O'Donnell, E.E., *The Annals of Dublin* (Dublin: Wolfhound Press, 1987).

O'Farrell, S.M.P., *Nano Nagle, Woman of the Gospel* (Cork: MA thesis, University College Cork, privately published 1996).

O'Flaherty, L., *Management & Control in Irish Education: the Post Primary Experience* (Dublin: Drumcondra Teachers' Centre, 1992).

O'Flynn, T., *The Irish Dominicans 1536–1641* (Dublin: Four Courts Press, 1993).

Ó Héideáin, Eustás, *National School Inspection in Ireland* (Dublin: Scepter Books, 1967).

Ó Maitiú, S., *Dublin's Suburban Towns 1834–1930* (Dublin: Four Courts Press, 2003).

O'Meara, Thomas F., *Thomas Aquinas, Theologian* (Indiana: Notre Dame Press, 1997).

O'Neill, Marie, *From Parnell to de Valera, a Biography of Jennie Wyse Power 1858–1941* (Dublin: Blackwater Press, 1991).

O'Neill, Rose, *A Rich Inheritance, Galway Dominican Nuns, 1644–1994* (Galway: Dominican Sisters, 1994).

Ó Tuama, Seán (ed.), *The Gaelic League Idea, Thomas Davis Lectures Series* (Cork and Dublin: Mercier Press, 1969).

Parkes, S., *Irish Education in the British Parliamentary Papers in the Nineteenth Century* (Cork: Cork University Press, 1978).

Paseta, Senia, *Before the Revolution* (Cork: Cork University Press, 1999).

Phillips, P., *The Scientific Lady; A Social History of Women's Scientific Interests 1520–1918* (London:Weidenfeld and Nicolson, 1990).

Pochin Mould, *The Irish Dominicans, The Friars Preachers in the History of Catholic Ireland* (Dublin: Dominican Publications, 1957).

Prunty, J., *Margaret Aylward 1810–1889* (Dublin: Four Courts Press, 1999).

Reed, M., *Educating Hearing Impaired Children* (Milton Keynes: Open University Press, 1984).

Southern, R.W., *Western Society and the Church in the Middle Ages* (Harmondsworth: Penguin Books, 1970).

Spender, Dale (ed.), *The Education Papers: Women's Quest for Equality In Britain 1850–1912* (London: Routledge and Kegan Paul, 1987).

Stevens, F., *The New Inheritors* (London: Hutchinson Educational, 1970).

Tierney, M. (ed.), *Struggle with Fortune* (Dublin: Browne & Nolan, 1954).

Tynan, K., *Twenty-Five Years; Reminiscences* (London: Smith, Elder & Co., 1913).

Turner, D.M., *History of Science Teaching in England* (London: Chapman and Hall, 1927).

Vicaire, M.-H., *Saint Dominic, His Life and Times*, trans. by K. Pound (London: Darton, Longman and Todd, 1964).

Vicaire, M.-H., *The Genius of St. Dominic, Study-Essays ed. by Peter Lobbo* (Nagpur, India: Dominican Publications, n.d).

Wall, Maureen, 'The Penal Laws', in G. O'Brien (ed.), *The Collected Essays of Maureeen Wall* (Dublin: Geography Publications, 1989).

Walsh, B., *Roman Catholic Nuns in England and Wales 1800–1937, A Social History* (Dublin: Irish Academic Press, 2002).

Walsh, P.J., *William J. Walsh, Archbishop of Dublin* (Dublin: Talbot Press, 1928).

Walsh, William, Archbishop of Dublin, *Statement of Chief Grievances of Irish Catholics in the Matter of Education, Primary, Secondary, and University* (Dublin: Browne & Nolan, 1890).

Ward, Margaret, 'Suffrage First – Above all Else', in A. Smith (ed.), *Women's Studies Reader* (Dublin: Attic Press, 1993).

Weavings: Celebrating Dominican Women (Dublin: Dominican Sisters, 1988).

Williams, N. and Roach, J., *Whooping Crones: God-Songs for Women* (Springfield, Oregon: Catherine Joseph Publications, 1996).

Wittberg, P., *The Rise and Fall of Catholic Religious Orders; A Social Movement Perspective* (New York: State University Press, 1994).

Wright, J. (ed.), *English Dialect Dictionary* (Oxford: Oxford University Press, 1961), Vol. 5.

Articles from journals, pamphlets and periodicals

An Old Convent Girl, 'A Word for the Convent Boarding Schools', *Fraser's Magazine for Town and Country*, 10 (1874), pp.473–83.

Anon., 'Convent Boarding Schools for Young Ladies', in *Fraser's Magazine for Town and Country*, 9 (1874), pp.778–86.

Anon., 'Dominican College, Fortwilliam', *Celebration of Dominican Education* (Dublin: private publication, 2000), pp.15–17.

Anon., 'The Dominican Convent', *Guide to Wicklow* (1870), p.24.

Anon., 'Jubilate Deo', *Lanthorn*, 7 (Dublin: Dominican College, Eccles Street, 1932), pp.165–78.

Anon., 'Proposed Changes in Intermediate Education', *Englishwoman's Review*, 16 (1885).

Anon., 'St. Mary's University College', *Lanthorn*, 7 (1932), pp.183–97.

Arana-Ward, M., 'As Technology Advances, A Bitter Debate Divides the Deaf', *Washington Post* (May 1997), p.A01.

Barry, P.C., 'The Holy See and the Irish National Schools', *Irish Ecclesiastical Record* (Maynooth: St Patrick's College, August 1959).

Benvenuta, Sr (MacCurtain, M.), 'St. Mary's University College', *University Review*, 3, 4 (Dublin: Newman House, 1964), pp.33–47.

Byers, M., 'Higher Education of Women', *Englishwoman's Review of Social and Industrial Questions*, 12 (1881), pp.457–8.

Byers, M., 'Higher Education of Women', *Transactions of the National Association for Promotion of Social Science* (1881), pp.413–33.

Daly, L., 'Women and the University Question', *New Ireland Review*, 17 (1902), pp.74–80.

Fenning, Hugh, 'Andrew Fitzgerald OP, Education Pioneer', *St. Kieran's College Record*, 15 (Kilkenny: Modern Printers, 1998).

Griffey, N., 'Educating Profoundly Deaf Children: Experience in Thirty Years Teaching Deaf Children', *Proceedings of the International Congress on Education of the Deaf* (Hamburg: 1980).

Golan, Lew, 'Dialogue of the Deaf; What Gallaudet Won't Teach', *Washington Post* Archives (10 March 1996).

Hayden, M. and H. Sheehy Skeffington, 'Women in University – A Reply', *Irish Educational Review*, 1, 5 (1908), pp.242–83.

Hayden M. and H. Sheehy Skeffington, 'Women in University, – A Further Reply', *Irish Educational Review*, 17 (1908), pp.410–18.

Hyland, Aine, 'The Treasury and Irish Education: 1850–1922: The Myth and the Reality', *Irish Educational Studies*, 3 (Dublin, 1983).

Kerr, D.A., 'The Catholic Church in Ireland', *Ireland after the Union*, Proceedings of the Second Joint Meeting of the Royal Irish Academy and the British Academy, London 1986 (Oxford: University Press, 1986).

Larkin, Emmet, 'The Devotional Revolution in Ireland 1850–75', *American Historical Review*, 77 (1972), pp.625–52.

Logan, J., 'Governesses, Tutors and Parents: Domestic Education in Ireland, 1700–1888', *Irish Education Studies*, 7, 2 (Dublin, 1988).

Luddy, M., 'Presentation Convents in County Tipperary', *Tipperary Historical Journal* (1992), pp.84–5.

McAleese, M., 'President McAleese Visits Villa Rosa', *Far and Near* (Dublin: Irish Dominican Province, June 1999), pp.3–4.

McDonnell, Patrick, 'Residential Schooling and the Education of Children with Impaired Hearing', *Irish Educational Studies*, 3 (1983).

Meade, N., 'Women in Universities', *Irish Educational Review*, 1, 4 (1908), pp.236–43.

Meade, N., 'Women in Universities, A Rejoinder', *New Ireland Review*, 1, 6 (1908), pp.355–61.

Mulvany, I., 'Intermediate Act and the Education of Girls', *Irish Educational Review*, 1 (1907), pp.14–20.

Newsinger, J., 'The Catholic Church in Nineteenth-Century Ireland', *European History Quarterly* (1995), No XXV, 2.

Ní Mhuireadhaidh, 'Scoil Chaitríona', *Iona News* (Dublin: Parish Magazine, May 1978).

Ó Canainn, Séamus, 'The Education Inquiry 1824–1826 in its Social and Political Context', *Irish Educational Studies*, 3 (Dublin: 1983).

O'Connor, Anne V., 'Influences affecting Girls' Secondary Education in Ireland 1860–1910', *Archivium Hibernicum*, 41 (Maynooth: Catholic Record Society, 1986).

Oldham, A., 'Women and the Irish University Question', *New Ireland Review* (January 1897), pp.257–63.

'Parliamentary evidence on National Education in Ireland', *Christian Examiner and Church of Ireland Magazine*, series ii (November 1937).

Sheehy, H., 'Women and University Education', *New Ireland Review*, 17 (1902), p.148.

Tod, I.M.S., 'Girls in National Schools in Ireland', *Englishwoman's Review* 20, (Sept. 1889), pp.394–7.

Toxe, P. 'Chronique d'Actualité Dominicaine', *Memoire Dominicaine*, 4, *Les Dominicaines et leur Histoire* (Paris: 1994).

Wilkenson, Raymond, 'The Educational Endowments (Ireland) Act, 1885', *Irish Educational Studies*, 3 (Dublin: 1983).

Unpublished theses and dissertations

Barry, Elaine, 'St. Mary's University College and the University Question for Women, 1893–1909' M.A. thesis, University College, Dublin, 1995.

Cunningham, Joseph, 'Father John Baptist Burke, C.M. 1822–1894' (Dissertation submitted for Diploma for Teachers of the Deaf, University College, Dublin, 1978).

Duggan, Regina, 'Evaluation of the Senior Cycle Curriculum and its Effectiveness in the Preparation of Deaf Students for Life after School' (M.Ed. thesis, University College, Dublin, 1998).

Heffernan, J., *Newbridge College Annual* (Newbridge: 2002), pp.34 and following.

Heffernan, J., *Newbridge College Magazine*, Summer 1900, p.91.

Flynn, T.A., 'The Involvement of the Dominican Sisters of Sion Hill Convent in Third Level Education, with special Reference to St. Catherine's College of Domestic Science, 1929–1962' (M.Ed. Dissertation, Trinity College, Dublin, 1996).

226 DOMINICAN EDUCATION IN IRELAND

Griffin, Seán, 'Archbishop Daniel Murray of Dublin and his Contribution to Elementary Education in Ireland 1823–1841' (M.Ed. thesis, Trinity College, Dublin, 1992).

Kealy, Mary M., 'The Dominican Nuns of Channel Row, 1717–1820' (MA Dissertation, Lancaster University, 1998).

Matthews, Geraldine M., 'Dominican Post-Primary Provision in The North of Ireland 1870–1995' (M.Ed. Dissertation, University of Ulster, Jordanstown, N.I., 1996).

Murphy, Edel M., 'The Contribution of Dominican Sisters to Education in the Town of Dún Laoghaire, Co. Dublin' (M.Ed. thesis, University College, Dublin, 1999).

O'Driscoll, Finbarr J., 'Dominican Convents in the Diocese of Dublin and their Contribution to the Higher Education of Women 1882–1924' (M.Ed. Dissertation, Trinity College, University of Dublin, 1982).

Rice, Breda, '"Half Women Are Not For Our Time": A study of the contribution of the Loreto Order to Women's Education in Ireland, 1822–1922' (M.Ed. Dissertation, University of Dublin, Trinity College 1990).

Roche, Camilla, 'Founded for the Future. The Educational Legacy of Mary Ward' (M.Ed. Dissertation, Maynooth College, 1980).

Rushe, J., 'Bishop O'Dwyer of Limerick 1886–1917 and the Educational Issues of His Time' (Master's thesis, University College, Galway, 1980).

ORAL HISTORY

Interviews with the following past pupils and staff members of Scoil Chaitríona, at intervals over the past eight years: Srs Cajetan Lyons OP, Acuíneas Nic Chárthaigh OP, (Sr Aquinas McCarthy), Sr Catherine Whelan DC, Máirín Iníon Ní Dhomhnalláin, and Máire Iníon Ní Mhuireadhaidh.

INTERNET

Anderson, G., 'Dominican Contributions to the Intellectual Life of the Church', in *The Dominican Story*. http://www.op.org/domcentral/trad/domstor2.htm

RADIO AND TELEVISION BROADCASTS

Ó hÉineacháin, T., 'Tuar Mhic Éide', Radio programme, Radio Telefís Éireann, 8 November 2000.

'Léargas', Television Documentary, Radio Telefís Éireann, 27 February 2001.

Index